CÉZANNE AND MODERNISM

SUNY Series, the Margins of Literature
Mihai I. Spariosu, editor

CÉZANNE AND MODERNISM
The poetics of painting

Joyce Medina

STATE UNIVERSITY OF NEW YORK PRESS

Published by
State University of New York Press

For information, address the State University of New York Press,
State University Plaza, Albany, NY 12246

Production by Bernadine Dawes • Marketing by Theresa Abad Swierzowski

Library of Congress Cataloging-in-Publication Data

Medina, Joyce, 1953–
    Cézanne and modernism : the poetics of painting / Joyce Medina.
          p. cm. — (SUNY series, the margins of literature)
    Includes bibliographical references (p.   ).
    ISBN 0-7914-2231-3 (alk. paper). — ISBN 0-7914-2232-1 (pbk. :
alk. paper)
        1. Impressionism (Art)—France. 2. Modernism (Art)—France.
3. Painting, Modern—19th century—France. 4. Cézanne, Paul,
1839–1906—Criticism and interpretation. 5. Aesthetics,
Modern—20th century. 6. Art—Psychology. I. Title. II. Series.
ND547.5.I4M37   1995
759.4'09'034—dc20   94-31716
                                                                    CIP

1 2 3 4 5 6 7 8 9 10

CONTENTS

ACKNOWLEDGMENTS

I would like to acknowledge the dedicated support from Angel Medina during both the thinking-through and writing processes of bringing this book into being. I would like to thank Professors Clark Poling, John Howett, and Robert Paul of Emory University for their helpful comments. Mihai Spariosu, editor of the series, and Carola Sautter, Bernadine Dawes, and Wendy Nelson of the Press are also deserving of my gratitude and appreciation.

INTRODUCTION

This book investigates the possibility of identifying the central features of the modernist movement in order to develop a unified theory of modernism. The underlying assumption is that, in modernism, profound changes in the nature and functions of the artistic image were the key to a new distinctive character of the art object.

Paul Cézanne is presented as a major master of the modernist movement because of his transformation of traditional pictorial images and his invention of radically new types of images. As a result of these changes, more fully attributable to Cézanne than to any other modernist, the mimetic (metaphysical and moral) motivation of the pictorial sign was replaced by symbolist, plastic, contemplative, and visionary motivations that yielded four corresponding types of images, all of which can generally be found together in all the great modernist masters. The current interpretation of these changes in the pictorial sign is that they either represent psychological states or are arbitrary signs of unconscious sexual, economic, social, and political motives. Thus Cézanne scholarship has been divided between traditional mimetic approaches and postmodernist textual readings of Cézanne's iconology and iconography; the creative, conscious, and artistic motifs of his work, particularly of the late period, have been neglected or distorted.

After surveying the transformation of the image in the psycho-logical theories of the nineteenth century, this investigation focuses on the Bergsonian philosophy of the image as a hermeneutical paral-lel of Cézanne's pictorial theory and practice. Within this parallel, the artistic devices of montage and collage, which are shown to cor-respond to contemplative and visionary images, respectively, receive a broader justification than that given to them by cubism and surreal-ism and subsequently accepted by postmodernist critics. The proposed interpretation of montage and collage as devices for the conversion of arbitrary signs into quasi-natural, or poetic, signs constitutes the ground for a new theory of iconology and iconography and allows for original readings of Cézanne's most important serial paintings, in particular the *Mont Sainte-Victoire,* the *Bathers,* and the *Cardplayers,* in the last two chapters of this study.

I

CÉZANNE AND THE UNITY OF MODERNISM

In a series of lectures in support of several exhibitions in 1909 of mainly postimpressionist works in the Grafton Galleries in London, Roger Fry attempted to explain to the public the new pictorial trends. In the process, he felt the need to isolate within these trends a "new movement," which eventually received the name *modernism*.[1] Although most of the concepts presented by Fry in these lectures had already been formulated in previous essays and review articles, he did emphasize that Cézanne's paintings embodied the "new spirit" of modernism, which he defined as the manifesting of the "visual language of the imagination."[2] The imagination, for Fry, was synonymous with "aesthetic experiences" and with "disinterested contemplation"[3] and ultimately associated by him and by Clive Bell (who at the time was working on the manuscript that was to become his book *Art*) with the "finding" and "making" of "significant forms." For these authors, then, the unified consciousness of "expressing" and the "emotional acts expressed" were signified by, and therefore only apprehensible in, "significant forms."[4]

Cézanne's ability to develop and use a similar language to embody aesthetic awareness and its creativity qualified him, for the English critics, as the point of departure for modernism. "The period

1

in which we find ourselves . . . begins with the maturity of Cézanne (about 1885)," wrote Bell in 1913; even though the works of Matisse, Picasso, Derain, and Vlaminck were shown side by side with Cézanne's paintings in the exhibitions Bell organized with Fry, Cézanne remained the central exemplary figure in their theoretical explanations. They found in his techniques an intentional abstraction of lines and colors in order to present patterns that could convey the "new" subject matter of the "new" movement: content that was neither imitative nor literary, but expressive solely of the artistic/aesthetic concerns faced and transcended by the painter in constituting forms that could signify these concerns. Cézanne best described this mutuality of aesthetic experience and creative act in his famous statement recorded by Joachim Gasquet from a "conversation" of 1896:

> Le paysage se reflète, s'humanise, se pense en moi. Je l'objective, le projette, le fixe sur ma toile . . . je serait la conscience subjective de ce paysage, comme ma toile en serait la conscience objective.[5]

According to Cézanne, the landscape and its consciousness exchange places in the development of the creating act that gives form to its aesthetic appearance. Consciousness might disappear altogether except for the objective signs on the canvas *of a life of the landscape that the painter lives* as he paints it. Hence Cézanne can claim that his picture is at the same time a sign of *the life of the landscape* and of *the aesthetically motivated contemplation* that arises as the landscape takes its own form (i.e., begins to endure on the canvas). The union of the life of the landscape in the *creating* painter and of the painter in the *created* landscape is what makes the pictorial synthesis, as a doubly expressive synthesis, a significant form. More precisely, in Cézanne's intentionally forceful language, that vital union is created in the signs of its own realization.

The emphasis by Fry and Bell on the late period of Cézanne's oeuvre as they developed the early definitions of modernism, together with the presentation of the Aix master's late works through the London exhibits and the famous 1907 retrospective at the Salon d'Automne in Paris, helped to focus the attention of the art world—artists, critics, and collectors—on the significance of Cézanne's works and theories *within a modernist context.* Also in the first two decades of the twentieth century, there appeared in the public presses "conversations" and "correspondence" with the French master; artists spoke of the "lessons of Cézanne" and of his "paternal" influences.[6] The lessons of Cézanne became the pivotal point for defining and redefining modernism; because of their lack of precision (no known diaries or theoretical pronouncements came from Cézanne's own hand), they were easily adapted through different and often contradictory interpretations. Cézanne was called a "classicist" and a "primitive,"[7] an "impressionist" and a "symbolist,"[8] a "late Romantic"[9] and "the father of Cubism,"[10] and all of these labels were applied to him during these first two decades of the twentieth century.

When isolated from their context, as was the case with the above examples, Cézanne's theoretical remarks contained in the letters and in the recounted conversations lend themselves easily to a critical "reading between the lines" and to the construing of narrow and exclusive precedents or sources for his inspiration. However, when carefully examined together as a narrative reconstruction of his artistic aims, his theoretical statements, sparse though they may be, can be more profitably used, not to establish his style within the narrow limits of a modern "ism," but to help define that vast and uncharted sea we identify as modernism. Through the unveiling of a unified sense of this movement it may become possible not only to deepen our understanding of new and exciting modern methodologies— psychoanalysis, phenomenological analysis, socioeconomic criticism, structural linguistic theory—as appropriate procedures for interpreting paintings, but to see within their depth and their connections with each other the existence of a deep structure of creation that found its most fully grounded power of realization in Cézanne's theories and his work. In sum, not only did the "landscape think itself" through Cézanne, but we can also find evidence in his oeuvre and his statements that modernism "thought" itself through him.

This study will attempt to uncover the language, the self-thinking, of modernism in both the practice and the theories of Paul Cézanne in order to prove him to be a modernist and thus cleanse his reputation from forced association with all the eccentric fashions of, and beyond, the fin de siècle. It will be necessary for this purpose to interpret his works as experimental applications of his theoretical statements. To this end, the master's famous and most precisely formulated aesthetic belief and goal, the elusive and constantly pursued "realization of the motif," will be used to characterize his paintings, especially those of his last decade, 1895–1906, which date from the statement of this goal, as the most pointed elaborations of his beliefs. But at the same time, Cézanne's statements and works will be reinterpreted as evidence of his efforts, in advance of but clearly in the spirit of modernism, to resolve and transcend his duality of concerns for the discovery of the most effective "pictorial" techniques ("representation" can no longer be the intent) and the circumscribing of new and fresh "subjects" for the art of painting.

MODERNISM: TECHNIQUE VS. CONTENT

These seemingly contradictory goals so prevalent in both Cézanne and modernism—the emphasis on technical advances and, at the same time, the discovery and presentation of new "modern" subjects—were but two sides of the same modernist coin. Experimentation with form (color, brushstroke, two-dimensional arrangement, etc.) could be seen as a collapsing of renewed aspects of content into sensory and signifying elements; at the same time, form itself collapsed into the contextual and existential (emotional, spiritual, social, communicational) aspects of content. Such alteration of the understanding of the pictorial constituents of content and form, with the consequent concentration on painting as a poetic language, a medium for the creation of meaning, was precisely the essential feature of modernism, as this study of aesthetic and art theoretical notions relevant to the peculiar style of Cézanne will show. More precisely, modernism will manifest its essential concentration upon art as a medium, a language, if the traditional conception of form is expanded and understood technically as significant form based on *motivated signs.*

Such an understanding of pictorial form as having signifying functions is indispensable for a fruitful reorientation and broadening of Cézanne studies; on the other hand, a broader view of Cézanne is indispensable for an adequate understanding of the conversion—not only perceived but achieved by him—of pictorial form into signifying form. Many modernist masters understood this conversion as Cézanne's major contribution and therefore saw his work as a more advanced realization of it than their own; yet somehow this "reader reception" of Cézanne's achievement and central contribution, the best path one can follow into the core of his creative struggle, has been lost in Cézanne studies.

Cézanne's own tangled pronouncements, though, exhibited a duality of concerns that were to become characteristic of modernism. The term *realization,* in his statements, was used in two seemingly contradictory ways: In a traditional sense he used it to refer to the finishing or completion of an artistic project; he also used the term, through the years, to indicate the substitution of formal equivalents first for the mood, then for fresh meanings or idealizations of emotion, and finally for the creative attitudes of the painter. The notion of a "substitution" meant, for him, that the mood, emotional idealization, and/or creative attitude must begin in, crystallize in, and end within the process of emergence of the pictorial "equivalent." There was for him no other extrinsic remnant in the motivation of the artistic act and its object. This manner of functioning of the pictorial equivalent of an aesthetic emotion differentiated it, and the emotion itself, from natural impressions and emotions. Artistic impressions came to exist in the strict correlation between creative act and created object, whereas conventional (i.e., psychologically identifiable) impressions and emotions were said to precede, both causally and as distinct consciousnesses, the objects that are made to represent them. This understanding, to which Cézanne adhered so adamantly, influenced very much the technical meaning he gave to the term *motif* in his statements.

The meaning of *motif* changes over the years in his theoretical formulations. In the early years of his artistic practice it meant a detail, outward design, or appearance that can be imitated and illustrates or stands for a subject. In later years it meant, in modernist parlance, the "essence," or "spiritual" quality, for which certain combinations of color and brushstroke formation could substitute while capturing, exposing, and presenting an "aesthetic emotion" or a poetic completion of reality and life.

Perhaps because Cézanne's paintings contained and compressed all of these constitutive variations, early modernist critics, in focusing on the prevalence of form over content and inspired by the richness of the painter's formal "equivalences," unwittingly restricted the understanding of form, and of Cézanne's forms, and converted it into a critical tool for a "formalist" characterization, perhaps inspired by Benedetto Croce, of the artwork (consider, for example, Roger Fry's and Clive Bell's concept of "significant form" and T. S. Eliot's and Ezra Pound's "objective correlative"). At the same time and by looking at the same works (*Mont Sainte-Victoire* landscapes, the *Bathers* series, and the still lifes) and examining the same theoretical statements, art historians and critics following the disciplines of contextual analysis and using the tools for analyzing meaning formation—from traditional iconography to psychoanalysis—have also added to our contemporary arsenal of critical instruments the possibility of reading a painting as a literary or poetic construction with metaphors and symbols, as do Fritz Novotny, Maurice Merleau-Ponty, and Kurt Badt.[11]

The opposing schools of Cézanne scholarship that arose from the multiplicity of interpretations of Cézanne's expressive forms appear irreconcilable.[12] *Mont Sainte-Victoire* is viewed by one interpretive school as a perceptual form with essential significance; for another school it presents "hidden, unconscious images" of a reclining female nude or of a self-portrait of the balding artist.[13] A sweeping diagonal brushstroke in the *Large Bathers* is, in some interpretations, a copy, or a citation, of the bending trees of Manet's *Luncheon on the Grass;* in other views, it is the wispy strands of hair of a portrait of Mme. Cézanne.[14] The still-life painting *The Black Clock* with its handless clock dial is, for some, a reference to Bergsonian nonlinear time;[15] for others it is a self-portrait informed by a pun: Cézanne's nickname "Le Pendu" is contained in the French word for clock, *la pendule.*[16]

Which interpreter is correct? Up to a point they all are. The strict formalists are especially sensitive to the limited repertory of Cézanne's images and have listed, categorized, and analyzed his formal "language" without understanding its *poetically linguistic* dimensions. The searchers for hidden imagery find it everywhere; their "vision" has become contagious and resulted in provocative disagreements on the motivation of Cézanne's imagery. The fascinating psychoanalytic "case histories" of Cézanne rival Freud's famous cases in the unequivocal evidence they locate of his "unconscious desires" translated into symptoms. But the psychoanalytic critics have not been speaking with the formalists, and vice versa. Indeed, Cézanne scholarship has fallen into an impossible mixture of formalism with naïve social or psychological content: The critics separate formal considerations from content, signifiers from signifieds, art from poetry, and philosophy from life, and then peculiarly reunite them just to show their own, not necessarily Cézanne's, originating biases. In fact, as a realized motif, *Mont Sainte-Victoire* is both a pantheistically conceived pyramid and a self-portrait; *The Large Bathers* is both a landscape with figures and a portrait of Mme. Cézanne; and *The Black Clock* contains both the personal and the theoretical references to an achievement of "realization."

My proposed interpretation differs from these partial approaches. I not only recognize a plurality of meanings and clearer stages, but I assign a proper role to the late period and allow it to appear as the ultimate synthesis that it was rather than as one more turn in a tortuous career. Therefore, one of the guidelines of this study, extracted from a hermeneutical juxtaposition of Cézanne with Bergson, will be that Cézanne's intent "realization of the motif" ultimately means for him to achieve the goal of attaining "The truth in painting," to the effect that *he must convey the harmonious oneness and creativity of being as operative in the craft of painting.* The famous mountain must thus have multiple appearances (the triangle, the human body, the face) all united by one creative intuition, the pyramid, as a "perfect structure" that sufficiently expresses and presents the *linguistic, poetic, or figural* unifiability of all the various levels of appearance.

If the psychoanalysts had spoken to the formalists about the validity of the "unconsciously motivated hidden images," the formalists could have offered a very important clarification: that if one bears in mind the limited repertory of forms, shapes, and images that Cézanne used (that the mountain and the face share, in Cézanne's oeuvre, the same essential motif), one must arrive at the conclusion that the "hidden" images were not unconsciously motivated but conscious elaborations and "realizations" dictated by a limited syntax of images. In this study, both of these viewpoints will be further qualified: The images in question are not necessarily hidden but could be said to be multiple, or consecutive, images. They are, in fact, generated by vital intentions and gain complexity through poetic tropes that function pictorially as passages, or "shifts," from one to another level of appearance so that the painting unveils itself like a poem to be completed, spatially and temporally, by the viewer.

CÉZANNE: THE LATE WORK

The most important turning point in Cézanne's theoretical development and his practice occurred in 1895. The highly acclaimed Vollard
exhibit of that year focused the art world's attention on the painter's
accomplishments, while Cézanne, the proverbial recluse, "retired" to
Aix—content, he said, to prove his theories. There he undertook,
during the remaining decade of his life, four major projects: the
Mont Sainte-Victoire series, the *Bathers* series, the *Cardplayers* series
and a series of still lifes from his Jas de Bouffan studio. His preoccupation with such a classical range of subjects (landscapes, nudes and
still lifes) was necessary, he explained,[17] to permit him the freedom
to experiment with his technical inventions (color modulation, condensation of forms, and abstraction of space). But many critics and
scholars have noticed, in the art of this last decade, changes not only
in his techniques but also in his theories and in his "style."

Indeed, as early as 1895, Gustave Geffroy noted that Cézanne's
paintings of that year, when compared with the full range of his
work as exhibited at the Vollard retrospective, was "a bifurcation
. . . a branch road . . . a new style" that is "neither Impressionism
nor Neo-Impressionism, Symbolism nor all three."[18] Maurice Denis
identified the "new style" as based on "free associations" and "contrasts" rather than on the "logical mimetic theory" of the earlier style.[19]
Lawrence Gowing has noted that in the "earlier style," before 1895,
Cézanne "painted objects" and that after 1895 he ceased to paint
objects and painted instead "abstract form"—form, he goes on to
say, that is

> voluminous without being solid, color that is luminous without
> light, representation that is apparently specific yet specifies noth-
> ing.[20]

Lilian Brion-Guerry[21] agrees with this distinction between "earlier"
and "later" practices and calls this later tendency toward abstraction
the expression of *passage*. By emphasizing the boundaries between
volumes and air, the transitions (shadows and reflections) become as
distinctly whole, she notes, as the apples once were in the earlier
paintings.

Others have noticed not only changes in technique and in subject matter but also changes in the motivation of his art. Meyer Schapiro locates within the later period a sublimation of erotic desire in the displacement of objects to form symbols: The "apple" entered his earlier repertory as an effect (a sign) and became, in the later style, a personal emblem that united his physical (bodily) desires with his artistic goals.[22] On the other hand, Kurt Badt[23] identifies Cézanne's psychological motivation as more spiritual than sexual and calls it "loneliness." He notes a destructive rebelliousness in Cézanne's "attack" on painting in the earlier period giving way, in the last decade, to a more resigned, meditative attitude with which Cézanne finds it possible to achieve an "inner divine melody."

A careful analysis of at least one of Cézanne's series undertaken during this last decade of his work should then be an appropriate device not only for disclosing the "changes" in his style, his techniques, and his subject matter, but also for showing the *conscious* (intentional) transformation of his motifs as they are realized into clusters of multiple poetic images in a single painting. This study will focus on the *Cardplayers* series and especially on the final version at the Musée D'Orsay. It will be pointed out that, in this final painting of the series, an image of a skull and the physiognomic appearances of a mask are "suggested"—that is, both visionarily present and absent. The inspiration for the motivation of this complex vision will be traced back to Cézanne's youth, as well as to numerous paintings of still lifes and figurative scenes, dating from as early as the 1860s, in which skulls appear as posed objects. In the final version of *The Cardplayers*, however, the skull ceases to be an object of contemplation, a memento mori, and it emerges, with its metaphoric twin, the mask,[24] as a fully realized motif that is both an abstract and an empathetic sign of the painter's deepest intentions.

The skull/mask can be recreated only in the final painting of the series, the Orsay oil (figure 6). In the subtle alterations of the consecutive paintings, the cardplayers and their positions at the table have been slightly shifted, simplified, and condensed through the progression of the series until the poses of the figures are gradually ordered to produce the structural metaphor of the cranium. In that final painting, the bent backs of the players and their converging knees frame the monumental outline of a skull, and the background of the earlier versions, as it is emptied of details and modeled more and more with flickering highlights, appears to be transformed from the stable solidity of a wall into the translucent depth and cavernous features of the death symbol.

The skull/mask/cardplaying motif realized in the final *Cardplayers* derives its evocative power from tropes or transformations in signifying functions. This study will trace the imaginative materials of this motif by establishing its connections within Cézanne's oeuvre, both painted and written, with such disparate elements as Dante's story of Ugolino from the *Inferno*, tarot card imagery, and the traditional associations of death and gaming in possible precedents of *The Cardplayers*. It will point to syntactic/semantic configurations, such as *montage* and *collage*, that transform pictorial technique and help establish the difference between the illusions and tricks of representation and the fusion of emerging, changing images that were invented by Cézanne and are still a mysterious side of his art.

In the clarification of the rise of "poetics" into the theory and practice of Cézanne's painting, a transition takes place. First it was considered from the standpoint of traditional aesthetic concepts such as form and subject matter, and later its levels of signification were understood more in conformity with the great conceptual innovations of modernism. Thus, the issue of the intentional or subliminal character of secondary images, and of their relations with the other of Cézanne's expressive and thematic concerns, was to be subsumed under a philosophy of the image more in keeping with the modernist character of his approaches to signification. In these developing approaches, it is possible to perceive, with some of the writers and painters that Cézanne inspired, a sharp awareness of *what* could be pictorially signified and of *how* the pictorial sign could function.

Chapter 2 of this study presents an exposition of premodernist concepts of the image (abstract and empathetic psychologism) and a reconciliation of these trends in Henri Bergson's theory of images. The conjunction of Bergson's theories with Cézanne's own images provides a hermeneutical horizon for the definition of modernist aesthetics. Chapter 3 will provide "other" backgrounds of modernism (optical science and color theory) that are blended by most modernist artists with an understanding, at least implicit (impressionism, postimpressionism, and symbolism). Chapter 4 explicates Cézanne's practice and theories, focusing on the progressive versions of his theory of "realization" and how they correspond, first, to the prevalent psychologism of the period, then to the color symbolism of the optical scientists, and, in the end, to Bergson's highest levels of images. The enhanced understanding of the pictorial sign and signification in Cézanne gleaned from the study of his theoretical development will be applied, in chapter 5, to an iconological and iconographic study of *The Cardplayers* in accordance with a modified modernist theory of iconography and iconology.

"Realized motifs" in modernism, whether they are Cézanne's or the avowed "cubist" novellas of Gertrude Stein or Kandinsky's synesthetic images, must be understood as pictorial and poetic, perceptual and spiritual, at the same time. In sum, we see in the greatest modernist works a most peculiar transformation of the doctrine of *ut pictura poesis*, which was introduced by Horace, recovered by Leonardo in the Renaissance and later by the Neoplatonists in the seventeenth century, and *finally reformulated by the modernists as the operation, in art, of the poetic sign: a sign that is perceptual in its silent, expressive values and spiritual in its visible form.* The "realized motif" of Cézanne was the first among such uses of the aesthetic sign in modernism; when successfully realized, it was, to quote Cézanne, "like a correct phrase of a new language to be completed."[25]

When the modernist movement appeared to have exhausted its creative foundations, Herbert Read, writing in 1933, aimed at defining modernism as a period concept and hinted at a revolutionary rather than an evolutionary significance of modernism in the context of the Western tradition in art.

> There have been revolutions in the history of art before today. There is a revolution with every new generation, and periodically, every century or so, we get a wider or deeper change of sensibility. . . . But I do think we can already discern a difference in kind in the contemporary revolution: it is not so much a revolution, which implies a turning over, even a turning back, but rather a break-up, a devolution, some would say a dissolution. Its character is catastrophic. . . . We are now concerned not with a logical development for which there is any historical parallel, but with an abrupt break with all tradition. . . . The aim of five centuries of European effort is openly abandoned.[26]

Read was careful here to distinguish the advent of the modernist attitude from the cyclical evolution of movements identified by him as generational changes; he characterized the former specifically as a "devolution," not the carrying forward of a "tradition" (the very notion of tradition was thus revised), but the development of a "new in a new way, almost in a new dimension," as C. S. Lewis notes.[27] When the modernists themselves spoke,[28] they muddied the waters even further by acknowledging that, though their "vision" was decidedly avant-garde, their visual apparatus was conditioned by the historical past. Their theoretical positions, "manifestos,"[29] often originated with a separation of their practices from conventional ones; then they slipped into polemical arguments and finally into programmatic statements of heroically worded goals. The terms *Reality, the past,* and *the self* appeared often in the slogans of these manifestos; their definitions were spiced up with hyperbolic oppositions, such as *objectivity/subjectivity* or *the internal/the external.*

One characteristic common to all modernist movements and stages was a desire for transcendence.[30] Historical transcendence, self-transcendence, transcendence of the material world, spiritual transcendence, technology as transcendence, and so forth, were all duly tested as means and ends of the avant-garde style of renewal. A similar impulse within modernism was a scientifically inspired desire for radical experimentation, a drive toward "new beginnings" that Émile Zola called "the aesthetic of experimentalism."[31] Gertrude Stein experimented with language patterns to invent "poem paintings";[32] Picasso pasted together newspaper fragments to fashion "collages"; James Joyce generated new syntactical structures with his "wave speech." In the attempts to characterize modernism by such appeals to critical breaks in historical continuity, to transcendence of the ordinary sense of reality, to radical experimentation, what is not generally noticed is that it is always the *art medium* that became the site of all retreats from reality as previously experienced. As evidenced in the three examples just cited, the expressive medium became the battlefield, the armaments, and the cause of the modernists' skirmishes. Artistic *language* was precisely what was reinvented, abstracted, transcended. Music, painting, art (even consciousness and history) began, with modernism, to exhibit a new, unique preoccupation with various means and levels of expression and eventually of new developments in linguistics, and more generally with semiotics, the theoretical and practical study of signs and symbols.[33]

FROM IMPRESSIONISM TO CÉZANNE
Psychological Theories

Although impressionism introduced and justified itself as a technique of representation on stricter physiological and psychological grounds than those implicit in traditional representational schools up to the 1860s, the discussions about impressions and their synthesis in conscious life went far beyond its initial implications within the context of representationalism. As the nineteenth century concluded and the twentieth century introduced new artistic concerns and an unprecedented interest in the origins of art, the issue of the conscious synthesis of sensations acquired momentous dimensions, involving not only the perceptual content and organization of pictorial scenes but a transformation of the very meaning of artistic content and of the relation between form and content.

THE IMPRESSION AS MEDIUM

Ah, there he is, there he is!" he cried in front of No. 98. . . . What does that canvas depict? Look at the catalogue." "Impression, Sunrise." "Impression, Sunrise—I was certain of it. I was just telling myself that, since I was impressed, there had to be some impression in it.

Louis Leroy's satirical review, "L'Exposition des Impression-istes,"[1] of the 1874 exhibition of the impressionists at Nadar's not only appropriates this new term, *impression,* into its title but comi-cally reenacts the fascination of the French with the scientific/mysti-cal possibilities of the impression for the new art. In tautological fashion, Leroy contends that if a painting contains impressions and, as the title claims, is an impression, then the viewer must have been led to "have some impressions."

The term itself had an intricate background.[2] It had been used pejoratively and as a plaudit; as we shall discuss in the next section, it had been the focus of psychological analysis in the late nineteenth century. It was described by the impressionists as "the only reality" and, conversely, by the symbolists as "the receptacle of the Ideal." For the former, it was nature itself speaking through the senses; for the latter, it was the language of the imagination and inner con-sciousness. Impressions were described as being "represented," "cap-tured," "achieved"; they were credited with initiating art and with becoming the means and the end of it.[3]

But for the artist, whether impressionist, postimpressionist, or symbolist, the "impression" was the focus of progress toward mod-ern art. Attention was centered on the impression by the technolo-gies of the modern age: Optical scientists, in exploring the seat and the workings of vision and the intricacies in the manifestation of light and color, studied the impression both as a mechanical and as an organic regulator of experience. Aestheticians and psychologists posited the impression as the mediation between the "self" and the "world," between "subjectivity" and "objectivity," by proposing "prin-ciples" (of association, of complementarity, and of empathy)[4] to ex-plain the complexities and the pervasive role of the impression. Art-ists, novelists, and musical composers exchanged views of its efficacy in inspiration, of its appropriateness as content, and of its expressive value as structure and form.

The impression became, then, for the premoderns and early moderns, the focus around which most changes in emphasis and label revolved. As was suggested earlier, for the impressionists the impression was still a passive response,[5] barely a "sign" of the con-scious character of sensibility; for the symbolists it was already sym-bol making and the manifestation of imaginative syntheses capable of expressing the permanent (the Universal, the Ideal).[6] As a sign, the impression of the impressionists was an integrated system of colored brushstrokes that contributed to structure and to expanding the field of appearances, the *phenomenal* reality of natural objects still being viewed as continuous with their causal reality.[7] For the symbolists, the impression was a collection of painted effects that stood for the synthesizing activity (consciousness) itself, or, what is the same, performed as the symbol, the unity, of an ideal coherence in reality and of ideal qualities in experience.[8]

In both schools, however, there were common factors that marked the early presence of certain modernist attitudes; the most important of these was the clear intent never to overlook the viewer's experience of the artwork, and also the explicit or implicit control of this experience achieved by the artist in manipulating "impressions."[9] The temporal nearness of the approaches of these schools to the sensory field contributed to hiding two widespread misconceptions about impressions:[10] that the impression is an imprint of an external stimulus on a receptive apparatus, and that sensations and impressions are two essentially different acts of apprehension.

Both of these misconceptions clouded statements by artists, critics, and philosophers. The various efforts in psychology and epistemology to be surveyed in what follows insisted that the "imprint" or "psychic matter," what is called the "stimulus" in empirical psychology, could not itself be an "object" of consciousness.[11] A conscious object is an inseparable mixture of the "psychic matter" and the "form" of the conscious response. The authority of Kantian critical philosophy had brought about a general recognition of sensory form in aesthetics as a cluster of spatiotemporal and affective properties, and perhaps of others as well (for example, differential and gestalt qualities).[12] The response itself, as a traditionally classified (i.e., perceptual, affective, imaginative, mnemonic, judgmental, or expressive) psychological intention, was precisely the "act" of consciousness. As such, the act could be abstracted (i.e., reflectively but not really separated) from conscious objects, because it remained implicit in the consciousness of them.[13]

It should be clear, then, that because psychic matter is not a conscious object, it is never perceived in itself (introspection is a questionable procedure at best) but only hypothetically described and measured by means of empirical models in science. The impression would emerge in aesthetic theory as a conscious object/act with greater or lesser spontaneity but always firmly distinguished from the idea of an imprint.

This conclusion clears the way for the resolution of the second misconception. Sensation and impression are not two different "acts" of apprehension but rather the same basic act. When a greater emphasis is placed on its empirical aspects in this study, this act will be called a "sensation"; and when a greater emphasis is placed on its synthetic and spontaneous aspects, it will be called an "impression."[14] As positivistic associationism was transcended in the last quarter of the nineteenth century, psychological and aesthetic theory discovered and emphasized *conscious* connections (including what is called the "unconscious" in psychoanalysis), not just among various apprehended qualities but also between the active stance of the whole sensibility (the body) and the *identical unities* of aesthetic or cognitive content that persist in the flux of our apprehensions and their contexts. Such conscious connections of objects to acts allow the objects, even at the sensory level, to become a clue, a *sign* (in the rising theoretical terminology), a structural stand-in for broadly conceived *ideal* contents. A repertory of such contents in modernism would include emotional, aesthetic, and moral qualities that were found to be as inherent in the experience of natural realities as they were in the existential and communicative experiences of human beings;[15] it would also include those consistent and recurrent aspects of phenomena because of which we talk about the "universally valid" meanings or truths that accompany the signifying presence of human reality in the world and, correspondingly, the dwelt-in character of the world itself.[16]

Whether they stood for the physical reality of natural things, for the harmony of an essential order that was said to permeate nature, or for the "spirituality" of the apprehending or expressive activity, impressions began to be understood at the onset of modernism as more than the individual effects of general causes. Artistic impressions in particular began to be treated first and foremost as *signs*, that is, as parts of experiential contexts more complex and encompassing than any representation and therefore subject to, as well as instruments for, the reading and interpretation of those contexts. However else the climate of modernism might be historically described, the centrality of these corrections and further definition of the idea of impressions for an understanding of the gradual overturning of traditional, nonlinguistic conceptions of human experience in general, and of art in particular, will be the key to modernism as a *period concept* explicated and applied in what follows.

THE REDEFINITION OF SENSATION:
PSYCHOLOGY AND EPISTEMOLOGY

It should be clear from the foregoing remarks that the concept of impression introduced in the preceding section is broader than the one that the impressionists themselves, or their critics and historians, could articulate. So understood, this concept encompasses a set of transformations of the reality and meaning of human experience that begins with the impressionists but that, as Pierre Francastel noticed, reaches down into the most diverse aspects of culture and to our own historical moment and beyond.

> Is Impressionism a fashion, a moment in the chain of forms that has no break in the centuries old cultural tradition of the Western world; or is it rather the rise of a style, the discovery, initially fragmentary, of a new mode of visual perception of the external world, a new analysis of optical sensations, a newly proposed field of sensory reflection for the spectator, and a problematic approach to the imaginative field? If one accepts the former, it is possible to think of an end of Impressionism; if the latter, these changes will be seen as *introducing a new type of signifying relations* if not at a world wide level at least at the level of what is conventionally called a civilization or culture.[17]

The depth of this transformation of the structure and function of the sensory field cannot be clearly established in all its scope and consequences by just looking at the progressive enrichment of the idea and the role of impressions in the special areas of science and theory that provided, still within the spirit of positivism or of its gradual replacement, a supporting and explanatory ground for art. Rather, to understand the newly emerging understanding of the sensory field as *the* medium of art, it is necessary to appeal to the clarification of the philosophical sense of this field, a clarification that, in the last quarter of the nineteenth century, took place ultimately in the context of psychological theory, since psychologism was precisely the philosophy (epistemology) of positivism.[18]

Such an appeal to psychology did not mean, however, that at this time changes in the explanation of the sensory field always took place within that science, nor that theoretical progress in the redefinition of the sensory field always needed to be causally legitimized by previous advances in the psychological theory of sensations. Psychology remained indeed more attached than aesthetics to the positivist principle that consciousness does not extend beyond sensations to the connections among them.[19] It would be more accurate to say that psychological explanations lagged behind, rather than that they preceded, advances in aesthetics.[20] Nevertheless, because psychological explanations of the changes in the theory of sensation provide the fullest understanding of those changes, I will summarize the pertinent psychological theories in this section before discussing the impression in aesthetics. Psychological redefinitions of the sensory field will be presented here more for their structural significance as parallels of aesthetic redefinitions than for their historical (causal) influence on the latter. Thus, such redefinitions will be available when the enrichment in the understanding of impressions in art theory and practice is surveyed in subsequent chapters.

Two remarks are in order here, before we discuss developments in late-nineteenth-century psychology concerning sensations and their relevance for art. First, changes in the psychology of sensations that emphasize their conscious character, both as single units and as complexes or conglomerates, will not generally occur in the field of psychology before similar changes in the field of aesthetics. Rather, in artistic theory in particular, to clear the way for their descriptions of the conscious depths of sensations (impressions), authors repeatedly must cut through the mechanistic prejudices of scientific psychology.

Second, even if psychologists and aestheticians themselves did not always fully realize this, to characterize sensations and other mental contents as "subjective" is to refer them to various kinds of *pure psychological activities of synthesis* rather than to the capabilities of a *substantial ego* (whether spiritual or material).[21] "Subjectivity" in the most clear-minded of these efforts, as in their counterparts in critical philosophy from Kant to Husserl, stood for a chain of conscious acts that were the strict correlates of conscious objects and propositions insofar as these were understood as *syntheses* rather than mere strings of associations.[22] The more these synthesizing acts were considered as powers of a substantial subject, the more they were made to fit within (reduced to) physiological or psychological teleologies. And, by contrast, the more this activity of consciousness was considered *in and by itself* as a phenomenon, the more its linguistic, that is, syntactical and semantical aspects, showed through together with those of the correlative conscious objects.

PSYCHOLOGICAL POSITIVISM: TAINE

Hippolyte Taine (1828–93) is generally identified with the denial of the conscious character of representational *syntheses*.[23] Taine would accept the phenomenal quality of elementary sensations (qualities such as color, extension, or touch), but he would claim that the integration of these into larger, meaningful units must be "factualized"—traced by observation to some regular tendencies or movements of the molecules of the nervous system:

> The words "faculty," "power," capacity," which have played so large a role in psychology are, we shall see, but convenient terms for gathering all the facts of a distinct kind into a distinct species. . . . Our major concern is to know what are the elements, how they are generated, in what ways and under what conditions they combine, and what are the constant effects of such combinations. Such is the method we have attempted to pursue in this work. In the first part, we have separated out the elements of cognition; by reduction after reduction we arrived at the simplest elements; then, we passed to the physiological changes which are the condition of their origin. In the second part, we have first described the mechanism and general effect of their combination.[24]

Taine was concerned both with the reductive analysis and with the synthesis of sensations, but as Sartre pointedly indicated in an insightful critique of the positivistic theory of the conscious image, for Taine "synthesis meant mere recombination."[25] Thus, when he confronted the active aspects of representation, Taine descended to the level of physiology:

> There is nothing real in the self save the series of occurrences. Of varying aspect, these are in their nature all alike, and can be reduced to sensation, which . . . reduces to a set of molecular motions.[26]

Mental images might exceed the level of "raw sensation," but they are reducible to "spontaneous repetitions of sensations."[27] And Sartre further noticed that Taine clung to the metaphysical point of view (a point of view the positivist was in principle bound to reject) by his all-embracing affirmation of an empirically unprovable postulate of the *double aspect of sensations*, that is, the axiom that "the physiological and the psychical are but two sides of the same reality."[28] This affirmation enveloped a contradiction that Sartre considered the Achilles' heel of the positivist: While the connections of images are, like all facts of consciousness, contingent, the connections of supporting molecular motions are, like all facts of nature, necessary; yet the latter was said to be apprehended by the former, the necessary by the contingent.

Several authors have noticed similar contradictions in Taine's professed integration of facts and laws, and in his use of idealist concepts in discussing the subject's contribution to art and history. Richard Shiff emphasized the ambiguities in Taine's characterization of the ideal: "Things pass from real to ideal when the artist reproduces them in modifying them according to his idea."[29] Ambiguities such as these arose for Shiff from the positivist unwillingness to "specify whether . . . the represented subject is a product of the artist's own particular experiences or somehow the essence of that subject itself."[30] Shiff seems to have been drawn by Taine's ontological haziness into attributing to him a recognition of genuine subjective life over and above basic sensations and the passive association of them. One must carefully guard against thinking that Taine could have acknowledged, under Hegel's influence, any active life of consciousness (spontaneous creative fantasies, for example).

Thus, to make Taine's position as clear as possible, one must point to his reduction of all elementary conscious units to their bare physical support through his postulate of the double aspect, physical and mental, of sensations, and also to his reduction of all complex levels of consciousness to effects of the three postulated universal and necessary causes: milieu, race and time.[31] With these reductions, truly autonomous consciousness was dissolved. As Ernst Cassirer has stated:

> The general causes, whose operation could always be demon-strated and which sufficed to explain every particular existence and development, were called by Taine the triad of race, milieu, time. The historian had done enough and completed his scientific task when he had succeeded in demonstrating the partici-pation of these three basic factors in all phenomena investigated. Thereupon an astonishing simplification appeared to have been reached: historical existence, so manifold at first glance, so het-erogeneous, so incalculably rich, revealed itself to the eye of the analyst as so simple and uniform that three concepts were enough to make it completely understandable.[32]

This exclusivist reductionism of the richness and variety of mental contents to three basic facts was the source of the bluntest attacks on Taine by his harshest critics:

> Taine's power of imagination saw [in his causes] something supposed to be original and supreme, but the critical mind knew nothing thereof, for critical thought requires that one should give reasons for the genesis of the facts or groups of facts that are called "century" and "race"; and in so doing at once make it clear that they cannot be either "universal" or "permanent," for so far as I know there are no universal and permanent "facts."[33]

For these reasons, it is not surprising that, in his later years, Taine became the straw man in the antimaterialist arguments of symbolist theoreticians.[34] Taine indeed left no room for any spontaneous con-scious activity for which noncontingent, logical, conscious wholes or essences, as well as linguistic or artistic formations, might stand as signs. It is important to emphasize in this respect that, in the general overturning and overcoming of positivism typical of the period dis-cussed here, the growing recognition of higher conscious activities did not result from the attribution of an enlarged role to an *introspec-tive faculty* that would put us immediately in touch with complex conscious activity. Introspection was widely used but, because of its privacy and relativity, never totally trusted in psychology. Instead, the wider acknowledgment of conscious activity and of its various levels depended increasingly on an implicit use of sign theory. Incipient as this theory might have been in the logic and linguistics of the time, it ultimately pointed to directly *intuited* objects and essential connections, and also to expressive and artistic realizations, as *signs of a free and spontaneous consciousness.*[35] Thus, a careful understanding of the use of the notion of *signs* in art theory must accompany the present study of the abrupt dissolution of the Cartesian separation of subject/object that was the consequence of the transformations of the notion of sensation in this period and would become the underlying and unifying feature of modernism. Indeed, the subject/object dichotomy was replaced in modernism by an expressive/conscious activity that, in its total immersion in world sense and in the sense of human life, social as well as personal, manifested with perfect immediacy both worldhood, not just nature, and persons in a fusion that was prior to the (representational) operation of traditional conceptual/perceptual habits and of conventional modes of artistic rendering.[36] It was at this level of fusion that Cézanne, as an initiator, placed himself.

PSYCHOLOGICAL ECLECTICISM: PSYCHOPHYSICS

The role of Gustav Theodor Fechner (1801–87) in the evolution of the psychology of sensation seems to have been equivocal. On the one hand, his *Elemente der Psychophysik*[37] opened the way to the mathematizing of psychology by establishing quantitative relations between "stimulus" and "sensation"; on the other, it can be said that, although correlated to the stimulus, the conscious contents of sensations, most importantly those contents that have aesthetic significance because they are accompanied by a special, nonutilitarian sense of pleasure, were no longer considered either copies of the stimulus or the immediate effects of it. In his *Vorschule der Ästhetik* of 1876,[38] instead of assuming a universal, whether factual or intellectual, definition of beauty, Fechner attempted to find experimental confirmation for the existence of "aesthetic feelings," which themselves would be primarily and distinctively characteristic of a realm of autonomous conscious activity.

He proposed several principles that could be taken as general criteria of distinctly aesthetic form, but as Katherine E. Gilbert and Helmet Kuhn point out in *A History of Aesthetics*,[39]

> Most of these are, however, broadly psychological rather than specifically aesthetic. They outline a psychology of mental activity in general and bear on aesthetic problems only in an indirect way.

Fechner's three supreme formal principles were (1) unified connection of the manifold of sensations; (2) consistency, that is, truth or agreement of the form with itself in its multiple presentations; and (3) clearness.

In contrast with Taine's positivistic stance, Fechner did not define his formal principles as translations into the psychological realm of any physical laws of motion of the organism. The positing of universal psychological causes of beauty would have been, for him, merely speculative and could not be subject to experimental confirmation, whether direct or indirect. Thus his principles were at best hypothetical postulations of a mental or spiritual sphere of energy whose existence and rules (i.e., the principles themselves) could be only indirectly confirmed. An indirect confirmation of aesthetically preferable ratios of dimension or division (for example, the 34:21 Golden Section over square and oblong shapes) involves the tacit recognition of two assumptions. First, as has been acknowledged by psychological theorists,

> Fechner does not contemplate any transmission of energy from the outer to the inner. The scale of changes in the outer sphere is and remains parallel to the scale of changes in the inner sphere.[40]

But this does not mean that the distinction between the spheres points to two incommunicable worlds. For Fechner, as G. S. Brett forcefully explains,

> In the end it may be true that inorganic, organic, plant, animal, man are all names for limitations; they may stand for divisions as artificial as the counties in a geographical map; nature may ignore them as the earth ignores its political boundaries.
>
> It is, therefore, not irrational to have more than one way of looking at things. . . . It is not irrational to co-ordinate the

psychical and the physical and yet maintain that the psychical is never wholly physical.[41]

Secondly, his methods of selection and construction of seemingly pleasant shapes, and of measuring manufactured objects used in daily life, all implied reports, on the part of the subjects of the experiments, about objects *as perceived.* The recognition of this fact forced Fechner to engage in considerations about the fate of elementary aesthetic forms when they enter into combinations with each other in larger aesthetically pleasing wholes. He faced this problem by pointing to the domination of a single form over a compound of elements, as a leitmotif dominates a musical score or a compositional scheme dominates an entire picture. In this way, aesthetically pleasing forms might preserve their values as aesthetic centers within complex wholes.

As soon as the perceptual whole was given a measure of unity and integrity *as perceived,* that whole began to be considered as the sign and bearer of meaning and of expressive intentions. It was not possible to say yet, as the psychology of empathy would eventually say, that the aesthetic whole constitutes an extension into nature of vital qualities of an embodied perceiver, but it was obvious that the psychophysical aesthetician, under the influence of the romantic postulate of the demonstrable continuity between natural and moral purposes,[42] was beginning to look in the perception itself for the grounds of a purposeful and qualitative equivalence or interchangeability between the perceived and the perceiver. As Gilbert and Kuhn pointedly noted:

> Contemplating some picture, we do not see merely a compound of particles of yellow, golden, and green color united into a certain shape, but we see a lemon. That is, the primary impressions are the carrier of a meaning. Owing, furthermore, to the connotations bound up with this particular fruit, its smell e.g. and the country of its origin, an expression may be embodied in the visual image. The lemon evokes the remembrance of a sky of dazzling blue, or dark foliage, of the charm of an Italian landscape. It has, to put in Fechner's own words, "mental color."[43]

The mystery of the *perceptual image*, as Fechner analyzed it with the help of mathematics and geometry, lay in the double direction in which the unification within it of sensations, concepts, words and expressive implications leads the viewer. On the one hand, the sensations in their different intensities and shapes seem to be harmonized, that is, given closure and distinctness, only as patterns confirmed by an aesthetic feeling that attests to their rightness and completeness *while being totally immersed in them*. This specifically aesthetic feeling, as buried in its correlative numbers and shapes, must be taken as the sign of a conscious activity or energy that cannot be reached directly; and it is as signs that numbers and shapes cease to be the iconic representatives of physical entities. The aesthetics of the period abounded in testimonies about the abstract signification precisely of the perceptual object. This abstract signification was increasingly seen as common to the percept, the concept, and the linguistic word; each in its own way was an accessible order, a pattern open to combination and rearrangement of its elements but that closed mysteriously upon itself as if motivated by an internal necessity. In the apparent arbitrariness of their opening and closing, as well as in the fact that they directly resembled neither things nor feelings, abstract patterns of perception/conception/language were said to share in the unique autonomy of musical form; that is, they signified only themselves, and did so as objects, not as acts within a universe of acts that would constitute objects within a lived world.[44]

On the other hand, in the process of perceptual experience, forms were coordinated with each other as expressive connotations. The "mental color" of a lemon was brought up as one of those connotations in the earlier example. When doubts began to arise concerning the sources of such coordination, Fechner responded by remaining at the level of "scientific" or experimental correlation. The continuous repetition and reinforcement of perceptual patterns within the perceiver's experience was ensured only by an additional objective principle, the "principle of association,"[45] which, like Fechner's other principles, must be subject to experimental confirmation. Thus the spanning and depth of the subjective or inner sphere were vouchsafed by a principle, association, for which one could find only signs in an analysis of perception. New postulations would be necessary to ground the functions of memory and creative imagination in the associative principle; this principle, with its automatism, would allow "associative energy" to reawaken or recombine images constantly sinking into unconsciousness.[46]

EMPATHETIC AND ABSTRACT PSYCHOLOGISM

The psychology of Fechner, with its precarious juxtaposition of elements of form and content, of synthetic units of extension, intensity, and recall, was widely influential not only in Germany but also in France and would constitute the underpinning for the most important aspects of symbolist poetics in literature, art, and music. Yet, because of the eclectic nature of their theoretical juxtaposition, the unity of the various components of the perceptual image cannot be explained within Fechner's approach. Gilbert and Kuhn clearly showed the extent of the inherent difficulties:

> The pleasure aroused by a simple form, for instance by a circle, is not a sum: the pleasure taken in the mathematical figure plus expressive value attributed to it by association. As object of aesthetic contemplation the circle is no longer the bare mathematical figure. Its roundness pleases because it is tinged, from the very outset, with specific expression attaching to things which are closed in themselves swinging round their own axis, self-sufficient. This expressiveness is not logically definable. It informs none the less the contemplated figure in a very distinct fashion. From Fechner's point of view, this phenomenon is unaccountable.[47]

The precarious coexistence of the elements of abstraction and association within Fechner's psychological theory of perception broke down in the last decade of the nineteenth century. Abstract perceptual patterns were increasingly considered signs connecting to form hypotheses, that is, *rules for the generalization or classification* of natural objects and facts. As such, these rules and generalizations had a syntactical or semantical role within the scientific methods of positivism, and thus the perceptual patterns that fell under them functioned as linguistic rather than sensorial wholes; encouraged by widespread perceptual experimentation, viewers and interpreters began to read, rather than grasp or "see," objects. Furthermore, because of its passivity, the principle of association came to be considered insufficient as the justification for the expressive accumulation of perceptual elements, that is, for the existence of a temporal depth in conscious experience that could somehow keep alive and resurrect receding or remote impressions and images.

To account for this survival and connotative overlap of images, the psychologism of the last years of the century utilized a notion of empathy that had roots in both evolutionary biology and subjective idealism. Emotional states that were previously understood to be correlated with particular intensities, qualities, and shapes in the presentation of things were now seen as infused into the things themselves, so that, as objects, realities were physiognomically molded by the characteristics of the emotion involved; hence later perceptions of objects thus penetrated and invested with emotions would bring about a recognition on the part of consciousness of the physiognomy of the invested object together with the affective charge attached to it.

The empathetic psychologism of, among others, Theodor Lipps in Germany and Victor Basch in France[48] had an interesting effect on the epistemology of perception that was, it should be remembered, brought about by the strictures of the positivists in reducing all consciousness to fact. Positivists had to struggle against their own postulates that forced them to acknowledge scientific (necessary) laws and stable percepts through the instrumentality of sensory (contingent) association, a paradoxical proposition that had burdened science from its very beginning. Zoology, ethnography, and scientific aesthetics had gradually transferred to the organic, subjective sphere the presence and stability of patterns; indeed, compared with the flux of sensory data and the instability of physical laws whose formulation was now subject to change with increasing rapidity, organic patterns of action and apprehension appeared to have a certain permanence, even if only on pragmatic grounds of adaptation.

In light of these facts the postulate of the necessity of natural laws finally collapsed. The selection of perceptual patterns manifesting physical objects and laws was seen in this school as having only a secondary pragmatic value linked to ordinary, habitual action and communication; hence the empathy psychologist began to look under them for perceptual images endowed with affective and expressive value that appeared to be much closer than ordinary perceptions to the stable purposes of the organism and hence to structure and type in reality. In short, the psychology of empathy gave rise, through its implicit recognition of the characteristic purposes and stability of the organic, to a privileging, unprecedented in its extent, of the affective and expressive object over the "abstract" object in perception. Such privileging of the affective and expressive object carried to the limit the signifying potential of the impression with respect to its synesthetic and kinesthetic links, and it granted to subjective responses a considerable measure of objectivity[49] that was not tied to the physical order of causes, as it was implicitly in psychophysics, but to a transcendent order that incorporated every possible mode of evolution and creativity, including moral and artistic creativity.

The consequences of this ascendancy of the affective, expressive side of the perceptual object could not be fully understood within psychologism, however. The psychology of the turn of the century in France, as represented by its most articulate spokesman, Théodule Ribot, was still subjectivistic about impressions and images. Both perceptual and imaginative objects continued to be for him mental representations, products of primary (impressions) and secondary (associations) forms of knowledge to which he now added, as an effect of evolution, the higher but unconscious mental activities of dissociation, apprehension of relations, and coordination (analysis and synthesis).[50] The more one ascended toward the higher analytic and synthetic objects, the more selective, arbitrary, and unreliable their contents and patterns would be.

There were, for Ribot, three levels of abstraction: (1) a lower level in which images of objects and other natural patterns such as simultaneity or succession are established with the help of metonymically connected signs but not words; (2) a secondary level in which the role of language in the determination of images emerges; and (3) a higher level where the image is totally replaced by words or sentences that stand alone as mental content or "representation." Paradoxically, these higher abstractions are no longer representable. The linguistic or theoretical third level helps circumscribe patterns and calculates their possible combinations and integrations, but it does not add any certainty to them; rather, in condensing and freezing the flow of observable data, this level of abstraction may help contrive artificial patterns without any verifiable connection with reality.

In his mistrust of abstraction, Ribot came close to romantic idealism and to empathetic theory by considering representations always to be a part, while experience (which for him, however, must be limited to the perceptual level) was the whole:

> L'abstrait est un cadavre. Il serait moins pittoresque, mais plus juste de dire un squelette; car une abstraction scientifique est la charpente osseuse des phénomènes. Donc, au fond, l'antagonisme de l'image et de l'idée, c'est celle du tout et de la partie.[51]

Science, "the abstract skeleton of the phenomena," was thus inadequate because of its incompleteness and lack of novelty and freshness. Nevertheless, Ribot criticized idealism and empathy because the higher experiences that they claimed to be able to enter into and define were backed only by vague emotions and pantheistic suppositions. In his view, the affective and expressive images that they appealed to (those that were so common in symbolist literature and art) were also abstractions; they were realized by evocation and suggestion and gave access not to evident objects but only to foreshadowings or adumbrations.

Searching for perceptual immediacy, Ribot concluded that this evidential quality could be found in the plastic images of the man of imagination, the artist. Plastic imagination was the only experience

> qui a pour caractères propres la netteté et la précision des formes—plus explicitement: celle dont les matériaux son des *images* nettes (quelle qu'en soit la nature) se rapprochant de la perception, donnant l'impression de la réalité, et où prédominent les *associations à rapports objectifs*, déterminables avec précision . . . c'est une imagination *extérieure*, issue de la sensation plus que du sentiment et qui a besoin de s'objectiver.[52]

Plastic imagination and its objects eventually became a feature in Cézanne and, through his example, in the modernists, whose will to believe in higher levels and contents of consciousness required the support of clear presences and of animated (action motivated), rather than merely expressive, symbols. In the philosophy of perception and mind, these attitudes central in Cézanne and the modernists would be paralleled and given a solid intellectual grounding by the greatest innovator of philosophical thought in those changing times: Henri Bergson.

As can be gathered from the foregoing survey, the rival psychological schools of the end of the nineteenth century, one centered on empathy and the other on abstraction, made considerable advances in the clarification of the contents of human experience and of its inherent modalities of evidence. Nevertheless, psychologism, in its double form, separated from each other crucial elements of experience and left experience hopelessly divided. In the course of the development of psychologism, the focus of this clarification of experience was the sensory field, because late-nineteenth-century culture was more concerned with facts than with methods or intellectual constructions. But as the process of clarification advanced, the emphasis, while still centered on immediate experience, gradually shifted, as noted above, from sensations and impressions to perception. And thus it was the understanding of perception, the keystone of consciousness and mind, that suffered most from the antinomies of psychological analysis.

On the one hand, the school of empathy moved beyond the study of psychophysical correlations (which were measurable, but tenuous and arguable because of the subjective reports on which they were founded) to a totally *objective* grounding of the expressive and emotive qualities of the perceptual image in the detailed investigations of zoology and ethnography. The synthetic and temporal depths of consciousness were thus extended from consciousness itself to the depths of nature, yet they were kept near the surface, in the perceptual object and in the bodily interaction of perceiver and perceived, where they could be neatly delimited and observed. Unfortunately, the more any scientific examination transcended specific biological functions and narrowly conceived cultural institutions, the more these observations and the corresponding images became vague and bound to postulated (subjective) forms of emotion and will.

On the other hand, the school of abstraction had changed considerably from its positivist antecedents. Contrary to them, it admitted of necessary synthetic forms and functions that were now said to accompany contingent association and to be apparent even at the perceptual level, where they granted perceptual objects a precision, solidity and "classic"[53] presence that they could not have had under positivist rules. Unfortunately, for abstraction, the perceptual object still remained a *subjective* representation, and was very shallow affectively, temporally, and reflectively, because further increases in abstraction only led, according to this school, to the formation of linguistically readable and mathematically controllable tokens whose general significance as theories could not be assessed, and whose applicability to the flow of experience would become questionable.

Psychologism, in both of its forms, sundered experience. In empathy, as has been noted, it preserved the unity of object and subject at the perceptual level, but it gave access to a tenuous higher subjective level, emotion and imagination, that could not be truly continuous with the first and had little more consistency than do healthy or unhealthy hallucinations. In abstraction, all experience is subjective. It is true that the resulting artificiality and formalism in this attitude were remedied in part by the poetic richness of images and by the logical manipulability of concepts, but pragmatic expediency of either kind did not compensate in the end for the sense of loss of reality, even in perception, and for the ultimate disorientation in which higher levels of theoretical abstraction were sunk.

The fragmentations of experience created by psychologism arose from an inability, traceable to the scientific method, to distinguish between introspection and reflection. Observation, whether external or introspective, takes consciousness away from activity and places it in images alone, because, as a method, it can perceive activity only when it is graphically or diagrammatically measured—that is, only in and as image. In empathy, the activity traced is evolution, and to attribute *significance* other than chance to such processes, this school had to assume (circularly, no doubt, given the increasingly higher spheres of being to be reached) emotive and expressive purposefulness in images as an equivalent of consciousness within the observed changes. In abstraction, the activity traced is always the physical work of organs, nerves, or brain that is both internally and externally observed through association of sensations. The associating *act* itself is contingent at its base and unconscious at its higher levels.[54] Thus postulated higher syntheses, such as the artistic and theoretical ones, have, *as forms and images*, no adequate motivation in action and must be supplemented by an extrinsic arbitrary act identified as convention. Such motivation makes the higher images less than necessary because of their relativity and less than *significant* because, in the end, those images are justified only by the existence of merely instinctive, basically mechanical, actions.

THE BERGSONIAN SYNTHESIS

It was the great contribution of Henri Bergson (1859–1941) to place consciousness back within activity[55] and to reconcile conscious action with the consciousness of images at all possible levels of experience; in so doing, he automatically ascended from introspection to reflection, and from stale epistemological justification of scientific practices and objects to an exploration and justification, not only inquisitive but performative in the brilliance of his own writings, of spiritual freedom and creativity.

Bergson and Cézanne can be said to have embodied, each in his own way, the metaphysics of modernism. As will be shown below, for both men metaphysics was not an esoteric dwelling on vague or mystical emotions and aspirations but an explication *through images*, that is, *through significant forms*, of the fusion of subject and object—namely, of the *dwelt-in* character of "world" as space and the narrative *value* of personal "existence" as time. In Bergson and, as will be shown later, in Cézanne as well, this justification could be said to emerge not only through the images but *in the images themselves*, which, as the philosopher explained them, *constitute the significant limit of* a *world* otherwise unlimited and *the fabric of* a *subjective existence* otherwise buried in the consuming depths of creative evolution.[56] Bergson made possible this theoretical transition from introspection to reflection by firmly placing consciousness among the properties of action as a form of tension that is at the same time attention and intention. It is attention, *attention à la vie*, in its concentration upon itself; it is intention in its direction toward objects or images. The concentration of action is duration or time as *projection,* which gathers the totality of an action or of an integrated set of actions in a span that flows from the projected future to the present; concentration is also duration as *memory*, which recovers images dropping, or dropped, from active attention to provide support to, and express, *dynamic schemata,* that is, projects of action that are virtual because of their transcendence of simpler actions and are therefore gathered in a temporal span that flows from the past to the present. It must be understood that duration is not a succession of separable moments or stages; instead, its concentration is such that the three phases of temporality—present, future, and past—and all of their possible divisions as well, interpenetrate each other in ways that the discontinuous presence of objects can neither match nor duplicate.

For Bergson, emotion, reflection, and intuition represented not additional faculties but strictly three different sides or components of attentive action. A summary of their meaning and role in his philosophy constitutes therefore a summary of his entire thought. As he painstakingly showed in *Time and Free Will*,[57] emotion is the quality, not quantity, of attention (duration) either as *projective* or as *recollective*. This psychic quality of attention is related to objects, not by being stirred or prompted by them but by attention's capacity for calling for, *and gathering*, appropriate equivalents in sensation and image, in action, in gesture, and in word. For Bergson, therefore, emotion, especially at the highest levels, is never vague, because in its intimate connection with action it is tied to very specific creative choices of action in the social, expressive, and moral realms. The kinds of emotion caused by things, or, as he said, "prefigured" in things, are very limited in number and always incline us to act toward the satisfaction of an urgent need; by contrast, emotions at the higher level of action "are real *inventions*, comparable to those of the musician." [58]

There are two reasons, very distinctive of and important within Bergson's philosophy that keep the reflective character of action from being confused with introspection. The first is that for Bergson images are not just *of* things but *in* things. Images are selective, abstract aspects of *events* (for him, *things* was only a commonsense name for events) attached to concentrated action upon an environment. The difference between perceptual, imaginative and memory images lay not in the images themselves but in their relations to immediate and habitual action (perception), virtual or projected action (imagination), and the totalization of existence (memory).

Thus, images never are nor can be, nor can they be represented or stored, *in a place other* than the world. They cannot be had or stored in the brain, because the brain is only afferent and efferent, strictly a conductor/selector of nerve impulses, and therefore a facilitator of choices and their application to impending courses of action. Nor can images be in the sensory organs, because these are just receptors of various impulses to be translated into nervous impulses. Finally, images cannot be placed in a postulated spiritual mind that would be their proper medium, because, for Bergson, mind is never anything other than action.[59]

Images could remain the subject of attention over the entire course of a human life if they were not neglected by brain activity in favor of objects of immediate concern for attention. Bergson pointed to cases of vivid predeath recall of a life course in full detail, a recall that might have some analogies with artistic creation. Images, when not attended to, return thus to the human environment and are kept there either in the form of objects of common use, or as signs, documents, and works, or as a part of the human body, *which is itself an image, the most central and resourceful of all.*

It is possible, then, after consideration of the relations between images and action, to state the second reason why reflection cannot be identified with introspection in Bergson: Action, he frequently claimed, grasps itself only in *actual, habitual, and virtual operation* (these straightforward characterizations of types of action that have already been mentioned will be fully clarified in the discussion of Bergson's theory of images that completes this section). It should be clear now that reflection, as *consciousness of action*, can never truly be the transformation of action into an image that could be then observed through introspection. It can be concluded therefore that if reflection is not a diversion of attention from an external to an internal space, it must occur not in space but in time: It can be defined only as the depth of attention, that is, as either projective or recollective duration.

These ideas lead directly to understanding Bergson's notion of intuition, the third major component or aspect of action. Intuition is action that, in its reflective attention, is empathetically tuned to the activity/passivity of events in the environment. Bergson vigorously protested against romantic and symbolist considerations of intuition as instinctive, emotional, and therefore irrational:

> Thus I repudiate facility. . . . How could certain people have mistaken my meaning? To say nothing of the kind of person who would insist that my 'intuition' was instinct or feeling. Not one line of what I have written could lend itself to such an interpretation. And in everything I have written there is assurance to the contrary: my intuition is reflection.[60]

The insistence on the reflective nature of intuition is of great importance in Bergson's work because, as a form of concentration (self-constitution) of action, intuition is *choice*, the choice of the multiplicity of components of projected action that can extend to the entire course of a life and also the choice of their order and orientation on the basis of their relative importance. This choice should not be arbitrary, and the above clarification from the author was meant to ensure this; also, it is not based on conjecture but instead on a submission to goals and values that is guided by life itself from the richness of its temporal experience.

The other side of intuition is, of course, the choice of images, a selection that at the most basic sensory levels amounts to *forming from the flux of cosmic energy*, and holding on to, the appropriate image to be attached to the intention of an action and thus directing it to its most urgent goals. From this understanding of the active core of the presence of images, Bergson anticipated the phenomenological insight that intuition is constitution; this insight brought about the final downfall of the empiricist understanding of sensation/perception, that commonly accepted conglomerate of the simplest units (data) of passively held presence, which had led to the Kantian denial of intellectual intuition in humans and to the consequent isolation of subject from world. Therefore, for Bergson, the conscious image could not be a *correlate* (either subjective or transcendental) *of* the interaction of perceiver and perceived; it was instead the immediate *field* created by that interaction, which is always immersed in it and thereby also in the environment itself.

From this perspective, it is possible also to understand that peculiar character of intuition as a seeing of things from the inside. The placement of intuition inside of things from its very start originates in this doctrine from the interpenetration, typical of interaction, between perceiver and perceived, in the course of which, as in Merleau-Ponty's famous example of the hand touching the hand, each takes alternatively and repeatedly an active and a passive role, so that the sensory (passive) and the motor (active) aspects of the action become interchangeable as they accumulate.[61] In its immersion in interaction, the intuited image *presents*, rather than represents, *the thing* (event) *from inside its own formative growth as an image*.

Two brief quotes can summarize this doctrine of intuition, which was so momentous for modernist aesthetics and paralleled Cézanne's theory of images to be explained in the chapters 4 and 5. The first quote, from Bergson, explains ontologically the ambiguity, the double root, of the intuitive image:

Spirit borrows from matter the perceptions on which it feeds,
and restores them to matter in the form of movements which it
has stamped with its own freedom.[62]

The second quote, from Ian Alexander's lucid book *Bergson,* explains
in clear technical language (which should be useful also in the analysis of Cézanne's theory of images) the ontological difference and
unity of subject and world in Bergson:

The 'subject' is the world in-tended and re-flected, the 'object' is
this re-flection ex-tended and pro-jected.[63]

This summary of Bergson's thought on the constitutive properties of action (viz., emotion, reflection, and intuition) has revealed
much about the nature of images (including the body image) and
their place, which is also the place of the subject, in the world. The
more explicit discussion of his theory of images that follows must
consider in fuller detail the classification of images in relation to the
modalities of action mentioned earlier. It must also be concerned
with the function of images in differentiating the structure of space
(which, as will be explained shortly, when separated from time con-
forms to the tactile, abstract, and metonymic potentialities of the
image) from the structure of time (which when united to space con-
forms to its visual, empathetic, and metaphoric potentialities). A
third and most important aspect of the discussion is the function of
images within Bergson's thought about significance—that is, the
meaning of meaning and its need for expression.

Two cautions about this brief survey of Bergson's theory of
images, which is so important for understanding parallel theories in
modernism and particularly in Cézanne: First, no effort will be made
in it to criticize the foundation or the logic of Bergson's arguments.
Whatever their empirical or logical weaknesses, in part rooted in the
controversy with the psychologism of empathy and abstraction from
which the doctrine originated, it will soon be seen that, when applied to aesthetics, the doctrine has intuitive and explanatory strengths
that do not easily yield to censure because of difficulties it may have
brought about in the explanation of other areas of consciousness.[64]
Second, some of the vocabulary and perspectives, particularly those
on signs and meaning explicitly used here because of their affinities

with present-day concerns, were only implicit in Bergson, whose treatment of aesthetics was always incidental to direct discussions of psychological, ontological, and moral topics. On the other hand, Bergson's use of the image in his thought was not just illustrative and didactic, as it was for major recent philosophers (e.g., Husserl, Heidegger, and Wittgenstein) whose concerns moved directly between perception and conceptualization/language. For Bergson perception and images were closer to intuition and duration, and therefore more central to experience, than linguistic and logical concepts would be. In this respect he qualifies as *the* philosopher of the image and consequently as the most pointed and relevant guide for contemporary aesthetics.

The key to the development of images as explained in the early chapters of *Matter and Memory* is the hypothetical introduction of two states of attention that can never occur in and by themselves: pure perception and pure memory. Between these two hypothetical states, Bergson placed memory images and perceptions, the only truly (re)presentational states of consciousness he accepted; all others either are reducible to these or are not (re)presentational. A pure perception would be an image of an event produced by an interaction of subject/event if the interaction could be hypothetically frozen and stopped in an extended present. This, of course, is impossible; because of the interpenetration of energy, all action is a continuous flow occurring partly in the future, partly in the present, and partly in the past. As for pure memory, it would be pure motor energy devoid of any sensory accompaniment. This is also impossible as long as there are in the world beings whose organically based capacity for choice allows them to interact with the environment by projecting their actions into it. Indeed, sensory images are but the tools or extensions of projection that develop in the interface of free (projectable) and contingent (cosmic) action.

Thus, because interactions between sustained and contingent actions take place constantly, sensory images would literally float and randomly reoccur in the flux of enduring energy. What prevents this randomness and transforms images into perceptions is the attentive accumulation of memory images upon sensations in the interest of the formation of complex projects of action. A developing "dynamic schema" of images, gestures, words, or other symbols makes possible the correlative growth of a "corporeal schema" of integrated motor impulses that in turn brings about the *realization*—that is the inscription or reinscription—of the images or symbols in the environment. What the images themselves bring about is the distribution of the motor impulses in a lived space, an antepredicative, concrete, and qualitatively diversified extension (Bergson called it "extensity") that should not be confused with amorphous, inert, representational space.

The convergence of dynamic schema and corporeal schema can become habitual when certain groups of images are mechanically reactivated for the sake of instinctual or routine practical concerns. But it can also become creative, in a very basic sense, when a perceiver succeeds in liberating natural images from their attachment to habitual action and thus recovers their spontaneity and freshness within lived experience. Fresh images are animated by an upsurge of spontaneous emotion in the corporeal schema and are therefore poetic in the simplest acceptance of this term.

The liberation of images from habitual action can lead to the artistic liberation, the intensification of emotions, as was the practice in symbolist art and poetry;, or it can be accomplished in order to recover, in regaining a sense of seemingly lost reality, the plastic perception that Ribot praised in the artist and that Bergson himself thought most characteristic of the relation of art to creative intuition. It is clear then that the liberation of emotion infuses new, fresh images, and their eventual interpretation, with empathetic significance, but because the focus at this level of personal reflection or of normal or repressed communication[65] is still on the process of liberation from straightforward habitual action, and because, as Ribot clearly pointed out, the emotions arising in this process are themselves vague and abstract in spite of the fact that they can be very intense, it must be concluded that, within these most basic of images, empathy is always subordinated and instrumental to abstraction.

In Bergson two types of poetic images break away from natural ones. Here we will give the label *symbolic* to those that accentuate emotion, whether fresh or repressed, and *plastic* to those that are the product of perceptual experimentation in which new patterns of perception, as well as a vocabulary of (re)presentational signs, gestures, or words/sounds to match these new perceptions, are "discovered."

It is important to notice also that, at this level, images are formed by contiguous accumulation of the inscribing action, as a line drawn in pencil juxtaposes in simultaneity the successive moments of the action of drawing. These images enter into living space along a metonymic axis or axis of combination.[66] A metaphoric substitution can already take place here, since an image can substitute itself for the concomitant action as a sign of it, but the reason for this exchange is the constant metonymic conjunction of action/image; therefore, in these basic poetic images the metaphoric axis is still subordinated to the metonymic. This early prevalence of contiguity leads to a selection and arrangement of the materials of images that, even when it is visual in its control over distances, approaches the patterning and the limitations of the tactile. The privileging of the metonymic and the tactile in basic projects of action manifests itself in Bergson's law of the correlation of action and perception regarding their free and spontaneous development:

> In a word, the more immediate the reaction is compelled to be, the more must perception resemble a mere contact. . . . But in the measure that the reaction becomes more uncertain and allows more room for suspense, does the distance increase at which the animal is sensible of the action of that which interests it. By sight, by hearing, it enters into relation with an ever greater number of things, and is subject to more and more distant influences . . . whatever be the inner nature of perception, we can affirm that its amplitude gives the exact measure of the indetermination of the act which is to follow. So that we can formulate this law: *perception is the master of space in the exact measure in which action is master of time.*[67]

If we translate this law in terms that might help us comprehend the expanding function of images in this theory, it would be appropriate to say that our survey of images in Bergson has reached a stage in which freedom can make possible the expansion of a dynamic schema of images up to the envisioning of the limits of the entire world, and freedom can make equally possible the expansion of a corporeal schema of actions up to the temporal boundaries of an entire project of life.

In the above analysis of the transformation of natural into basic poetic (whether *symbolic* or *plastic*) images, the *realization* (selection and inscription) process is still tied to the contingencies of evolution and organic need, except for the fact that the discovered images acquire a certain qualitative fixity connected with the *essential* novelty and concentration of the related emotion. This emotion indeed gains an existential/temporal *distance from contingency* in accordance with Bergson's "law" or principle of indetermination cited above.

Do these facts mean that the principal function of art for Bergson was the establishment and expression of high emotions? This question has often been answered affirmatively by friends and foes of the philosopher who noticed above all his organicism and what they thought was a Rousseauistic, optimistic outlook concerning the effects of freedom in society. Those critics, who linked him favorably or unfavorably to romanticism, were unable to recognize the tendencies in his theory toward a qualified modernist "elitism" of the artist, the sage, and the saint. However, the most important point regarding his aesthetics is that, beyond the emotions, it was concerned with the explication of the depths of time and meaning, and followed, *without abandoning the perceptual, imaginative, and emotional planes* in which it is firmly planted, the path toward the realization and presentation of higher levels of temporality and significance.

The new perceptions and emotions "discovered" or "found" by reformers of perception, particularly the artists, constituted in accordance with the above analysis a vocabulary of visible signs, gestures or sounds for actions that attempted to break away from the mechanical and habitual accomplishment of basic intentions. Yet, as long as such attempts remained themselves experimental, the essential unity and completeness of the discovered images was merely formal and depended still, at a nonformal level, upon the regularities of habit and ultimately upon the contingencies, the infinite possibilities of synthesis of natural energy. The potentialities of free action remained thus, at the edge of the world, infinitely multipliable but unintegrated and incoherent. In and by themselves, the basic images, gestures, and words that accompany such free actions constituted a wonderful vocabulary for a language that, like the purely relational "systems" of signs that were soon to emerge in linguistics, existed only to multiply itself, hence only to speak, or "write," itself.

Thanks to art, however, the realm of significance can be found to extend even farther, and a new species of images that contain and express these farther reaches of significance takes its place *in* the world. As will be shown below, the action and the images that lie open this realm of significance are not just at the edge of the world, they are the edge of a proper world—of a bound, perspectively oriented, and qualitatively differentiated spatiotemporal world. The poetic value of the world thus bound justifies a painstaking study, long as it may be, of the next two types of images to be found in Bergson's work. As Alexander states, in Bergson "the problem of art is, in fact, to infuse into disconnected symbols mental duration."[68] Sustained artistic intentionality and art "making" meant for him more than the addition of different events, or marks, or signs onto nature (more than imitating nature); they meant sustained concentration on *virtual* action, that is, on an intention/action relation that surpasses, in the making of a work, even the experimental transcending of the purposes of instincts and habits.

If the terminal effect of transcendence was merely to "find" new actions and new images and expressions for them, no ontological difference would exist between the still-contingent realm of basic poetic perceptions and images, on the one hand, and the higher purposes of art, on the other. What distinguishes the higher realm of art making from the intoxicating bursts of inspiration typical of the basic discovery of new perceptions and emotions is more than its initial detachment from the habits and instincts of natural and conventional life. Because of a generalized oversimplification of the ideas of mimesis and expression, the aesthetics and criticism of the turn of the century mistakenly believed that such detachment did not exist in traditional allegorical or realistic art; thus many voices were raised calling for pure art, dehumanization, and other formulas to produce aesthetic distance from life. For Bergson, as for Rilke a few years later, such detachment should not be brought about by disposing of life or by substituting travesties of it in its place; instead, what was needed was *a reflective-productive absorption of the widest possible rhythms and intentions of life in and through time.*

In *Matter and Memory*, the liberation of perception and emotion from the urgent activities and the habits of ordinary life is, in the end, positively brought about through a very disciplined and very difficult process of (1) dissociation of movement from quantity and (2) the consequent intuition of *movement as quality*. Through this process, (3) a true understanding of the *spatiotemporal* unity and *totality* of the rhythms of action and (4) an understanding of time itself as a *qualitative variety of rhythms of duration* finally become possible. In such a difficult endeavor, art and ethics can exercise a guiding role for science and philosophy, both of which would, without their help, fall prey to the quantitative, homogeneous, undifferentiated "perception" and imagining of space, time, and quality that result from habitual action.

The main intent of *Time and Free Will* was to help the person biased by the modes of experiencing qualities fostered by modern mechanistic philosophy to understand that the *intensity* associated with the perception of a quality in this (and in common sense) philosophy is not an effect of physical causes; *it is the quality itself.* By separating intensity from quantity in *Matter and Memory*, the philosopher dissociates intensive qualities (color, figure, solidity, etc.) from geometrical extension and attaches them to "extensity," that is, to the mixture of duration, purpose, and freedom that make up the consistency and virtual reach of an action.

Bergson was fully aware of the demands that these radical adjustments would impose on ordinary perception. He called them "the *turn* of experience," and to correct our point of view he insisted, as Ribot had earlier, on the symbolic and diagrammatic rather than empirical, the conceptual rather than truly perceptual, character of mechanistic space, time, and sense data.

> Certainly, it would be a chimerical enterprise to try to free ourselves from the fundamental conditions of external perception. But the question is whether certain conditions, which we usually regard as fundamental, do not rather concern the use to be made of things. . . . More particularly, in regard to concrete extension, continuous, diversified and at the same time organized, we do not see why it should be bound up with the amorphous and inert space that subtends it—a space which we divide indefinitely, out of which we carve figures arbitrarily, and in which movement itself, as we have said elsewhere, can only appear as a multiplicity of instantaneous positions. . . . It might, then, be possible, in a certain measure, to transcend space without stepping out from extensity.[69]

This retreat from biases in perception opened the doors of experience and lay before the perceiver the full reach of visibility or circumspection. The viewer proceeds here from *tactile vision*, with its modulations and modeling of near and remote objects as fields of crafty manipulations, to a *visual vision* that ranges in its freedom over all the actions a newly created action encompasses. But visual vision is not just a panorama; it is the experience of *extensity as articulated by a free combination of actions* in which spatiality (i.e., the territory of our habits) has been transcended.

There will be emotion connected with this transcendence, but an emotion that is itself invented, immersed in the created actions and in the works that orient them.

> Thus mountains may, since the beginning of time, have had the faculty of rousing in those who looked upon them certain feelings comparable with sensations, and indeed inseparable from mountains. But Rousseau created in connection with them a new and original emotion. This emotion has become current coin, Rousseau having put it into circulation. And even today it is Rousseau who makes us feel it, as much and more than the mountains. True, there are reasons why this emotion, sprung from the heart of Jean-Jacques, should fasten on to mountains rather than any other object; the elementary feelings, akin to sensations, which were directly aroused by mountains must have been able to harmonize with the new emotion. But Rousseau gathered them together, gave them their places, henceforth as mere harmonics in a sound for which he provided, by true creation, the principal tone.[70]

If before these changes in our understanding the biases in our perception forced us to immobilize qualities and to "see" mobility as attached to separate bodies in space, our education in spatiotemporality would lead, as indicated above, to the *realization* of the constant *mobility of qualities* and of the qualitative character of all motion as the *change of state of an active whole*. The philosopher then proposed a series of perceptual variations in which he explored the consequences of changes in the spans of duration related to ordinary action and considered the consequences of such a change on sensations.

If two colors appear irreducible in one of our moments in which we grasp billions of vibrations that they execute, would we not, if we lived at a slower pace, "see these colors pale and lengthen into successive impressions, still colored, no doubt, but nearer and nearer to coincidence with pure vibrations?"[71] And conversely, a division of an act and of the interval of attention that goes with it may quicken the circulation of phenomena, yet the perceiver will remain behind in counting the millions of appearances that overrun the act of attention. On the other hand, could not a mind of greater concentration than ours "watch the development of humanity while contracting it . . . into the great phases of its evolution?" Such variations in attention are not, however, hypothetical:

> Do we not sometimes perceive in ourselves, in sleep, two contemporaneous and distinct persons, one of whom sleeps a few minutes, while the other's dream fills days and weeks?[72]

Now that he had educated perceivers in controlling the synthesis of space, time, and sensation, Bergson entices them to a spatiotemporal experiencing of the objects of the human environment "at long, very long, intervals, and by as many leaps over enormous periods of the inner history of things." Such views "are bound to be pictorial" and their most vivid colors "will condense an infinity of elementary repetitions and changes." His conclusion was that this constructive serialization of controlled views would have a decisive effect on our familiar conception of the things themselves and of their relation to their environment:

> That there are, in a sense, multiple objects, that one man is distinct from another man, tree from tree, stone from stone, is an indisputable fact; for each of these beings, each of these things, has characteristic properties and obeys a determined law of evolution. But the separation between a thing and its environment cannot be absolutely definite and clear-cut; there is a passage by insensible gradations from the one to the other: the close solidarity which binds all the objects of the material universe, the perpetuality of their reciprocal actions and reactions, is sufficient to prove that they have not the precise limits which we attribute to them.[73]

A disciplined perception that has passed through all of these stages is capable of perceptual-intuitive awareness, *in each of the serialized experiences*, of the totality of the world as an integrated articulation of the achieved perceptual variations. The world will no longer be experienced as simultaneous and successive extension, but as a continuity that moves qualitatively as a whole with every step taken in the integration of its parts:

things wear a very different aspect when we pass from . . . the abstract study of motion to a consideration of the concrete changes occurring in the universe. Though we are free to attribute rest or motion to any material point taken by itself, it is nonetheless true that the aspect of the material universe changes, that the internal configuration of every real system varies, and that here we have no longer the choice between mobility and rest. . . . We may not be able to say what parts of the whole are in motion; motion there is in the whole, nonetheless.[74]

It can thus be said in summation that the experience of Bergsonian extensity is characterized by *its bringing the totality of the world upon every situation in which a new "qualitative perspective" is achieved;* the world totalized in this manner is the unity of the continuous series of its previous "presentations" with the added awareness that, with the inclusion of the new actions and works, the emerging whole can no longer be evolving in the same direction nor present the same aspect.

Because of the recollective and virtual unification of earlier action and images in the projection and creation of new ones, the images that are produced at this level of experience can properly be called "contemplative" even though there is no room in Bergson's psychology for a pure imaginative viewing that is not attached to one form of action or another. This understanding of *contemplative* images emphatically indicates the importance of art, for Bergson, for the creation of new meaning *in* the world; it is also in perfect accord with his theory of "universality" and "individuality" of concepts and terms or, what is the same, with his explanation of the intersection of the metonymic and metaphoric axes of synthesis of signs.

It is necessary to understand the peculiar way in which these axes intersect in Bergson in order to achieve a logical clarity, consistent with his metaphysics of things, about the derivative nature of the "singular concrete" and the "universal abstract" meanings of identity that constitute the basis of our biased logic and of our biased seeing. Together with a sense of the importance of the role of the artwork in logic, we gain in this context an insightful approach to the *contemplative* image, a key image in modernist abstract, as well as expressionist, form, as *an ideal typical unity constituted by the intersection between the concerns of action and the concerns of the dream.*

In explaining the formation of these images, Bergson begins with his previous characterization of the image as arising from action and preserved in the world confronted by complex or virtual actions. In relation to the needs of action, images acquire a brute identity that gathers the same aspects as correlative to the same needs. This identity, neither universal nor individual, is the product of an "association of simplicity," the one that gives animals the color and smell of grass *in general* or, as he says, "experienced as forces (we do not go so far as to say, thought as qualities or as genera)."[75] Such brute images are the components of the field of pure memory, alluded to earlier as a purely hypothetical one, still in need of clarification. This field indeed is the world of humans as a collection of raw images that would remain so except for their unbroken connection to habitual or virtual actions[76] that are always in progress.

The spectrum of these actions determines the gradual emergence of the reflective identity of images. At the most basic level, beyond the hypothetical one already indicated, is found the plane of dreams. Here the urgency of the needs is relaxed and the motor impulses are merely inchoative; memory is close to complete recall, as in the life of the primitive and the child. Bergson cites in this connection the example of the astonished missionary in seeing his long sermon repeated to the last detail in word and gesture by the local peoples.[77] Curiously, images that had no individuality when related to common pragmatic need subsequently acquire a strange and peculiar identity when placed in a long sequence of contiguous events such as a dream, or in the "search for lost time," to use the Proustian terms for our reactivation of memory. At the other extreme, actions are automatic or habitual; here association and recall are barely necessary, because only one or a handful of narrowly focused images are connected with habits.

But Bergson claims that these two planes are themselves close to hypothetical existence. Actions that are properly human always combine the perspectives of both planes in an infinite variety of degrees, and *contemplative* images arise from such combinations:

> It would seem, then, that we start neither from the perception of the individual nor from the conception of the genus, but from an intermediate knowledge, from a confused sense of the *striking quality* or of resemblance: this sense, equally remote from generality fully conceived and from individuality clearly perceived, begets both of them by a process of dissociation.

Reflective analysis clarifies it into the general idea; discrimina-
tive memory solidifies it into a perception of the individual.[78]

Our images, then, first have a confused, *contemplative*, intermediate
identity, while logical identity, individuality in the percept and universality in the concept, arise subsequently from a reflective process.
In the above quotation, Bergson calls that process "reflective dissociation"; thus we come to understand the gradual sedimentation that
settles on any one of the possible intermediate *contemplative* images,
and in relation with it on an entire series of them, as a converse
process of *reflective association* that Bergson opposes to the contingent and, to him, inexplicable associations of the positivists. Because
they are formed by a dissociation whose end can be controlled, the
universal idea and the individual image are fixed and can be used in
the stable articulation of signs and language. On the other hand, the
general, *contemplative* image is for Bergson both evanescent and personal, and "goes on indefinitely without ever reaching its goal."[79]

Reflective association can thus settle on or create different degrees of similarity, all of them analogical rather than identical; it can
also settle on or create narrower or broader combinations by contiguity. In both cases similarity and contiguity work together, showing
their common reflective origin. When general images are closer to
action and the tactile, "contiguity tends to approximate to similarity
and to be thus distinguished from a mere relation of chronological
succession." Conversely as our actions become more relaxed, visual,
or ranging over more actions, the possible repetitions of our past life
become "cut up" from each other, and

> the cutting up is not the same when we pass from one copy to
> another, each of them being in fact characterized by the particu-
> lar kind of dominant memories on which the other memories
> lean as on supporting points.[80]

Thus these contiguous images rest on the similarity of the dominant
memories, "shining points round which the others form a vague
nebulosity."[81]

These remarks sum up the qualitative changes of the visual or
contemplative world as it unfolds through the analogical crossings of
the two axes of synthesis; and thus it is possible logically to understand

the fluidity and flexibility of all identities in the world. At this level, metaphoric synthesis works poetically as *identity through difference*. A transition from the third to a fourth plane of Bergson's theory of images is provided by these observations:

> Everything happens, then, as though our recollections were repeated an infinite number of times in these many possible reductions of our past life. They take a more *common* form *when memory shrinks most*, more *personal when it widens out*, and they thus enter into an unlimited number of different "systematizations."[82]

Such "systematizations" portray with total precision the formal process of artistic "making"; they also announce new metaphoric equivalences that will become possible in the course of the widening of our experience up to the boundaries of our full biographical span.

The depth of consciousness seems up to now strictly tied to providing qualitative transformations and limits to the world, so it would be legitimate to ask at this point how the qualitative temporal *intensity* of a free life is structured in its inner formative stages. The answer to this question was still tied to poetics in Bergson, and although in his later work it became the basis of an aesthetic ethics, it represented for him (as it would represent at the roots of the coincidence of the major modernist styles: abstraction, expressionism, and surrealism) the summit of poetic significance.

From this summit all the fragments of images, speech, and action, which at the first three levels of constructive perception and imagination have crystallized into a vocabulary of fixed communicative symbols, will receive their animation and *motivation*. Only because of the syntheses that occur at this fourth level will all the others become truly significant discourse and meaningful expressions of existence. It can be stated without exaggeration that in Bergson's theory, in opposition to all formalist and purely structural theories of meaning, there is *really no meaning*, however articulated actions or signs might be, until an *intention* (motive, motif) is constituted at this biographical level and flows from it down to the rest.

Bergson has produced a definition of the nature of inner life with the claim that it resides neither in the exercise of a power or faculty, nor in a store of fixed habits or images, but always in the reciprocal relation of projects of motion and action, his "corporeal schemata," to concomitant and even prefiguring complexes of images, his "dynamic schemata." As seen earlier, the latter constitute the field of orientation of the former. It would be wrong to assume that this reciprocal relation is always practical rather than narrative, that it is just oriented to the constitution of complex actions destined to emerge in, and fill our future relations with, the world. Our actions do not always follow the cosmic élan; to be sure, we not only have empathy with the rhythms of the world, but, the philosopher states, "we sympathize with ourselves," and "our whole life, from the time of our first awakening to consciousness, is something like [an] indefinitely prolonged discourse." As "artisans of our lives, we work continually . . . to mold a figure unique . . . as unforeseeable as the form given by the sculptor to the clay."[83]

The flow of our conscious human life, then, does not proceed as a linear stream or with a fixed pattern. Outwardly, one can perceive the stream of practically oriented life with its perceptions, memories, habitual and virtual actions. But "beneath these clear-cut crystals and this superficial congelation is a continuity of flow comparable to no other flowing I have ever seen." The temporality of our inner life is not just "like the unrolling of a spool," for it is "just as much a continual winding, like that of thread into a ball." Unhappy with these simple analogies, Bergson looked for images of qualitative change:

> We must therefore evoke a spectrum of a thousand shades, with imperceptible gradations leading from one shade to another. A current of feeling running through the spectrum, becoming tinted with each of these shades in turn, would suffer gradual changes, each of which would announce the following and sum up within itself the preceding ones.[84]

Still, the rich plurality of this inner duration cannot be presented by a single image (even less by concepts) and must be refracted like light through a prism to show its kaleidoscopic composition. A variety of images, "taken from quite different orders of things, will be able, through the convergence of their action, to direct the consciousness" to the recovery of the intuition of our life as a whole from a certain point of view. The skillful painter of the inner life will collect images as dissimilar as possible to prevent any one of them "from usurping the place of the intuition it is instructed to call forth, since it would then be driven out immediately by its rivals.[85] Yet this super-imposition of images is neither contingent nor casual; in another spot, the philosopher warned the "painter of mental scenery" never to *indiscriminately* juxtapose images formed at different levels of attention to life:

> We know, for instance, when we read a psychological novel, that certain associations of ideas there depicted for us are true, that they may have been lived; others offend us, or fail to give us an impression of reality, because we feel in them the effect of a connection, mechanically and artificially brought about, between different mental levels.[86]

Bergson wanted, then, the convergence of different images and scenes in the interior narrative to be based on a lived *emotional and poetic equivalence* that is deeper than the formal definition of poetry as the overlaying of the axis of similarity on the axis of contiguity and, for this reason, had the vital effect of turning existence upon itself:

> By seeing that in spite of their differences in aspect [all these images] demand of our mind the same kind of attention and, as it were, the same degree of tension, one will gradually accustom the consciousness to a particular and definitely determined disposition, precisely the one it will have to adopt in order to appear unveiled to itself.[87]

We have now, with Bergson, reached time-qualitative life in its depths without any help from introspection. The multiple imagery illuminated at this level transcends both the tactile and the visual, of course, and can most appropriately be called "visionary." It may be the case that in other respects important to his doctrine the author changed his mind as he matured. Regarding his intuition of the reflective life as a qualitative, free, creative flow that provides *narrative* consistency to the *élan vital* that subtends it, it can be easily verified that his grasp was firm from as early as *Time and Free Will* and never abandoned him:

> But if, digging below the surface of contact between the self and external objects, we penetrate into the depths of the organized and living intelligence, we shall witness the joining to-

gether or rather the blending of many ideas which, *when once dissociated*, seem to exclude one another as logically contradictory terms. The strangest dreams, in which *two images overlie one another* and show us at the same time two different persons, who yet make only one, will hardly give us an idea of the interweaving of concepts which goes on when we are awake. The imagination of the dreamer, cut off from the external world, *imitates with mere images*, and parodies in its own way, the process which constantly goes on with regard to ideas in the deeper regions of the intellectual life.[88]

It is thus clear that the idea of our whole life cannot shift as easily as our contemplative points of view; indeed, the dissociation of the intermediate ideas of a life into their presentational images intensifies and thus transcends the metonymic montage of diverse views associated through action and time that was typical of contemplation. Bergson was sure that the conversion of the sense of a life into images originates from a synthesis that, in its "concentration," or, to use the existentialist term, in its "concern," is prior to, and *more adequate than, contiguity and similarity, manipulation (touch) and circumspection (vision), abstraction and empathy as motifs*. Instead of a metaphoric grouping of equivalent images from different moments in life, the *visionary* "mental scenery" is a collage in which each one of the parts can be both qualitatively and narratively the equivalent of the whole:

> The associationist reduces the self to an aggregate of conscious states: sensations, feelings and ideas. But if he sees in these various states no more than is expressed in their name, if he retains only their impersonal aspect, he may set them side by side forever without getting anything but a phantom self, the shadow of the ego projecting itself into space. If, on the contrary, he takes these psychic states with the particular colouring which they assume in the case of a definite person and which comes to each of them by reflection from all the others, then there is no need to associate a number of conscious states in order to rebuild the person, for the whole personality is in a single one of them, provided that we know how to choose it.[89]

As the preceding synopsis indicates, the most basic images analyzed by Bergson were the product of symbolist aesthetics. In accordance with his views on the theory of association, these images would be comparable to metonymic conglomerates of impressions of various senses linked to an abstract emotion and physiognomically recognizable as related to some practical or repressed vital needs. If repressed, they would be in some respects visionary because of the intensity of the related emotion(s); but their metonymic structure suggests that they are primarily readable as patterns and therefore tactile.

The second group of images in Bergson are those to be found in most of the postimpressionist schools and experiments, which are themselves indebted in part to the impressionists and in part to symbolist aesthetics. Their psychology and epistemology correspond to various mixtures of positivistic associationism, Fechner's "scientific" psychophysics, empathetic ideas, and late positivistic psychologism (Ribot). Their plastic motivation is still a metonymic connection of data from various senses to be read as abstract, musically inspired patterns still suggestive of vague emotions. Thus their empathetic component is always subordinated, even subservient, to abstraction. And insofar as they can become fixated through repetition of recognizable units or motifs, these patterns become contingently closed, and thus "found" ensembles of part-whole relations.

The contemplative and visionary images have some aspects in common with those found in empathetic and abstract psychologism, and they extend the signifying potential of the highest varieties of the symbolist image, but their theoretical core is neither romantic organicism nor associationism. Their justification and analysis is possible only in terms of Bergson's reflective theories (later to be reinforced by phenomenological and existential refinements); the loss of this reflective core in subsequent philosophy seems to have only impoverished more-recent aesthetics and theories of meaning. These images, precisely because they are human creations, work within the context of concrete, personal, and ultimately narrative viewpoints, thus neither their elements nor they themselves as wholes can be considered abstract. More specifically, in them abstraction is always at the service of empathy, of empathetic individualization of the world as a dwelling place, or of existence as a narrative whole. As effects of dissociation of a previous synthesis of concentration or concern, contemplative and visionary images must be both metonymic and metaphoric; the first are montages of "metonymic" equivalences, the second collages of "metaphoric" diversities. Finally, their unequivocal visuality must be attributed to the openness or unlimited virtuality of the freedom in which they are founded.

THE BLENDING OF HORIZONS:
BERGSON, CÉZANNE, MODERNISM

Important as this rough Bergsonian synthesis of the artistic medium, the image, may have been for contemporary art and eventually for modernism, its role should not, and will not, be considered in this enquiry within the framework of cause-and-effect relations, that is, of "historically demonstrable" influences it might have had on them.[90] The appropriate assessment of the significance of the Bergsonian synthesis depends on the possibility of *establishing it as a historical present*, as a point of convergence and authentic union of all the diverse and even contradictory ideas that preceded it. When the importance of synthesis and of reconciliation is ignored, the historical process has the appearance of the confused and disorganized advance of an army of marauders. When the importance of Bergson's synthesis is neglected, the movement of history before and after him remains a proliferation of initiatives and proposals that intertangle and separate without producing movement in any discernible direction.

But a historical present, a point of convergence and synthesis, cannot be established by the authority of a single person. Indeed, most often the greater the authority of a person the more ephemeral and transitory it is. The hermeneutical method proposes the use of intellectual or spiritual dialogue among several "contemporaries" (it is precisely their dialogue that makes them so) as a means of determining a truly enduring, rather than ephemeral, present. An enduring present has for hermeneutics the function of an intellectual line of sight, or horizon, and the "dialogue" that constitutes it is thus seen as a blending of horizons. This dialogue need not be direct; or rather, it is not a direct impact, or influence, or contact through a medium that counts for the purpose of constituting parallel lives; what is required is that two or more minds be formed by parallel efforts in constituting analogical syntheses out of a confused and disorderly mass of chronological precedents.

Ironically, personal syntheses are generally, as was the case with Bergson, rough and fragmentary. Thus in a strict sense a systematic overlap of parallel syntheses is always the result of subsequent hermeneutics. But the proximity to each other of great synthesizers is sufficient to create a magnetic field in which a multitude of preceding and subsequent creative initiatives find an alignment. For the purposes of subsistence within a nurturing cultural zeitgeist, that mode of alignment is sufficient; yet hermeneutics remains necessary for reactivating the synthesis, that is, for giving experiential validity to its antecedents. This "questioning backward," this effort of reactivation of antecedents *as* antecedents of a historical present, is implicit in the attempt to make two or more authors dialogue and converge even if they did not demonstrably do so. Carefully and persistently pursued, reactivation constitutes what in hermeneutics is called the delineation of "effective historical development."[91]

It can be made clear now that the preceding survey of the development of the notion of the image in the late nineteenth century was not traditional history, nor even "history of ideas," but a hermeneutical "effective history." What is meant by such a characterization is that a "developmental" tracing of the progress of the notion would not have been possible without a hermeneutical preunderstanding of the theory, and the variety, of images in Bergson as the horizon toward which that "effective history" was moving. With the help of such a preunderstanding, the various images and their epistemological explanations began to appear as integral parts of a system or whole of meaning, which is what they eventually are shown to be in Bergson. The movement from whole to parts, and vice versa, together with the reciprocity of reactivation and preunderstanding, is precisely what constitutes the well-known "hermeneutical circle."

But this is not all; it can also be stated now that the extrication and understanding of a "theory of images" from a mass of references to the image in many different contexts in Bergson would not have been possible without a similar preunderstanding of the various examples and systematic unity of the image in Cézanne. It is precisely the parallelism of both theories of images that constitutes a historical horizon for the muddle and anarchy of their precedents. And there is more: As an enduring present, this horizon extends both backward *and forward*. The following surprising conclusion leads deeply into the heart of this enquiry: *modernism itself cannot be understood, except as a mass of confused and contradictory ideological and stylistic positions, without a basic understanding of the systematic unity of the diverse types of images established simultaneously by Bergson and Cézanne.*

When these images are understood as a spectrum of efforts of association in search of their deep reflective origin and unity, one can see that they cannot exist in total independence from each other, and one must also admit that the different aspects and trends within modernism that emphasize one or more of these images could not possibly exist in total independence from each other. The systematic diversity and unity of images constitute the core of the "poetics of painting" in Cézanne and his legacy to the poetics of the great modernist masters, not only in painting but in other arts and in literature as well. The modernists stretched this poetic core in various directions, but all the great masters understood and used all of the images systematized at their historical horizon, and when the implicit unity of the core broke down, so did modernism.

The central and concluding chapters of this study discuss the development of the above circumscribed poetic core in art theory and practice before and in Cézanne. They also offer an explanation of the premier example of visionary images, *The Cardplayers*, as an illustration of the meaning of the painting itself and of the validity of the established mode of interpretation.

III

FROM IMPRESSIONISM TO CÉZANNE
Aesthetic Theories

Bergson believed that the ultimate source of the cultural crisis of the late nineteenth century that brought about, as a reaction, the initiation of modernism was the mistaken assumption that sensation is already "pure knowledge."[1] This identification of knowledge with the sensory faculties was, he proposed, an attempt, within the latter stages of romanticism, to reconcile idealist and realist impulses by affirming that the impression was both absolute and true. The strong emphasis that this belief placed on perception as the epistemological regulator of reality caused a deep separation of perception from human action and forced impressions to remain incomplete and "virtual."

The art movements that developed from this belief tested the various ways in which perception can extend into the world and subsequently intend itself back out of the world in the form of art. The impressionists, for example, privileged tactile vision as "knowledge" that for them reflected the contingency of the world and expressed their mistrust of the organic.[2] The symbolists, on the other hand, experimented with increasingly diverse synesthetic and kinesthetic syntheses as constitutive of the impression. Impressions, they claimed, precisely because of their synthetic nature, can be related only indirectly to the contingency of the world, and thus their artistic presentations must be considered *correspondences* "with," while impressionist art works claimed to be *equivalences* "of," reality.

This progress toward a new "content" and toward the "form" in which to embody that content gave rise in contemporaneous art movements to considerations about the motivation of art making. Influenced by outdated, scientistic ontologies, artists and theorists questioned whether perception is of "the eye" or of "the mind," whether the obtained "knowledge" is real or symbolic, and whether the art that is produced is imitative or autonomous.[3] These contradictory enquiries pointed to perspectives that would gradually emerge in the aesthetic theories of the time, as the focus on impressions gave way to a new concentration on perceptual and imaginative syntheses capable of integrating empathetic projection with abstracting simplification.

To motivate these syntheses, whether (in their terminology) "subjectively" or "objectively" grounded, impressionists/postimpressionists and symbolists turned to scientific models of collecting, classifying, and transforming "perceptual knowledge." Predictably, these models paralleled and responded to the prevalent psychologism discussed in chapter 2. Developed chiefly within the fields of optics and color science, the new scientific models provided artists with data ("concrete" and "immutable," they claimed) for *constructing images*.

However, as Merleau-Ponty noted, the models of these pseudoscientists were a form of scientific thinking that looks on the world from above.[4] The principles, laws, and facts that they accumulated produced models of aesthetic activity as if "incoming data" (i.e., "impressions") could be transformed into masterpieces through the careful control of sensations/impressions by an "operational" apparatus that would intervene at all of the necessary stages of their transformation and function as a storehouse, signal-changing station, and dispatcher.[5]

Certainly the impressionists, postimpressionists and symbolists produced works that far exceeded the simplicity and rigidity of their starting point (viz., "perception is knowledge"); and perhaps we can describe their ability to transcend a very limited epistemology as another example of the overarching influences of the revolutionary aesthetic advances that were to become the intellectual horizon of the times. Thus, within the curious struggle of movements and styles that made up this period, we can also witness the subtle interpretative presence of the great artists.

By studying the major synthesizing transitions of the last few decades of the nineteenth century, leading up to Cézanne's mature period, it will be possible to foresee the gradual emergence of a modernist theory of images as it occurs, not through appropriations and influences, but in the brilliant anticipations of the impressionists and symbolists as they, like Cézanne, let modernism "think itself" through them. It is indeed characteristic of Cézanne's genius that he did not remain outside or "above" his contemporaries, but, in using the same language, he participated in *their* dialogue while he was creating an entirely new poetic core.

The theories and practices of the impressionists/postimpressionists outlined below will be shown to concentrate on the plastic image. Their experiments with abstraction and principles of design will then be considered within the context of the formulation, in optical science and color theory, of the formal language of art. The symbolists, on the other hand, derived from these "scientific" theories evidence for the development of an ambiguity in their motifs that had its equivalent in Bergson's "symbolic" and "contemplative" images. The following summary of the art theories of impressionists and symbolists, together with the practical rules of the optical scientists, will point to the horizon of the modernist theory of images, and will thus set the stage for the discussion in chapter 4 of Cézanne's aesthetics, including all four types of images (symbolist, plastic, contemplative, and visionary) introduced above.

THE IMPRESSIONISTS:
FROM SENSATIONS TO SIGNS

In his review of the Salon des Refusés of 1863, Castagnary pronounced about J. B. Jongkind:

> He is an artist to his very fingertips, possessed of true and rare sensibilities. His work is all impression.[6]

The sensibility that Castagnary admired in Jongkind, he went on to say, was his willing obedience to the "appearances of nature," to the seasonal and atmospheric conditions that illustrate their ephemerality, as opposed to the more stable *essential* qualities of their permanence. Appearances are the outwardly manifest conditions and effects of the changeable presentation of the environment, of time and chance, as they illuminate and darken, erode and cleanse, multiply and condense the components of the natural world; and they, and they alone, are "perceivable."[7]

These conditions and effects are apprehended in human "sensibility" (perceptual knowledge) as impressions. The impression determines its constitution in the form of perceptual units, coded bundles of sense data (i.e., units of light, color, texture, rhythm, difference), and larger articulations (such as attitudes and moods) formed by consciousness during the process of being "impressed." Impressional moods result, for example, in visual/tactile syntheses such as "warm" and "cool" colors, "deep" shadows, and "soft" clouds.[8]

The process is both passive and active: In experiencing the appearances of nature, consciousness is the passive collector of "impressions" *and* simultaneously reacts to these impressions by actively coordinating their similarities, or their contiguity as apprehended either immediately or in association with the whole of past experience. One is thus both conscious of impressions and conscious of the consciousness of impressions.[9]

Some impressionists' remarks reflected an awareness of the receptor/reactor duality of the conscious experience of impressions. In a letter to Bazille dated 15 July 1864, Claude Monet wrote:

> [I]t seems to me, when I see nature, that I see it ready made, completely written—but then, try to do it! All this proves that one must think of nothing but them [impressions]; it is by dint of observation and reflection that one makes discoveries.[10]

The impression, for Monet, required the synthesis of both observation and reflection. For Degas the synthesis was an idea, an idea that explained effects by associating them consciously with other effects. "I can," he wrote in his *Notebook* of 1863–67,

> for example, easily recall the color of some hair, because I got the idea that it was made out of polished walnutwood, or else flax, or horse-chestnut shells. The rendering of the form will make real the hair, with its softness and lightness or its roughness or its weight out of tone which is almost precisely that of walnutwood, flax or horse-chestnut shell.[11]

As both a passive sensual experience and an actively associative conscious synthesis, the impression is ultimately a *content*. The hair of Degas's ballerina is associated by his sensibility with the similarities in the impression of the walnutwood. Passively he lets these qualities converge, and consciously he synthesizes them into a "deeper" truth, a more profoundly veristic reality, the ultimate recognition of the walnutwood/hair as the content of his experience. The following beautiful lines from Marcel Proust's *Le temps retrouvé* exemplify, in impressionist literature, the same recognition of the simultaneity of the sensuous association and the consciousness of it.

> Une heure n'est pas qu'une heure, c'est un vase rempli de parfums, de sons, de projets et de climates. Ce que nous appelons la réalité est un certain rapport entre ces sensations et ces souvenirs qui nous entourent simultanément.[12]

As can be seen in their statements, both Degas and Proust comprehended that the content of the experience of the world is the impression and also recognized the possibility of making it the content of paintings and novels as well. "Impressed" before nature, they in turn tried to impress their public. But in order to convey their impressions to their viewer/readers, they had to use a subjective terminology, which, because of their indebtedness to psychologism, could only be the terminology of impressions. A painting, like nature, is accessible through impressions, and therefore, to be *made* accessible, the *form* of the painting as an integration and presentation of its content must also be a form of impressions.

As the following evidence will bear out, the impression, as both the new subject matter for painting and its desired formal language, was indeed the line of demarcation of the new modern styles from the past historical ones. As early as 1860 Baudelaire noted in *The Painters of Modern Life* that modernity is the "transitory," the "fleeting," the "contingent";[13] in other words, modernity was the celebration of the impression. And again, to celebrate the impression, the painters and novelists required an expressive form, a language, that would communicate precisely this content.

To communicate impressions through impressions, to actualize the content of Degas's walnutwood/hair through visible means, to translate the Proustian vase into a plastic equivalent, required that the impressionists devise a *syntax* of impressions—a structure for the ordering of the components of the experience of impressions, *and* a system of *semantic units*—fixed, meaningful units that would fit within the orderly linking of impressions. Thus, they turned to the scientists, first to the optical scientists, for an understanding of the syntax of impressions; and next, although almost simultaneously, they looked to the psychologists for an understanding of the content of impressions. Toward the end of the century both scientific schools worked on the components of the "language" of impressions; whether they thought of them as "perception," "imagination," or other mental faculties, they shared a belief in the interdependency of the perceiving, impressed subject (consciousness) with the impressing cause, or fact.

Indeed, André Gide's variation on the Cartesian cogito—"I see, I feel, I hear, I smell; therefore I am"[14]—placed the experience of being itself within the scope of the conscious experience of impressions. Colors, scents, sounds fill up the Proustian vase with immediate sensations that constitute the data of the impressionistic consciousness. However, while the experience of being is the absorption in the plenitude of impressions, this plenitude cannot be *directly* expressed. The Proustian vase cannot be emptied onto the canvas, and the walnutwood/hair cannot be recreated in all its evocative exactitude in two dimensions. Because neither the painter nor the novelist can "paint" sounds, moods, or even light, they must resort to the use of an *indirect language* still of and about impressions.

As we have seen, the impressionist chose "signs" as meaningful units to translate some actual impressions into others and these signs (for the painter: colored, patterned brushstrokes) were not only adequate equivalents for the conscious content of an impression, but they also *presented* themselves as evidence of the conscious activity of an impression. One could say that the concept of a painting as a "Renaissance window on the world" was modified by the impressionists to show the painting itself also present as a surface that reflects and refracts light, and distorts and multiplies images.[15]

As indicated earlier, the impressionists' techniques, practices, and theories for indirectly expressing this plenitude by means of signs relied on the "facts" of the optical sciences for a deduction of the categories that would render the impression as a synthesis. Laws on the "behavior" of impressions, canons of visual operations, and principles of pandemic design were quickly utilized by the painters as a syntax of impressions. These sciences trusted the impression to be as analyzable and measurable as pure scientific facts, though it itself is by nature an ephemeral and phenomenal "reality." The "factualization" of the impression was undertaken in the same spirit as the peerings of biologists into a microscope and their theorizing about the mysteries of the cell or of brain function.[16] However, its purpose, as far as the painters were concerned, was not to speculate about reality but to present the layman with uncontestable facts that could be subsumed under categories, and the categories under broader relational structures, so as to provide their impressionistic works with a discernible, even predictable, grammar or syntax.

FROM TRUTH TO SYMBOL:
OPTICS AND COLOR SCIENCE

One of the earliest of the optical scientists of the modern age[17] to open the way for the consideration of sensations as signs was Michel-Eugène Chevreul (1786–1889). His wool-dyeing experiments at the Gobelins tapestry factory led to the publication in 1839 of his *La loi de contraste simultané des coleurs,*[18] which examined the behavior of colors interacting spatially with each other. In it, he proposed certain color combinations that produce predictable perspectival effects that can operate as signs for plethoric impressions. He also proposed that colors are perceived simultaneously as both value and tone: that red transmits not only redness but also effects of light and shadow.

Chevreul derived from his studies certain principles of harmony, which could be put into practice to take advantage of the simultaneity of color and tonal values. Analogous colors (adjacents on the color wheel, such as red, red/orange, orange), he found, start to blend together when juxtaposed, because of their shared tonal values; and in the spatial intervals between the color areas are generated additional optical blends (such as reddish red/orange). Because of their multiple components, these generated colors have a decreased value range and they appear darker, obscured, almost as shadows; and due to their proximity to the purer color areas, they appear to recede. On the other hand, Chevreul discovered that colors that are not close in value (complementary pairs like blue and orange) produce no blending or generation of additional colors and instead contrast with each other so sharply that, in their contiguity, they brighten and intensify each other, almost as if they both radiate light. This brightness caused by simultaneous contrast is called by Chevreul "harmony of contrasts," and is produced by the impossibility of optical blending.

Chevreul's "laws of simultaneous contrast," which produce spatial differentiation and generate light and dark effects, were influential on the impressionist painters. His experiments incorporated earlier findings in the field of optics that proved that the behavior of light rays, an additive process, is dissimilar to the subtractive behavior of paint pigments. Aware of the impossibility of painting actual light, the impressionists found in these theories that not only did the signifying colors for spatial signs operate to generate the spatial contrasts of advancement and recession, but they could also substitute for light as well. Chevreul's color formulas also incited the generation of darkened, shadowed areas within the harmonic blends, and of bright, "lighted" areas, with the disharmonic complements thus providing signs for, not actual light, but the conscious experience of light apprehended in the form of light "effects."

The signs for space and light effects provided by Chevreul's laws represented the first step in an expanded artistic assessment of the impression. Rather than painting a pastoral scene in which the natural world prepares an allegorical stage for the moralizing story of a subject matter, the impressionists subsumed the content of their art, consciousness of impressions, in their settings and ultimately in their manner of painting. Thus, one could say that they, unlike their immediate forebears, achieved the collapsing of content into form or, using the terminology of sign theory, a collapsing of the signified into the signifier that reversed the romantic collapsing of the signifier into the signified. This convergence of signifier and signified and the heroic endeavor to "capture" the full workings of the impression became possible for the impressionists only because of the experimental theories of Chevreul and the other optical scientists who turned away from the search for more and better ways to *imitate* objects and make them real to scientifically inspired adventures in inventing substitutes for perception, consciousness, and moods.

Rather than resembling objects, like a tree or the sun, the signs used by the impressionists and invented by the optical scientists stood in for, and made present, the apprehension of consciousness, the motor activity of the sensory organs, the accompanying affective dispositions, and the multiple sensual effects resulting from active and passive interaction of consciousness with physical realities. And Chevreul's scientific facts about the complex determination of colors provided the impressionist painters with a nonallegorical, nonideational and nondirect language that could express the evocative, transitory, and self-conscious impression.

In Monet's painting *Impression: Sunrise*,[19] the harmonies of the blues and violets gather the impression of the shadows not yet dispelled by the entrance of the protagonist, the sun, and the blues and greens clustering close to the blazing orb intensify its brilliance. Thus Monet's initial impression, let us rather say receptive-creative impression, of the sunrise was incorporated by him into a series of signs that fully determined his experience in paint. The signs were the blue-violet units that signified deep shadows and the red disk with green halo that produced the "ascendancy of the sun." Monet had painted, therefore, not light or objects, but his materialized impression of their effects.[20]

To immunize himself against the distractions of "real" objects and "real" light and to focus his sensibilities on the impression, he advised:

> When you go out to paint, try to forget what objects you have before you—a tree, a house, a field, or whatever. Merely think, here is a little square of blue, here an oblong of pink, here a streak of yellow, and paint it just as it looks to you, the exact color and shape, until it gives your own naïve impression of the scene before you.[21]

The allegiance demanded by the romantics from sublime Nature lost its mesmerizing hold on the early moderns, and the search for a perfect imitation of its grandeur by the salon painters became subordinated to a new fascination with its physical and physiological laws. Instead of painting a tree, and thus celebrating its objecthood, the impressionists painted a streak of yellow and celebrated instead their own "naïve" experiencing.

The techniques of the impressionists thus required not only a way of gathering impressions but also a way of focusing on this elusive experiencing, and capturing it, in painting. The subsequent scientific experiments on optics and color initiated by Chevreul provided the painters with the much-desired new "facts" about impressions. As René Huyghe noted, both science and impressionism sought to apprehend the same thing: "rational sensualism."[22] Rational sensualism, an appropriate oxymoron for the ironies of the impressionist's aim, is a very fair statement of this goal: to isolate and "factualize" the impression.

In six articles entitled "Les Phénomènes de la vision" published in 1850 in *L'Art*,[23] David Sutter (1811–80) continued the theoretical experiments on the signifying power of complementary pairs and provided more "facts" to the impressionists seeking to rationalize their perceptual experiences. He noted that if there is no interval between the pairs, one color will "radiate" more than the other, and that a relieflike illusion, one should say phenomenon, is created. Spatial recession and advancement using complementaries is thus also manipulable, and the decisive factor in this aspect is the size of the colored area: The larger area of the complementary pair appears to advance in front of its opposite. Adding to Chevreul's laws of spatial and light effects, Sutter offered yet another spatial sign: The red sun will radiate, ascend, and separate from its surrounding shadows if the "shadow" areas are of smaller proportions and green; and the violet water lilies will appear to float above the viscous pond if it is amber and composed of smaller elements.

After interviewing Eugène Delacroix in 1854,[24] Charles Blanc (1813–82) took the next logical step in the invention of new, modern signs for the impression of light effects. He proved that one need not actually paint the shadows surrounding the red sun with green paint, as the red patch itself will scientifically generate its own shadowy greenness. Delacroix had recounted in his diaries an observation that the yellow cabs of Paris *produce* their own violet shadows, and Blanc expanded this observation to propose that painters should leave bare intervals, or interstices, between color patches and apply the color patches in rhythmic formations (dashes, dots, stripes) in order to allow for a space into which can be projected or generated the complementary color.

Blanc's proof that one need not paint the shadow, because it will be optically manifest, became the origin of a theoretical position of his concerning the necessary focus of artistic consciousness. He recommended in his treatise "Grammaire des arts du dessin" of the 1860s[25] that one need not paint what one sees *(ce qu'il voit)*, nor should one paint what one knows or expects *(ce qu'il entend)*, but one should paint one's humanness, one's doubts and uncertainties about reality, one's discomfort with physical laws and space, and one's individuality, by painting always and only, *ce qu'il se sent* (with emphasis placed on the reflexivity of the verb).[26] This substitution, recommended by Blanc, of "that which one is conscious of" for "that which one sees" was a subtle anticipation of the revisionist goals of the avant-garde impressionists to do away with the laws of imitation of the French Academy[27] (characterized by Blanc as *ce qu'il entend*) and replace them with a more "truthful" form of (what he identifies as) realism that incorporated the uneasiness and doubts of human existence by making human consciousness the appropriate access to reality.

Émile Zola's definition of impressions as "nature seen through the eyes of a temperament"[28] also expressed this grounding of reality in consciousness. Sight, privileged by Zola as sensual contemplation, internalizes the physical realities of nature by transforming them into effects that fill up the active-passive medium of consciousness, the Proustian vase. The temperament is the consciousness of consciousness and is composed of the many contents of individual and unique experience. Cézanne called the temperament "a veil"[29] through which one experiences the world—a veil with its distorting properties, its obscurities, its tears and stains, but also its emphases and markings that not only represent individual life but also define it. The temperament and its operative "agents," the senses, would therefore control *ce qu'il se sent* by limiting or expanding, depending of course on the predilections of "the veil," the interpenetration and fusion of living consciousness with the lived world. If "reality" and ultimately "the world" are believed to have a determinate significance only *for* consciousness, that must be because consciousness constitutes itself (*se sent*) as it selectively internalizes, that is, analyzes and synthesizes, only those impressions that "the veil" can "rationally" incorporate into its texture.

Often-quoted statements that the impressionists painted "what they see" (Blanc's *ce qu'il voit*), and that the impression is "what one sees instead of what one knows is there," as well as Cézanne's famous remark that "Monet is nothing but an eye, but what an eye,"[30]

continued to enhance the false opinion that the impressionists ren-
dered only *visual* perception, that sight is internalized perception,
and that human perception and consciousness are the slaves of visual
data. The purity and certainty of *ce qu'il voit*, the visual field, was
muddied, for half of the century, through the stultifying control on
the part of the French Academy with its imposition of indisputable
"rules of seeing." These rules were aimed at achieving results, such as
decorum, beauty, the ideal; and they used imitation, trompe l'oeil, and
other illusionistic devices as a means to instruct the viewer in the *ideal*
forms of reality, which of course were, for the Academics, "out there."
Thus the painters were indoctrinated in the *imitation* of reality.

The impressionists' revision of the positioning of "reality" from
being "out there" to being there *for consciousness* (particularly an awake
and working one)[31] resulted in very different "rules" for the new
school, based on quite distinct beliefs about the relationship of the
self to the world. The beliefs were metaphysical in the Academics,
naïvely realistic in the positivists; as impressionism advanced, they
became progressively critical and, as the increasing use of the notion
of signs indicates, modeled on the genesis and elements of linguistic
expression. The Academic painter, however, saw *objects* in the world
and painted them as objects: objects that the painter *knew*, understood, and was acquainted with, through conceptual presuppositions
the painter considered well founded. The sun was a yellow orb; shadows were dense gray. The impressionist, on the other hand, refused
to acknowledge the Academic formulas about "known realities" and
"rules of seeing" and proposed a more veristic positioning of the self
in the world, as *consciousness of it*.

Baudelaire's prophetic review of the salon of 1859 introduced
the opposition between these two worldviews, one of them positivistic, which he identified with the Academic painter, and the other
"Imaginativistic," which he assigned to the impressionists:

> The immense group of artists . . . may be divided into
> two very distinct camps. In one, we have those who call them-
> selves realists, . . . and to bring out more clearly their error, we
> will call them positivists. The positivist says: "I want to repre-
> sent things as they are, or on the assumption that I did not
> exist." The universe without man. And in the other camp, there
> are the imaginative ones who say: "I want to illuminate things
> with my mind [*esprit*] and cast its reflection upon other minds."[32]

Armed with these intimations of the critic, one can better grasp the full extent of the critical stance against Academicism that will became a point of departure for all modernists.

The normalizing vision of the Academics resulted, according to Baudelaire, in the representation of a "universe without man"—a world that could manifest itself independently of a perceiving consciousness—and the salon painter was relegated to mechanical reproduction of visual rules, to produce merely their imitated objects, to represent autonomous reality without any references to his own activities of seeing. When the impressionists reinstated the "activity of seeing," they stressed "activity." The activity of seeing was an animation of the objects of the world by the consciousness of the perceiver (Baudelaire's "illumin[ation of] things with my *esprit*"), so that all sensual elements—the contents of the Proustian vase—are activated with respect to a full self-manifestation. Thus for the impressionists the "activity of seeing" was not just sight but active sight, sight that experiences the tactile pleasures of shadows and the evocative scents of walnutwood/hair.

Baudelaire's precision in recognizing the interaction of "things" and the perceiving *esprit* was matched by his formulation of the purpose of the activity of seeing for the impressionists: to "cast its reflection [of illuminated things] upon other minds." Within the scope of Academic aims, the communicative purpose must not be incongruous (because things can manifest themselves) and excessive (because the enhancement of such manifestation must be "artful" or contrived). While impressionists painted the real *appearances* of things, the salon painters represented not so much the essences of the things or events as *some* permanent and perfect *concepts* by means of which we traditionally understand them: Their beauty amounted, then, to the ease of such understanding and was celebrated as the natural connections, which can be gathered in rules, between things and their concepts.

This not-so-subtle didacticism on the part of the Academic painters was intentionally connected by them with the intellect, the reasoning, moral side of human beings; the impressionists, in contrast, wished to enhance and extend consciousness *as* experience, and to display this experience so that it could be actively completed by other minds. The signs used to project the activity of seeing were aimed at the consciousness of the viewer and made up a language of impressions that could be most readily made present to all who were not over-whelmed by inherited "concepts." The sharing of experiences among two subjects or minds would thus be a translation of the operation of signs at the individual level: The sign "speaks" the language of consciousness, but only if and when consciousness articulates itself through its impressions. Therefore, not only must signs be about impressions; they must themselves be impressions.

To return to Blanc's use of Delacroix, the latter's observation about the behavior of certain light rays in a three-dimensional world was converted by the former into an awareness of the two-dimen-sional, metonymic values of a sign (viz., color). Furthermore, the multiple value of the sign allows us to relate it to changing circum-stances of impressions so they can unfold temporally and spatially for the viewer. Instead of seeing a completed object, the viewer ex-periences an object in the making of its concrete presence through the filling up of the boundaries by the generated shadows, their re-cession in depth around the object, and the vibrancy of the object "trembling" in the spontaneity of its manifestation.

While Delacroix was fascinated by the impressions of the yel-low cabs in the Parisian sunlight, the viewer who stands in front of Monet's *Impression: Sunrise* is also fascinated, not by a mere thing but by the spontaneous conversion of a sensation into a sign. This spon-taneous conversion—the impression—"luminizes" the sensation. As signs, the sensations become correlatives for human consciousness. They are obviously animated and even personified, and so also are the expressive signs (warm, cool, soft . . . colors and brushstrokes) that stand for them. They are all charged with the background of the feeling, smelling, thinking, remembering acts (or syntheses) of hu-man consciousness. Painters who were particularly skillful at form-ing this humanized correlative—Monet for example—were praised for their "eye," but this praise applies not so much to their ability to see as to their ability to create an act of seeing that embodied in itself all of the abundance of consciousness.

This ambitious aim not only was promulgated by the French theorists; it was also the subject of scientific experiments by English and German aesthetic scientists. The German physicist Heinrich-Wilhelm Dove developed a "theory of luster" based on the contrast of complementary colors.[33] He proposed that, because the eye is un-able to blend complementary colors, it moves back and forth between the two, attempting to reconcile them. This involuntary movement of the eye produces a vibration, as if the colors are both moving together and repelled apart. Influenced by these findings, Ogden Nash Rood took up in 1879 this discovery in his book *Modern Chromatics* (translated into French in 1881)[34] and, in extending the findings of Sutter and Blanc to suggest industrial uses for colors, he concluded that when painted impressions are "scientifically" ordered, something unpredictable and indeed "unscientific" is evoked. In his experiments, he became increasingly more interested in studying not how colors react to each other but how they create a reaction in a human viewer. Rood thus initiated a shift in scientific focus away from the rules governing the manipulation of colors and patterns as signs to a concern with the "facts" of human perception. The color sciences thus became infected with the positivistic bias toward psychologistic explanations.

Charles Henry in his book of 1885, *Introduction à une esthetique scientifique*, formulated a scientifically ordered explanation of the role of impressions as *perceptual units,* thus utilizing both the theories of his predecessors in optical research and those of the positivists.[35] Like Rood, he also found that within the formal elements of the impression—the intervals, vibrations, and colors—"feelings and emotions" are evoked, feelings that he could not connect with the activities suggested within the abstract patterns. He identified these feelings as constituting certain "abstract emotions," which he categorized as pleasure and displeasure and called, respectively, "dynamogeny" and "inhibition."[36] He proposed that certain colors are pleasurable (red, pink, yellow) and others inhibitory (green, violet, blue), and lines evoke the same emotional values: "dynamogenic" lines, arranged left to right, moving from below and upward; and "inhibitory" lines, which follow the reverse pattern.

Henry's "aesthetique scientifique,"[37] as he called it, identified signs that can signify "dominant sentiments." In his experiments at the Laboratoire de Physiologie des Sensations at the Sorbonne, he tested the "anatomy" of colored linear configurations by questioning his subjects about the emotions they felt while viewing certain patterns. Through this process, he discovered certain harmonies that always evoked the same responses in his subjects. Abstract patterns of descending, ascending, or horizontal lines given either cool, warm, or neutral coloration "suggested" to his clients what he considered to be "abstract emotions"—moods without any individual or personal content. These abstract emotions were thus said to have been *caused* by the patterns instead of being vestigial "emotional confusions" from the interviewee's life. As a positivist, Henry believed he had discovered, in his abstract patterns of dynamogeny and inhibition, *facts* of psychological associationism that could be elevated to laws of aesthetic emotional response.[38] To verify his aesthetic laws, Henry was encouraged by his friend Gustave Kahn, a symbolist poet and art critic, to test his findings by looking for supporting evidence for their facticity in patterns found in nature. The natural patterns that Henry incorporated, however, were not selected from organic and/or landscape forms that he witnessed *in nature;* they were appropriated from Humbert de Superville's work on human gestures and facial configurations. The Dutch painter-theorist's *Essai sur les signes inconditionnels dans l'art*, from 1832, categorized the patterns formed by the lines of facial features into those that he specified as being "pleasing" or "pleased," and those that signified "displeasure."[39] Henry borrowed these categories to expand his own theories of dynamogeny and inhibition, and he worked out their veracity using algebraic formulas derived from the angles of a protractor. He justified his reliance on applied mathematical theory by appealing to the need for rationalism in aesthetic design:

> It is evident that these angular distances [of the faces] should be determined if one wishes to arrive at a rational classification [of lines] and colors and a knowledge of the laws of their harmony.[40]

Using these "aesthetic protractors," he specified, in "Aesthetique rapporteurs" (1888),[41] the application of these principles of rational harmony to design. A painter could determine how to utilize "only a small degree of sadness" by use of a certain angled ratio, but also the other angles that could rhythmically harmonize and thus fortify each other. The protractor was used to replace the unpredictability of intuitive design with formulas that were, in the words of the positivists, "true" and "clear."

Henry's laws of dynamogeny and inhibition held true, in his estimation, for all the arts: For music, the principles specified the limits of emotional provocation; for architecture, he provided information concerning the issue of the relation of form to function; and

for painting, he sought to clarify with a psychologistic bias the signifying functions of painterly signs. However, the direct application of
Henry's theories by modern artists was at cross currents with his
intentions.[42] Painters, such as the postimpressionists Seurat, Signac
and Pissarro, and the early symbolists van Gogh and Gauguin, as
well as the symbolist poets, were well ahead of Henry in determining universal, permanent, ideal patterns of harmony and disharmony
that emerged in the personifications and symbols they were testing
in their works.

Indeed, a reference by Paul Gauguin from 1885 to Henry's
theory of inhibitory lines disclosed its inadequacy and narrowness in
fully exploring the potential of an abstract line to *evoke* rather than to
rationalize an emotional response on the part of a viewer or reader.

> Why are the willows with hanging branches called "weeping"?
> Is it because descending lines are sad?[43]

In this inquiry, Paul Gauguin skeptically questioned the "truth" of
Henry's theory of sad lines by proposing a complex personified association that far exceeded a line's ability to formulate sadness. "Weeping," Gauguin seemed to hint, is much more complex than the path
of a line. The "weeping" of the willow, with its bowed and quivering
attitude, far surpasses the evocative consummation traced by a linear
pattern of the human *mood* of sadness and substitutes instead a chain
of *acts* of sadness.

The assumption that the arbitrary sign of perceptual constitution is connected iconically, rather than in a chain of contiguity or
constant conjunction, with aspects of nature was steadily losing cur-
rency. Therefore, the inhibitory line would be seen as containing
within itself the spontaneity and experiential depth of the conscious
response, the *act* of sadness, by assuming the role of a direct embodiment or reenactment of the psychic counterparts of that emotion—
for instance, sobbing and sighing. In this way, the line and volume,
shading and boundaries, and many other features carefully selected
from nature as suggestively filled with tension or balance, became
the direct heirs of the romantic symbol as particulars that contained
a universal, spiritual purpose or "intention." Thus Gauguin's comparison of the intention, "weeping," with the sign (now elevated to
symbol) "sad, descending lines," pointed in an exemplary manner

not only to the "corrections" being made to the positivist/optical scientist stance but also to the profound differences that were emerging between the theories of the impressionists and those of the symbolists. Gauguin's "weeping" line illustrated a revised role (the role of supporting symbols, rather than just accompanying sensations) for the sign within symbolist thought.

THE SYMBOLISTS: FROM SIGNS TO IMAGES

In his "Definition of Neotraditionism" of 1890, Maurice Denis[44] qualified the differences between the schools of impressionism and symbolism as based on two opposing definitions of "nature." Impressionists, he proposed, relied on a perceptual experience of "nature," while symbolists experienced it aesthetically "as painter[s]." The "painterly temperament," he went on to say, produces art that is

> the sanctification of nature, . . . the disguise of natural objects
> with their vulgar sensations by icons that are sacred, magical
> and commanding.[45]

Thus as perceptual fulfillments of natural objects, the signs of the impressionists/postimpressionists were "deceits" based on an analytic conversion of perceptual states into patterns. Symbolists, on the other hand, adopted images that did not refer to natural effects but were quasi-figurative "suggestions" of vital correlatives or equivalences, and of conscious states, such as aesthetic emotions and attitudes toward the world. As signs, the images of the symbolists accentuated the abstraction and stylization already present in the impressionist sign and converted them into forms that were liberated from the need for perceptual fulfillment. This liberation had momentous implications because it created for the images that were possible within this aesthetics a broad range of significance that spanned from intensified emotions to pure and spontaneous experiences of dwelling in, completing, and elevating the purposes of nature. With these theoretical changes, the romantic notion of the sublime was pared down to the modernist endeavor of situating artistic creation within the ultimate horizons of living.

The images of the symbolist thus surpassed simple and limited representationalism of natural effects and became the synthesis of patterns of experiencing that the symbolists called the "ideal." The ideal was the unified essential "form" in which the "things" of the world participate; and Denis specified two categories of Ideal forms: the beautiful and the sacred.[46] These categories constitute both the "world as spirit" and the direction of the individual symbolist's "painterly temperament."

The Ideal was thus universal, cosmic (world delimiting), and, most importantly, vital. The imaginative configurations that expressed it were no longer simple signs of things, or of ordinary events, but rather they were empathetically animated symbols of the highly autonomous activity of consciousness as it makes up the realm of the "Spirit." By abandoning the exploration of their contingent merging, the symbolists made possible the participation of the impressions in a world of meaning that had an essentially poetic reality, a reality that arose not from the scientific or commonsense justification of sensory experience but from the poetic or aesthetic activity of world actualization or world making. These artists circumscribed the realm of the spirit from within by using imaginatively condensed abstractions in which consciousness, conceived as an activity that captures and elaborates upon the harmonies of nature, signified and externalized itself. As Gustave Kahn pronounced in 1886 in defense of the symbolist project and against the positivist/impressionist approach:

> [T]he essential aim of our art is to objectify the subjective (the externalization of the Ideas) instead of subjectivizing the objective (nature seen through the eyes of a temperament). Thus we carry the analysis of the self to the extreme, we let the multiplicity and intertwining of rhythm harmonize with the measure of the Idea.[47]

Ideas were the organizing imperatives for the actualization (realization) of "the ideal." As constructive intuitions, they made manifest an "intertwining" rhythm of the ideal realm, a demand for lawfulness with which any possible world presents itself as possible to a consciousness.

Because ideas were motivated by such an intuitive participation of conscious beings in a structured reality, they constituted a world;

the primary expressive device both for a constituting world structure and for its aesthetic presence to a conscious being is metaphor. While the impressionist's sign was metonymically motivated by the natural effects that it signified and constituted itself through metonymic effects of association and division, the symbolist's sign was primarily motivated through its characteristic signification of imaginative presence in absence and absence in presence.[48] The trademark of symbolism was a proliferation of images whose juxtaposed meanings might be ambiguous to common sense yet coincide with each other by virtue of a precise and disciplined grammar of equivalences. Many of these juxtapositions of images were still "impressionistic" and thus the product of association, but many complex symbolist images manifested a free and reflective activity of substitution that ranged over the experience of a lived world or a unified course of existence.

G.-Albert Aurier, in an 1891 article on symbolism,[49] used a very powerful analogy to explain the new signifying potency of the symbol: Plato's myth of the cave. In his analogy, the flickering reflections from the fire dancing on the wall are presented as impressions, and the "reality" that the slaves confront at this stage is the glimmer of appearances, of insubstantial ghostlike effects of a shadowy, firelit world that is full of empty signs and abandoned signifiers without their signifieds. However, when the slaves leave the cave of impressions and enter into "the world," they encounter Platonic Forms as images. Images are, Aurier noted, a "sublime alphabet to express Ideas," and ideas are filled with the essential "truths" of the world.

> Thanks to this gift, symbols—that is, Ideas—arise from the darkness, become animated, begin to live with a life that is no longer our life of contingencies and relativities, but a splendid life, the life of Art, the being of being.[50]

This drama of ritualized symbol making, enacted by the symbolists, celebrated "the being of being" by elevating the being of human consciousness, the medium of images, above contingent reality.

This liberation occurred through stages of comprehension—the operation of the metaphor—and also through and in the attainment of the supereminent completeness of the symbol. The symbolist painting must, Aurier went on to say, present this liberation in all of its stages of "finding," and of "making," by narrating the attainment of "the being of being" while achieving it. Indeed, Paul Gauguin expressed this dual focus when he remarked that the symbol must "create a story" and *be* the story itself;[51] and Stéphane Mallarmé's definition of symbolist poetry as always being about itself[52] also affirmed the reflexivity in the depth of the creative experience of the symbol.

A remarkable confirmation for Aurier's symbolist translation of the myth of the cave can be found in earlier poem by Mallarmé, the sonnet "Ses pur ongles," which is one of the few for which the poet himself offered an explanation.[53] Mallarmé gathered the poetic power of metaphor in a richly redundant elaboration of the images of night. The symbol of night develops in a subtle narrative based on the juxtaposition of three cavernous images in which absence is perceived only in its traces.

> Ses purs ongles très haut leur onyx,
> L'Angoisse, ce minuit, soutient lampadophore,
> Mainte rêve vespéral brûlé par le Phénix
> Que ne recueille pas de cinéraire amphore
> Sur les crédences, au salon vide: nul ptyx,
> Aboli bibelot d'inanité sonore,
> (Car le Maître est allé puiser des pleurs au Styx
> Avec ce seul objet dont le Néant s'honore).[54]

A room opens onto the night, framing, through its window, nature as a funereal carrier, *lampadophore*, of burned-out possibilities that dissolve in the void without an amphora to collect their ashes. Anguish flows out of the room and crystallizes in the outer darkness as the "blackened nails" of nature, the carrier of dying dreams. Inside the nocturnal drawing room, no human presences, no sounds, no tears are found. The room is thus metamorphosed into a conch shell filled with the imaginary sound of the ocean; and the doubling of the human shelter into the conch produces a compound image of Hades as a river or flux of tears and sighs, which the conch could never gather together because they are only the traces of the nothingness of human absence.

> Mais proche le croisée au nord vacante, un or
> Agonise selon peut-être décor
> Des licornes ruant du feu contre une nixe,

Elle, défunte nue en le miroir, encore
Que, dans l'oubli fermé par le cadre, se fixe
De scintillations sitôt le septuor.[55]

The inside/outside relation is reversed and doubled again in the vague appearance next to the window of a mirror frame whose center is, for the moment, empty as it reflects only the dark. But in the frame itself the world of poetry and mythology is foreshadowed in the form of a relief of unicorns rushing "from the fire towards a water nymph." The nymph is the past, dead and naked, in the frame. But now the inside of the mirror, *l'oubli* (oblivion), is vaguely lit up with the "fixed scintillation" of the stars of the Great Bear.

In this profusion of suggestive mirrorings that accompany or mark potential and abolished presences, poetic activity "gives" a body to consciousness and a ghost or soul to nature; also in this seemingly uncontainable progress of circles or dialectics, poetic activity "gives" the reader a constantly delimited world, enclosed by the equivalences of the symbol. In those equivalences, as in the reciprocal relations of form and content in the poem, nature repeatedly animates the spirit and, conversely, the spirit animates nature.

This same ability of a symbol to unfold its polysemic potential is also exemplified in Paul Gauguin's *Self-Portrait* of 1889,[56] in which a halo acts as the symbol that both "forms" and expresses the "content" of the painting. It floats above the head of the image of the painter, thus assigning to him divine status. But this image, made sacred, also contains other attributes that extend its symbolic allusions: A nearby tree branch with hanging apple establishes a reference to the temptation of Adam and Eve; and a coiling snake together with hornlike curls of the self-portrait confirms it as an image of the tempting and conniving Satan. Thus the halo unites the metaphoric references (Gauguin to Christ, Gauguin to Adam, and Gauguin to Satan) by expressing the paradigmatic links of similarity within the code of "divinity." However, once the metaphoric equivalences are realized, the "idea" behind, or liberated by, the substitutions is revealed and the ironic truth (that the divine may be conspicuous even in evil, in the satanic, in sinfulness, in Adam, or in artistic creativity, in Gauguin) is made explicit by the presiding of the halo over the "discourse" of its various references.

IN CONCLUSION: CÉZANNE,
THE POTENTIAL SYNTHESIS

In the conversion of sensations into perceptual signs by the impressionists and into imaginative signs by the symbolists, "new and fresh"[57] images were freed from the conventions and habits of common experience. In both schools these images were the correlation of spatial, and thus "external," syntheses with durational, and thus "internal," syntheses within a pictorial display that was not yet clearly understood as a spatiotemporal whole. Because these correlatives had to capture or convey the interaction within experience of consciousness and the "world," the artistic language of the two schools had pronounced differences that derived from the dissimilarity of their understanding of that interaction and of its consequences.

In impressionism, the embodiment of the sensation in metonymic associations constituted a deliberate avoidance of the possibility of placing the synthesizing act within the fabric of the world, and at the same time a subordination of empathy to the psychological workings of abstraction within the economy of sign making. Although the subordination of empathy to abstraction appeared to be less pronounced in symbolism, the images of the symbolists favored, nonetheless, the abstract *configurations* of their artistic language (patterns and rhythms, juxtaposition and repetition) and expressed the deliquescence of consciousness above the world. The contemplative images of the symbolists, which in the end would add metaphoric suggestion to their already typical metonymies, began to emphasize the empathetic component, but as still subordinated to, embodied in, and awakened through the relations among abstract forms.

To surpass the uncritical notions of "perception" and "imagination" that made up the theories and practices of the impressionists and symbolists and fully to transcend the limited signifying potential of their vague abstractions and intense, ambiguous emotions, a new and more poetic image was required. This image, unlike those tied to associative signs and suggestive symbols, had to blend abstraction and empathy in conveying the self-realization of the inner life of the artist as it creatively attunes itself to and reflectively channels the forces of circumstance.

One can detect in the coexisting aesthetics of impressionism/post-impressionism, on the one hand, and symbolism, on the other, the same fragmentation and contradiction of potentially complementary attitudes that were found in the opposition between empathetic and abstract psychologisms. Thus it is clear that, up to the turning point of the fin de siècle, the emphasis lay on the opposition of contiguous associations to the suggested presence/absence of equivalents both in psychology and in art theory.

These poetic devices were in fact, as has been repeatedly indicated, not mutually exclusive in the art of the period, but their systematic complementarity cannot be seen within the scope of their founding theory, associationism. Hypothetically the transcending of this foundation might have occurred either in psychological or in aesthetic theory, but the proper visualization of the transcending step would not truly be possible until new examples of different and more-encompassing images were provided by daring and persistent "image makers." In fact, as has already been stressed, the artists were ahead of the philosophers all through this historical period.

The contribution of Cézanne in constructing, and giving aesthetic grounds to, contemplative and visionary images marked the revolutionary step that transcended the experiential and poetic poverty of associationism. This contribution remains hidden and unrecognizable as long as his images are explained with the tools of those associationists who preceded him or of those who succeeded him (formalists, Freudians, structuralists and poststructuralists). In the ensuing chapters, the philosophical and aesthetic tools of interpretation afforded by a hermeneutical pairing with his contemporary, Bergson, will be used to unveil the distinctive existence and significance of contemplative and visionary images in Cézanne, and the new creative and interpretative horizon that, within that distinctive significance, these images opened up for modernism.

Fig. 1. *Maison de Pendu*, ca. 1873, Musée D'Orsay. (V133)

Fig. 2. *Still Life with Compotier*, 1882, private collection.

Fig. 3. *Mont Sainte-Victoire*, 1902-4, the Philadelphia Museum of Art. (V798)

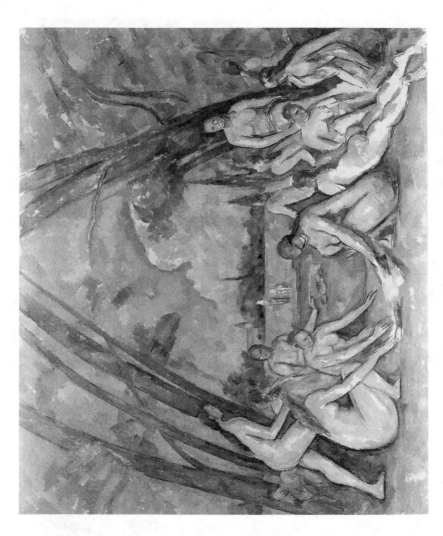

Fig. 4. *The Large Bathers*, 1898–1905, the Philadelphia Museum of Art. (V719)

Fig. 5. *The Cardplayers*, 1890–99, collection of V. Pellerin, Paris. (V536)

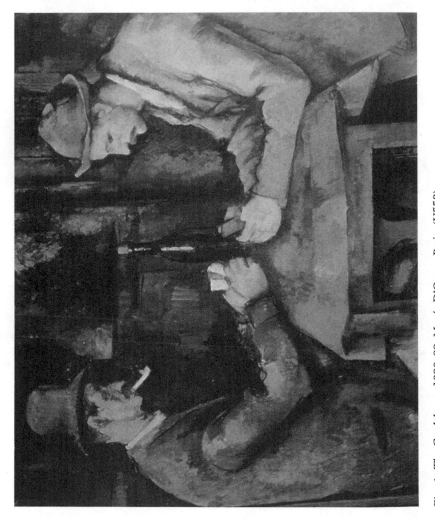

Fig. 6. *The Cardplayers*, 1890–99, Musée D'Orsay, Paris. (V558)

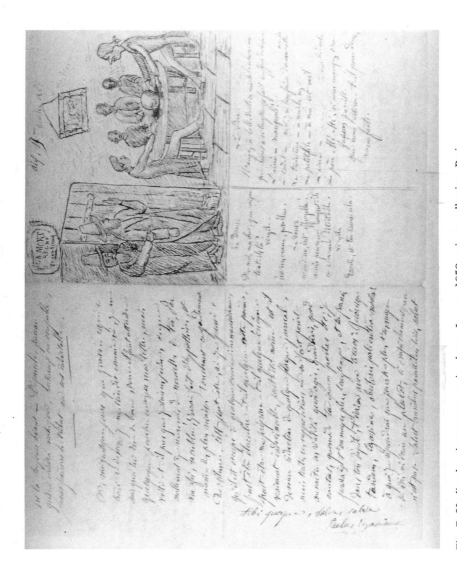

Fig. 7. *Ugolino* drawing accompanying letter, January 1859, private collection, Paris.

THE PATH INTO MODERNISM
Four Modalities of Imagery in Cézanne

Frenhofer, c'est moi!
—Paul Cézanne, 1904

Two years before his death, Cézanne confided to Émile Bernard that when he read Balzac's novel *Le chef d'oeuvre inconnu*,[1] the story of the painter Frenhofer who is unable to "realize" successfully his artistic goals, he was moved to tears and considered himself to be the incarnation of that tragic hero.[2] Although Balzac probably had modeled the character after Delacroix,[3] in his identification with the character, Cézanne could point to the fact that he shared with Frenhofer the goal of "express[ing] life with color."[4] Frenhofer's repeated complaint is that successful "realization" eludes him, and that by failing to realize his artistic goals he is dooming himself to unhappiness in life. Life and art are united in Balzac's novel as the motivation and attainment of each other. Frenhofer's theories about art and his practice of it derive from his perception of the significance of his life as a painter, and the paintings that he produces aspire to be the embodiment of his aesthetic concerns and also an aesthetic fulfillment of his existential concerns.

As a late product of the romantic obsession with the tragic hero, Balzac's Frenhofer is predictably unable to realize his art, and thus his life, and finally ends his suffering by committing suicide in front of his last work, tragically an unrecognized masterpiece. The element of the novel with which Cézanne might have identified most are the speeches in which Frenhofer describes his theories and practice. The unfortunate painter considers his major artistic problem to be the "modernization" of Leonardo's techniques of *chiaroscuro* and *sfumato* to render "plasticity" not with line and shading, as did the Renaissance master, but with color. After years of studying colors and experimenting with "solids and voids," Frenhofer believes he has finally accomplished his goals in a painting of a woman in which "a cloud" of color expresses the plasticity of both the solid human figure and its surrounding open spaces.[5]

> Upon showing it to two younger painters, they remark that they could only see colors placed together in chaotic confusion, held together by a mass of strange lines and forming an impenetrable wall of painting.[6]

Only after lengthy viewing did one of them say that he saw in a corner of the picture "a piece of foot which emerges from this chaos of colors, shades, and undifferentiated hues" as a "kind of mist without shape." In answer to this, Frenhofer exclaims:

> A hand (or foot) is not simply part of the body but the expression and continuation of a thought which must be captured and conveyed. . . . That is the real struggle! Many painters triumph instinctively, unaware of this theme of art. You draw a woman, but you do not see her [in context].[7]

Cézanne's aesthetics, like Frenhofer's, strove to reach beyond experimentation with new techniques and reaction to stylistic trends. Cézanne, too, sought to "capture" and "convey" poetically the fabric and accidents of human existence. Like Frenhofer, he was a mysterious, secretive introvert who guarded his privacy and his progress; unlike Frenhofer, however, he did eventually achieve his goals.

THE "LEGENDARY" CÉZANNE

In *Le Figaro* in December 1895, Arsène Alexandre wrote: "One might have doubted whether, like Homer, Cézanne really existed."[8]

Cézanne's artworks are undeniably a part of our culture and are admired, faithfully copied, and praised, yet Cézanne is not a pervasive historical presence. He recreated the form and content of his medium but did not publish a theoretical treatise and did not bequeath his "inventions" to responsible disciples. Aestheticians and art historians, from his day until our own, have had only a "legendary" or partial Cézanne as a source for their interpretations of his style and inventions. Only a few painters of the next generation who never knew him have pointed to "the Cézannesque" as a major influence in their own practices. Picasso, for example, expressed his appreciation of the artist by proclaiming him "the father of us all,"[9] and Paul Klee called him "the teacher par excellence."[10]

For today's interpreter, the greatest critical problem to be solved arises from the fact that the spokespersons for Cézanne (Émile Bernard, Maurice Denis, Joachim Gasquet, Georges Rivière, J. F. Schnerb, Ambroise Vollard, Gustave Geffroy) have often redefined Cézannism to suit their own aims. Unlike Delacroix, Cézanne did not keep a journal (or at least none has been discovered), and his correspondence is largely composed of salutations and requests for painting supplies. And unlike the flamboyant Picasso, little about his personal life was ever made public. We are fortunate, however, to have some letters from the painter's last years that present enough of his theoretical concerns, if not of his actual theories, to offer us some directions for research into his works; also available are published "conversations" or interviews from this last decade, which were either confirmed or clarified by Cézanne in his letters and thus can be used to support clues that can be found elsewhere in his correspondence.

The language that Cézanne used in his letters, and evidently in his conversations, to describe his theory and his practice represents an elaboration of the ideas, presented in the previous chapters, of both impressionists and symbolists and of some of the late-nineteenth-century academic painters as well. He made frequent use of that volatile term *realisation,* already mentioned in connection with Balzac's Frenhofer, as the means and end of his art. The term first appeared in Cézanne's letters in the 1870s,[11] and in his earliest remarks he referred to the need to realize "sensations" and "impressions." Around 1895 he spoke of *realisation sur nature* as practiced in the techniques of modulation and condensation; and finally in 1900 he arrived at the phrase "realization of the motif" and used this formula to explain not only his current practice but also to defend earlier methods and to explicate earlier paintings. "Realization of the motif" eventually became the most precise statement of the main concern of his theory and his practice. Although he had much earlier, and quite often, spoken of the importance of the *motif,* the two terms *motif* and *realisation* were not unified until the last decade, when, in Aix, he found himself besieged by younger artists who posed questions developing out of their late-impressionist education and out of the emerging symbolist tendencies. To balance their misinterpretations of his out-of-date language, he condensed and substituted words until he arrived at the final formula, which seemed impervious to intellectual distortion. Bernard, Denis, Gasquet, R. P. Rivière, and Schnerb all received this formula from the master, and in conversations and letters they asked for more clarification of it. After Cézanne's death, Matisse continued the discussion of the phrase and deeded its terms to the twentieth century. Other users of the formula, Picasso among them, refined its theoretical intent and its exacting translation into practice.

The term *realisation* was neither invented by Cézanne nor first applied to painting by him. Delacroix used it to refer to aesthetic attention to an artistic "idea" such as the romantic "sublime";[12] in his *Philosophie du salon de 1847*, Castagnary referred to "realized works" as the "subjective productions" of symbolist "dramas";[13] for Émile Zola, the term was synonymous with the "realistic" impulses of naturalism.[14] As can be discerned from just these three sources, the concept has a multiple history, and Cézanne's appropriation of it inherited many of the problems attached to its ambiguous antecedents.

"REALIZATION" IN NINETEENTH-CENTURY AESTHETICS

Only the greatest artists successfully achieved a realization of the problem of mass and of the plasticity which gives the effect of being alive.

—Eugene Delacroix, *Journal*, 21 October 1860

Self-effacing *trompe l'oeil* images, while fulfilling the requirement of decorum for the previous generations, were inadequate expressive means for the newly awakened imagination of the romantic painter desiring to use and explore intense painterly sensations, experimental optical and color ideas, and the new subjects—emotions, moods, personality types, and qualities—so common in contemporary literature and music. *Realiser,* for Delacroix, was to imitate something real and to transcend it in the process of imitation. Such transcendence could be achieved by substituting for the real thing a painted or sculpted equivalent when the latter itself had an autonomous physical presence. The transcending presence would mark the degree of accomplishment in *realisation* by an artist and must be his aim in selecting an appropriate medium and content for *realisation.* But to attain this, the formula for equivalence would have to adequately render the presence of the original object to such an extent that one could say that it was fulfilled in the plastic image; the new physical presence would have to combine its elements with such plasticity that it brought its theme to life independently from the imitated qualities of the original object.

In his above remarks, Delacroix concluded by referring to Peter Paul Rubens's use of glazes of oil paint, which adhered to the linen by the merest dab, enabling it to project away from the surface and catch and reflect the spectrum of the colored light rays striking it.[15] Thus the splash of sea water from the oceans agitated by the frolicking sea nymphs in Rubens's *Marie de'Medici's Embarkation at the Port of Marseilles* was imitated realistically—"realized" according to Delacroix—by the linen-oil-brushstroke formula that reproduced the same splashing image. But so corporeal was the painted effect that it itself actively glistened, interacting with the light and space beyond the canvas surface as an actual physical phenomenon. Although tenuously three-dimensional, the oil drop was nonetheless as distinct as an object as was the real, imitated object. In the Flemish painter, Delacroix found an intentional avoidance of illusionistic devices that concealed and disguised the materials of art making and their effects. Thus he was able to follow his predecessor's efforts in deliberately disclosing the means of art production so that the choices made by an artist and the stages of the making became almost a subplot to the content or theme of the work.

The influence of Rubens on Delacroix in inspiring him to perfect the formulas for *realisation* are well documented. However, *realisation* was not one of Rubens's stated beliefs or aims, and indeed one must keep in mind that there were fundamental differences in their respective "formulas" and in their subsequent *realisation*. Delacroix's attempts to *realiser* tended to explore most fully how the plasticity of the painted surface could express "the effect of being alive," and thus, more than Rubens, he subordinated the rendering of a referential object to his study of painterly effects. In another passage of the *Journal*, Delacroix meditated on the tenuousness of the twofold relations (of an object to its imitation and of the imita- tion to its painterly signs) inherent in *realisation* by discussing the related issue of "finish," or completion.[16] He presented two different types of "realizers" which he contrasted as artistic temperaments: The first were "impetuous, undisciplined genius[es]" who "obey only their instinct[s]" and "do not guide their genius but are guided by it"; and the contrasting type were "the divine geniuses who follow only their own nature, and who also command it" and who "never fall into abnormalities" or "contradictions." He cited as examples of the first type Shakespeare, Michelangelo, Rubens, and Beethoven, all of whom use *le piquant,* which resulted in *realisations* that were more aesthetically "alive" than imitatively correct. For the second type, he cited Racine, Raphael, Poussin, and Mozart as examples of the alternative form of *realisation,* in which the "lack of flaws and incongruities" resulted in what he called *la forme achevée,* a perfect rendering without exaggeration. Delacroix, of course, preferred the first type, with its "sublime" spontaneity and contrasts that expressed, he said, "the pathos of a successful trial of strength." The second type of genius, he found, was too concerned with beauty or the "ideal," rather than with "ideas," and was thus slavishly ruled by Nature and its de- mands for perfect imitation. Therefore, he recommended, and as a ro- mantic he practiced, a process of *realisation* that was more spontaneous than exacting and more expressive than imitative, that retained the disorder and felicitous accidents (*heureuses negligences*) of the sketch and allowed the viewer to share in *la chaleur de son execution.*[17]

But Delacroix was criticized for his attempts at *realisation* by the conservative French critics, who noted a new tendency in his works, a tendency they identified as "abstraction."

> The time is near when, if Delacroix does not get cured, he will wear himself out linking up shades of color without worrying about what they may portray; he will paint bouquets in which one can no longer find flowers.[18]

It is just this type of *realisation* that would be evident in modernism: the "linking" together of color and forms given as much, if not more, importance than any concern for what "they may portray."

Delacroix's *Journals* were published in 1895, that decisive year in Cézanne's career that marked the end of the "earlier" style and the beginning of the "mature." Cézanne read and extensively annotated them. Not only did he change his palette organization in keeping with Delacroix's recommendation (from seven colors in a wheel pattern to eighteen shades in a linear passage ranging from warm to cool tones), but he also began using the word *realisation* to explain his own practice. Indeed, rather than apply this remark to Delacroix, one could say, more correctly, of Cézanne that his later paintings were "bouquets in which one can no longer find flowers."[19] Cézanne's appropriation of the concept of *realisation*, however, did not truly embrace Delacroix's romanticizing of the Rubens type of *realisation* to attain sublimity in expression. Although the Rubens-Delacroix-Cézanne lineage is a provocative outline of influences, one more issue must be considered: the additions made by Émile Zola to the concept of *realisation*.

L'Oeuvre, written by Zola in 1885,[20] was the sad story of Claude, "un genie incomplét, sans la realisation entiér" who, like Frenhofer, commmits suicide in front of his "oeuvre irrealisée." Fully to *réaliser*, Zola explained in his novel, was to work "with the formula of painting in light colors boldly and powerfully," a formula that he identified with the style and technique of the impressionists. But their mistake, he believed, was that they painted fleeting moments observed without reflection. This criticism, though aimed at the *plein air* group, addressed again the issue of finish, or what Zola calls *faire sortir le reste*. In his defense of the style he referred to as "naturalism" (in the preface, written in 1868, to the second edition of *Therese Raquin*),[21] he specifies what finish is: it is "scientific curiosity" that observes with meticulous clarity but without "being touched by the slightest . . . feeling."

> While I was busy writing *Therese Raquin* I forgot the world and devoted myself to copying life exactly, meticulously, giving myself up entirely to precise analysis of the mechanism of the human being. . . . The human side of the models ceased to exist, just as it ceases to exist for the eye of the artist who has a naked

woman sprawled in front of him but who is solely concerned with getting on to canvas a true representation of her shape and coloration.[22]

To attain finish, then, is to rid the narrative, or the painting, of any vestiges of the presence of the author, to record dispassionately, analytically. However much Zola appears in these passages to be favoring a type of *realisation* that avoids the expressive elements of art in favor of more imitative intentions, and thus to be far from the early modernist position, it must be noted that the novelist was instead still attempting to establish the potential and, more important, the limits of expressiveness (or of impressions, since he was criticizing impressionism). According to Zola, what must be recorded are the *effects* produced on a "mechanism" or "organism" (e.g., "shape and coloration" and, to recall his advice in *L'Oeuvre*, "light colors"). One had to therefore paint light reflections and refractions, relations among various color surfaces and among types of structural configuration— the ultimate permanent, stable, and analyzable elements that can be translated into paint. Skin, hair, or fabric, and seasonal and atmospheric conditions and changes, should not be themselves the objects of imitation. In other words, Zola advised avoidance of representational imitation and favored instead paintings or narratives that presented (completed, fulfilled, accomplished, finished) the mechanics of pictorial/perceptual synthesis by *recording definite causes of conscious effects*.

Zola's advice on finish, when united with Delacroix's, constituted the margins within which the concept of *realisation* as theorized by the early modernists would take shape. Zola agreed with Delacroix's focus on the art-making process, the "formula," as a source of expressiveness and independence from subject matter in the artwork, and he also specified, as indicated above, that use of the formula must be limited to presenting accurately identified responses (effects) rather than representing objects. Stéphane Mallarmé's theory of "equivalences," dating from the 1860s, required similar limitations concerning *realisation* in his famous advice, "Peindre non la chose mais l'effet qu'elle produit."[23]

Thus, by the 1870s when Cézanne appropriated the word and the concept, it was necessary for him to select from its usage the aspects of the definition he wished to emphasize. He accomplished this not so much by redefining the term directly (indeed he never did so) nor by citing any of his sources; he proceeded instead to a cautious selection of additional terms to accompany the word in order to specify the limits operative in his own practice of *realisation*. His first use of the term *realisation* was in his letters in 1878, in the phrase "the realization of wishes," which apparently referred to the consummation and fulfillment of desired goals and aims (the traditional meaning of "finish"). He later expanded and refined the meaning of the term *realisation* by combining it with certain modifiers—specifically, "of sensations," "after nature," and "of the motif," which suggested a substantial and original elaboration of its meaning well beyond the traditional understanding of it as "finish" that is still the most commonly recognized definition by critics.

CÉZANNE'S EARLY PERIOD (1863–80)
Symbolic Images: *Realisation des Sensations*

In a letter to Zola of November 1878, Cézanne remarked that they should discuss how their respective arts were "means of realizing sensations."[24] In his letters of 1876 to 1886, Cézanne frequently referred to Zola's books, articles, and theories and occasionally made references also to the characters of Zola's novels. His remarks indicate that, at least until 1886, Cézanne agreed with Zola's definition of *realisation* as a synthesis of perceptual and aesthetic experiences that transformed sensations into impressions.[25]

However, in other letters to his friend, Cézanne often spoke of some special difficulties of his in "realizing sensations" that arose from his peculiar sensitivity as a painterly "temperament." The problem, he found, was centered on his rising need to extend his discoveries of painterly effects, that is, to collect more adequate signs for natural appearances, by finding a greater number of correlations between natural mechanisms and the aesthetic temperament impressed by them. A letter written in 1878[26] contains remarks concerning how the temperament, "or creative force," must be appropriately matched to and fulfilled through the works produced by it; the works, indeed, must be "pregnated with the passion that agitates the persons." Thus instead of accepting the conversion of conventional emotions and established aesthetic moods into plastic "impressions," as Zola called for, Cézanne appealed for a more deep and enduring, a biographical, significance to permeate all paintings.

In working toward its creative development, the painterly temperament must persistently engage in two modes of active/synthetic experience, identified by Cézanne as "the eye" and "the mind."

> Dans le peintre il y a deux choses; l'oeil et le cerveau, tous deux doivent s'entre-aider: il faut travailler à leur développement mutuel; à l'oeil par la vision sur nature, au cerveau par la logique des sensations organisées, qui donne les moyens d'expression.[27]

Cézanne analyzes here the activities of consciousness as it clarifies and intensifies its intentions amidst the contingencies of the flux of the world. The "eye" and the "mind"—working together as temperament—establish the range and duration of intuitive and memory processes as they project themselves into the receptiveness and resistance of the natural world. Within this experience of participation, the artist's temperament unfolds its structures of meaningfulness, which invest with their own significance both worldly situations and *les moyens d'expression.*

The "eye" accumulates sensory data and concurrently orders and magnifies them progressing from simple and conventional syntheses of experience to more abstract and comprehensive ones that continually add significance to perception. In this enriched perception, the "mind" can intensify its intentions and also achieve its own liberation by a greater understanding of its own activities and directions. Like the eye, the mind also concentrates on itself in the twofold act of making and acquiring meaning.

Cézanne had more to say, in this quote, about the active character of intuition and projection as "mind" than about the results of their applications to sensory experience; what was important, though, was that because of their mutual interaction in every engagement of consciousness, he could conclude that aesthetic understanding is the process in which eye and mind interpenetrate in order to realize sensations. As mind, the temperament reveals to itself a dynamic schema, that is, a formula for organizing sensations. Cézanne called this meaningful schema a "logic," and spoke of it as constituted by relations of and between sensations making up patterns. It should be clear from these symbolic perceptions that the artistic temperament was itself a "realization" that manifested itself in its own aesthetic "matter." For Cézanne the matter for the artistic temperament was constituted by the drift and the affective burden of our habitual sensations as they offer themselves for elaboration by the freedom of our enduring experience. In the end, as was claimed above, to "realize" sensations was to make them adequate expressive instruments of the manifested and manifesting fusion of eye and mind in prolonged activity.

In a letter to his son, Pissarro described Cézanne's practice of "realizing sensations." He recalled that Cézanne painted with "sweeping brushstrokes" of thick paint that set up dramatic contrasts of tones and textures, and that his obvious devotion to these dramatic contrasts had precedence over any concern with subject matter or impressionistic truth.[28] According to Pissarro, Cézanne did not emphasize the ability of colors and brushstrokes to convey adequately natural effects or perceptual states; he stressed instead their logic of abstract relations of painterly means, as inferred from his temperament.

Regarding these "sweeping brushstrokes," Pissarro went on to say, Cézanne erred in not presenting impressions as impressions and in showing too much of his artistic temperament. Indeed, Pissarro criticized Cézanne for this and called the paintings produced at that time "color reliefs" of temperament; consequently he advised his student to organize the textures and forms of his composition with underlying geometrical abstractions (cone, cylinder, sphere). These latter would, Pissarro hoped, crystallize *the scene* into an impression.

In fact, the plasticity and luminosity of Cézanne's colored brushstrokes animated as "dramatic contrasts" by his temperament were not used to convey the natural effects or even his conscious analysis of a scene (Pissarro's geometricized organization). They were used *to form a site for realization.* Thus the painting, instead of being a scene from nature, was in reality an abstract site to be animated by an empathetic projection of Cézanne's artistic temperament; and the colored brushstrokes were the signs of his temperament, *which was itself realized in that animation.*

A famous work from this early stage of Cézanne's development, the *Maison du Pendu* of 1873 (figure 1) can be analyzed in order to unravel the stages of the activity of the artist's consciousness forming and signifying itself in painting. At a primary level of analysis, the colored brushstrokes could be read as natural signs (impressions): "Local" colors are used to reproduce the most mechanical effects—rich "organic colors" for the fertile natural growth, "deep" blue for the sky, and "dusty" brown for the dirt track—and the brushstrokes are used to reconstruct the textures of the natural "objects"—sweeping, commalike brushstrokes for the leaves, palette-knife swirls for the sky, and parallel, slashing brushstrokes for the ruts in the road.[29]

Although these apparently natural signs, "deep blueness" and "dustiness," appear to be similar to Monet's impression "ascending luminosity" in the painting *Impression: Sunrise*, they can also be read as *relations* of the painterly elements—that is, within a "logic" that transcends the impressionist sign. The linear brushstrokes of the road, of the houses, and of the trees associatively connect the patterned rhythms as spatial signs that mark the dynamism of the pictorial space. The rising verticals of the trees lead upward from a ground line to the open space of the sky, while the slashing lines of the road in the foreground "lead" or recede to the horizon line of the background. And the horizontal linear rhythms repeated in the houses line up alongside the road and substantiate its recessional path through these planar levels.

A logic of color relations is also evident in the scene: Warm colors, including a reddish brown with orange highlights, are used for the linear patterns that convey the spatial relations—the road, house, and trees—while their complementary contrasts, a cool green and blue, are used for the curved patterns—shrubs and grass and the softly swirling sky—and serve to relieve the strong warm colors of the linear patterns and qualify them as different vital forms.

Within this context of contrasts (linear/curved, warm/cool), Cézanne attempted to modify the impressionist presentation of a scene ordered in such a way that it would evoke a similar moody experience in the viewer or recreate a deep and overwhelming sensorial memory. He instead went beyond merely stabilizing material identities and apprehending them in a scene by beginning to structure a situation in which he could project his intuitions as images that have already made sense out of a "moody experience" and "memory" and crystallized them into dematerialized forms dynamically expressive of his emotions.

Thus the prevailing abstract language in the painting *Maison du Pendu* could be read as an articulation of logical or relational concepts that found and formed meaning within the compass of the painter's aesthetic experience. These relations of contrasting dynamism embodied in the linear patterns, colors, textures, and spatial indices might appear to imply a division of their concrete effects (curved/noncurved, stable/unstable, etc.); but beyond this division, they could also be understood as expressing, in their juxtapositions, the full range of the vital indivisibility, the "flowing togetherness," of the world and the perceiver. Thus these abstractions could be said to reveal the reciprocity, the initial reflectiveness, between the activities of the artistic temperament and a world that can only come together *for* that temperament. The contrasting elements could thus be said to be plastic equivalents of the cosmic tensions, rifts, and mysterious harmonies that Cézanne had transcended by painting them as the unified empathetic projection of his own *élan vital*.

This world of the painting that Cézanne brought forth into being[30] through these reciprocal contrasts also contained, dispersed within its "abstract" rhythms and tensions, a variety of meaningful images of the activity, emotion, and freedom of his artistic temperament in the process of creation. These "images" showed the mark of temperament through *distortion*. Thus they lay outside the realm of pure abstract relations and indeed were present only within the limits of the pictorial space through explicit signals that emphatically pointed to, and made meaningful, their absence.

In this scene of a fork in a road there are no people, there is no activity; no clouds float in this immense blue sky, there are no flying birds, no scampering animals. What "things" are conspicuous in it efface themselves in a looming deadly calm that allows only patterns, colors, rhythms, and qualities to be shown through them. The road goes nowhere: It disappears to the left, and its turning to the right is also hidden. There is much that is absent in this scene, but there is also much that is mysteriously present in the disguised, the hidden, and the distorted. The ruts in this road make all the more present the absent wheels of the cart that dug them and marked their depth and their thrust in this space. The blank, staring windows of the rhomboidal houses look blindly at us, empty of the humans behind them, the folk who inhabit this village and who trod the road, pushed the cart, built the houses, and were neighbors of the man who killed himself.

The linear patterns, while appearing to construct the logic of the visual space, in effect fragment it. The trees along the road that mark spatial continuity have no stabilizing ground, no actual source; and the trees on a distant hill, which should have opened up spatial depth, appear to sprout incongruously from the slanted eave of a roof that lies in a different spatial plane. The colors, while appearing on one level of analysis to describe natural effects, can be seen on another level as limiting the diversity of organic profusion to the simpler contrast of arbitrary complementary pairings.

These distortions, then, order the abstractions and their rhythmic manifestations into an expressive unity that no longer describes a scene, relates natural effects, or realizes impressions. The distortions prevent the painterly elements from acting in the service of representational vision and empower them instead to express certain aesthetic intuitions on the part of the creator. Thus the *Maison du Pendu* is not the collection of fleeting, spontaneous events that constituted the *sensation forte* of the impressionists. It is a canvas filled with tensions in color and pattern that project (not evoke, nor convey) a tense world; indeed the space of this world is so charged that we can neither move within it nor escape from it.

Cézanne holds our attention captive within this space, making it the site of his transcendence of the instantaneous impression. The painting is thus the vehicle for, and the realization of, his dismissal of the ephemeral, the transitory, and the fleeting in the natural world. At the same time, it captures, arrests, and makes transparent, fixed, and stable the uneasy intensities of his temperament. His goal of "realizing sensations," together with the great emphasis he placed on the spontaneous and logical, the abstracting and liberating tendencies of the artistic temperament, matched his desire to transcend the limitations of objectified, devitalized, and, in the end, ghostly impressions and compelled him to realize the vitality of his own enduring aesthetic responses and activities.

As Bergson noted, the work of art brought forth by such aesthetic activities was the "outcome of an emotion unique of its kind, which seemed to baffle expression and yet had to express itself."[31] Emotion, for him, was the attention of consciousness "in-tending" itself into images. In the case of the *Maison du Pendu* the emotion seems to stir within the agitations on the surface of the canvas and in the distortions that express the deep-seated concerns of the artistic temperament. These distortions are thus correlates for persistent and particular emotions that, as Merleau-Ponty discovered, contain intuitions about the breadth of existence.

> We live in the midst of man-made objects, among tools, in houses, streets, cities and most of the time we see them only through the human actions which put them to use. We become used to thinking that all this exists necessarily and unshakeably. Cézanne's painting suspends these habits of thought and reveals the base of inhuman nature upon which man has installed himself. This is why Cézanne's people are strange, as if viewed by a creature of another species. Nature itself is stripped of the attributes which make it ready for animistic communions: there is no wind in the landscape, no movement on the Lac d'Annecy, the frozen objects hesitate as if at the beginning of the world. It is an unfamiliar world in which one is uncomfortable and which forbids all human effusiveness. . . . [Cézanne's is] a vision which penetrates right to the root of things beneath the imposed order of humanity.[32]

The impetus of the aesthetic ideas of the painter is thus infused into the relations amongst the abstractions, so that they and not objects, or shadows, or sunlight, or the typical icons of the Academics, make evident his being-there with all the intensity of his temperament.

> Only one emotion is possible for this painter—the feeling of strangeness—and only one lyricism—that of the continual rebirth of existence.[33]

This lyricism is totally imbued and realized in the patterns; they, not the trees, houses, or road, move and extend, multiply and connect, to create a tactile space that is consistent with the uneasiness and scrupulousness of abstraction.[34] Similarly, the vibrating colors, and not the window glass or the moist air, recreate the immateriality of the world. As his highly charged emotions empathetically supported and animated his abstractions, Cézanne transcended the dualisms of subject/object and self/world and revealed the rightful location of the subject *in* the object. As Bergson noted, this coincidence of subject and object "is the mind finding itself in things." Or as Cézanne was later to say in a letter to Émile Bernard, "One must penetrate what lies before."[35]

Like Bergson's philosophical quest, this quest of Cézanne's, of which we have only traced the very earliest stage in the 1870s, was metaphysically motivated. In his special situation, between impressionism and symbolism and between abstract and empathetic psychologism, he strove to go beyond the materializing activities of art making, to realize the creative intention of the art-making process, and to paint that process that was as much the concern of his life as it was of his painting. Thus, rather than being like the impressionist works, which introduce feelings into us, Cézanne's works introduce us into feelings, into his temperament.

In the next stage of his development, Cézanne focused on creating new and "fresh" patterns (images) that could make up a repertory of rhythms expressive of "the lyricism of the rebirth of existence" and could be used in turn as more precise correlates for his own aesthetic temperament "living" through this lyricism. The new images were developed not by studying nature and its effects, but by the most minute investigation of the effects produced by his painting materials—the colors and textures of his color reliefs—aimed at discovering the synthesizing, stabilizing, ordering, and signifying tendencies of his temperament *in transcending* nature. During this next stage of his theoretical development, he referred to his experiments as attempts to *realiser sur nature* even though the resultant realization was attained by and through, as well as *dependent* on, his medium. This designation *sur nature* points to the increasing importance given by the painter, at this stage of his stylistic development, to developing abstracting techniques that will reveal the "truth" of his empathetic technique.

CÉZANNE'S EXPERIMENTAL PERIOD (1880-95)
Plastic Images: *Realisation sur Nature*

The phrase *realisation sur nature* has been incorrectly translated in the English editions of Cézanne's *Letters*, and by those who use these translations, as "realization of nature" instead of "realization on nature" or "realization in nature."[36] This misinterpretation, along with many others, such as the recurring translations of *realisation* as "accomplishment," "achievement," and "expression," has contributed to conceptual looseness in Cézanne scholarship in several ways: It has resulted in a widespread assessment of Cézanne's style, whether of the early or late periods, as based on an obedience to nature as the source and content of his art and in a consequent identification of Cézanne as the impressionist par excellence, as the culmination or "end of impressionism." Consequently, Cézanne's search for a unique relation of art to nature has been made to look like the slavish dependency of a naïve naturalism based on an unreconstructed attitude toward perception and, therefore, as a point of view that is decidedly premodernist.

However, in numerous instances the master reacted with horror to pronouncements like these, made during his lifetime. His statements, which exhibited a new understanding of the signifying rather than representational functions of realization, reached further than similar statements by the symbolists and constituted, as shown in previous chapters, the turning point of modernism. "Que penser des imbéciles qui vous disent: le peintre est toujours inférieur à la nature?" he said to Gasquet.[37] And his often-repeated statement about the autonomy of art, "L'art est une harmonie parallèle à la nature,"[38] further confirmed this belief and also implied that, though independent, art shares with nature in eliciting harmony. According to Cézanne, "the Pater Omnipotens Acternae Deus"[39] is the "realizer" of nature, and the artist, the "realizer" of his own aesthetic ideas.

The use of the preposition *sur,* in the phrase *realisation sur nature,* might imply also an impressionist bias—that is, that the resulting *realisation* may be a variation on a theme, pattern, or motif taken from, or inspired by contact with, nature. Themes, such as those developed from moods and attitudes, patterns of contiguity, contrast or similarity seen in nature, motifs of essential qualities of things and relations within the natural world, were indeed the subjects for the impressionists' attempts at *realisation sur nature*. But for Cézanne, contact with nature was not necessary in order to realize "after" it. "Nature is on the inside," he proclaimed to Gasquet;[40] the colors, textures, spaces, and light reflections from nature extend into the artist's conscious bodily activity, arousing internal equivalents and awakening intuitions.

In one of the accounts of Cézanne's practice, we find another example of the master's emphatic recognitions that the subject and object, the self and the world, the artistic temperament and operative "stimuli," are inextricably conjoined and coalesced within aesthetic experience and artistic activity. To "realize in nature" is not to imitate, capture, or stabilize it, but to participate with it in its coming "to be." Indeed, in this account, which will be discussed presently, Cézanne further modified the range of his aesthetic experiences to include the history of art as a horizon of his intuitive projections.

In 1899, the gallery owner Ambroise Vollard sat for a portrait with Cézanne. After over one hundred agonizingly long and tension-filled sittings in which the painter frequently threw down his tools and pronounced himself unable to continue, Vollard, wishing to complete the commission, called attention to two patches of bare canvas in the center of the composition where the "hands" were. Quickly Cézanne explained that he had noticed them as well. However, he remarked:

> Si ma séance de ce tantôt au Louvre est bonne, peut-être demain trouverai-je le ton juste pour boucher ces blancs. Comprenez un peu, M. Vollard, si je mettais là quelque chose au hasard, je serais forcé de reprendre tout mon tableau en partant de cet endroit.[41]

Instead of studying the light and dark effects playing on the skin of his sitter's hands and matching them, like an impressionist, to the colors on his palette and the textures of his brushes, Cézanne steered clear of all naturally evoked perceptual experience and, turning away from the sensual immediacy of the scene, he went to the Louvre. There he redirected his active/reflective consciousness to the "effects" of the paintings—their signs—in order to find a tonality *juste pour boucher* this unique pictorial situation.[42] The "nature" to which Cézanne turned in forming signs and motifs during this period of his development was even beyond the "uncomfortable" world projected into the tense landscape of the *Maison du Pendu;* it was a different, "inhuman" world,[43] the world of art as embodied in its history. He studied this world, this collection of constituted reconstructions, a ready-made conversion *sur nature* that agreed with his most perceptive predilections. Thus he directed his studies at the Louvre toward synthesizing within his own experiments impressions he extracted from past works and reactivated in his own.

Vollard's description of Cézanne's careful considerations of how to complete the blank section of his portrait also reveals the theoretical concerns in this stage of Cézanne's development. The painter's insistence on part-to-part integration and part-to-whole consistency in the painting indicated that he was still concerned with analyzing the *relations* of his painterly elements; but in this stage of his development, he began to emphasize the diversity, the vitality, and the magnitude of his abstractions instead of utilizing them, as before, to reveal the "unfamiliar." As has been repeatedly indicated in earlier contexts, these revised abstractions, now realized *sur nature*, were even more ideal crystallizations of the ideal harmony of the "world" inhabited by the painter's temperament.

By realizing *in the context of the activities of painting*, his own and those of his predecessors, the master was released from the necessity of intuiting, in and through the inhuman world, "the vital" and the "true." He was now set free to concentrate on finding and producing *the language of the human*, the poetics of an aesthetic existence. During this period, the focus on the techniques of painting was directed at discovering that language of action, the expression, Cézanne explained, of the *logique* of the painterly relations and of their ability to signify the lived rhythms of his practice. *Logique* revealed to him the *principles* of organized sensation, and in order to realize it he developed two techniques that presented ideal structure through patterns proper of a "grammar" of (syntactical) relations; these techniques were called "modulation" and "condensation."

Modulation

Modulation was used by Cézanne as a technique for ordering his "colored patches" into a syntactical arrangement of analytic parts making up the harmony of the whole painting as a synthesis.

> Il n'y pas de ligne, il n'y a pas de modelé, il n'y a que des contrasts. Ces contrasts, ce ne sont pas le noir et le blanc qui les donnent, c'est la sensation colorée. Du rapport exact des tones résulte le modelé. . . . On ne devrait pas dire modeler, on devrait dire *moduler*. . . . Quand le couleur est à sa richesse, la forme est à sa plénitude. Les contrastes et les rapports de tons voilà le secret du dessin et du modelé. . . . L'effet constitue le tableau, il l'unifie et le concentre; c'est sur l'existence d'une tache dominant qu'il faut l'établir.[44]

In the modulating of single objects, such as an "apple" or a "mountain," the colors and brushstrokes were organized and controlled by careful gradations of tone based on scientific color relations and applied in patterned arrangements;[45] as indicated above, the modulated *taches colorées* were subordinated to a total synthesizing organization so that they not only expressed individual effects but also were integrated within a tactile fabric of color.

A good example of such intentional part-to-part and part-to-whole integration can be found in one of Cézanne's most luminous and tightly organized still lifes, the *Still Life with Compotier* of 1882 (figure 2). The canvas is covered with strokes of basically the same shape, texture, and size, producing a homogeneous, mosaic-like surface. These slightly arching strokes are fitted together, as if hinged, into a screenlike design; like screens, the strokes form the surfaces of each object, whether concave, convex or flat, by altering their parametrical direction.[46] Not only does this neutralizing *facture* render all "objects" alike in their surface and compositional qualities, but it also prevents any qualitative distinction in the treatment of "non-objects," like empty space, shadows, or reflections. Whether inanimate or animate as presences, the hard metal of a knife blade or the fragile flesh of an apple, the stationary glass bowl or the slightly shifting grapes, the mechanically printed wallpaper or the coarse grain of the wooden table receive the same treatment in their qualitative formulas. All "objects" are converted into patterns of tactile vision and presented as *plastic images* whose interpenetration is achieved in the homogeneous texture of the canvas surface.

No diverse repertory of color formulas is used in these patterned strokes; the colors all perform the same function of hinging together the tactile space so that it, and not the assemblage of "objects," composes the *situation* to which the world is reduced by the painter's aesthetic activities. The colors here do not describe independent and substantial aspects of things; they are used to articulate the world's *qualitative* response to a concentrated act of aesthetic attention. Colors fill in the tactile space with sequences of modulated tones that visually preserve the objects at a proximate distance as if sculpted. In this painting, the graduated arrangements are organized by using adjacent blends from the colored spectrum of the rainbow. The "apples" are patterns of rainbow-arch-shaped strokes filled with warm colors (red/orange/yellow in various combinations and tonal emphases); the "pears" are formed with quite another chromatic range, that of yellow/yellowish-green/green adjacents; and the glass "compotier" is patterned with large white strokes modulated by contiguous purple/blue and yellow/orange complementary pairings that create a vibratory translucency.

As was said above, all of these individual patterns are harmonized within the integral structure of the composition. The location of individual patterns can affect their color formulas, as can the equilibrium of the quadrants of the composition require the repetition of certain colored patterns at certain sites. The pervasive symmetry of the tonal patterning is most evident in the imagery that takes up the largest areas of space, such as the draped cloth and the wallpaper. These areas are made to appear different in their overall color arrangement as contiguous patterns come into contact with each other.

While the color formulas in the painting are derived from careful and logical plotting by locality and spatial symmetry, the overarching compositional plan is just as apparent. The limited repertory of colored patterns (essentially restricted to cool or warm adjacent blends) results in the creation of a subtle rhythm of chromatic repetitions and counterrepetitions throughout the painting. Like the homogeneity produced on the surface of the canvas by the repeating brushstrokes, the colors themselves are by necessity distributed rhythmically throughout the surface; consequently they too transcend mere descriptive analysis and become expressive of an interpenetration of all the elements of this tactile space that characteristically illuminates the objects from the inside.

Thus modulation can be seen as arising out of a *logique* of painterly effects whose development Cézanne initiated during the 1870s in order to organize his abstractions within a syntax of surface relations. In the *Still Life with Compotier*, however, the technique of modulation was an attempt to control logically not only the constituted images (abstractions) of his paintings but also the constituting intentions (empathetic projections) within the images. By presenting the abstractions as pure patterns, arbitrarily textured and arbitrarily colored, he restricted their emotive excesses so that they could come alive *as the corporeal schema of the painting*.

The closed rhythm of rainbow patterns in this still life avoids the perceptual/emotional qualities of earlier patterns found in the *Maison du Pendu*, in which the brushstrokes and colors are so specific, independent, and provocative that they can be said to make up *the* physiognomic tensions of the painting. The rainbow patterns of the *Compotier* emerge from an abstraction that closes and restricts expressiveness without limiting its expressive *value*, an abstraction that avoids excessive subjectivity and perceptual effulgence and that, by virtue of its nonconventional status, can be said to arise from a preexisting imaginative schema that *contains* all its correlates. These correlates emerge within the "logic" of the modulations as poetic equivalences gathered together in the collection of rainbow patterns. Within their range of selective and combinatory tactile/visual relations, the rainbow patterns can be read as a syntax of colored strokes based not only on contiguous (and thus syntagmatic) connections, but also on comparative (paradigmatic) connections that can be added to, and accentuate, the metonymies of similarly modulated objects.

A very interesting rainbow pattern to trace in its metonymic dispersal, in this still life, makes use of the full color spectrum of the rainbow. It appears within the shadowy depths of the folds of draped cloth, as the prevalent pattern of the crystalline wine glass, and on the artificial leaves and flowers in the wallpaper design. By sharing the same modulated pattern, all of these images are connected within a dynamic schema. The cloth, the glass, and the artificial flowers all participate in the cosmic perfection of the complete rainbow pattern, with its otherworldly luminosity and vaulting arch that surges from the earth and encloses the sky. The rainbow, in its own ethereal form, affirms that the objects in the still life have both transitory and enduring qualities; like the rainbow, they are more than mere inanimate objects, for their qualitative intensity identifies with the perennial energies of life. These rainbow patterns do not depict the bruise in a petal of a dying flower or the curling edge of a leaf in a harvested vine, nor do they assign ephemeral qualities to the slow drip of wax from a burning candle or to the sheen of dust on an open book. The rainbow patterns find embodiment instead in common, man-made things, tools for living. The cloth spreads its length and mediates between surfaces: covering, protecting, consecrating the site with its presence. The glass embraces the unembraceability of the liquid: holding, preserving, and presenting it. The wallpaper, like the linen cloth, provides a new, unfamiliar setting that in this case introduces a collection of images from another world. The "leaves" and "flowers" of the wallpaper fill the interior space of the still life with presences from an exterior realm, with the clutter and excess of organic growth.

Like the carefully modulated canvas, the wallpaper presents orderly, denaturalized abstractions of organic shapes.[47] These repetitive rhythms of the organic find resonance in the other metonymic references: The folds of the linen are aligned and drawn with such regularity that they seem as motionless and pervasively plastic as a mountain range, yet as malleable as a bank of clouds;[48] and the smooth, translucent/transparent surface of the glass/liquid appears to hesitate between the heavy calm of the ocean and the volatile density of a gossamer sky.

As a metonymic chain, these images activated by the shared rainbow patterning suggest another set of references, this time metaphoric, that are present only in their traces, that is, in the constitutive pattern of the rainbow that is their common analogue. The rainbow thus frames an imaginary landscape and makes visible the mountain in the cloth and the ocean in the glass. The rainbow is operative within this setting as an underlying dynamic schema that makes present the vital forces of the interior/exterior world; in the equivalence of the interior and exterior forces, Cézanne realized a set of metaphoric implications that overflow the metonymies, *but* without superficially vitalizing colors and textures. The metonymies in this still life activate the schema of modulated abstractions by enhancing and multiplying their signifying potential, but always within the limits that the painter drew by subordinating his empathetic projection of metaphors to a restrictive, though still poetic, abstracting purpose.

Meyer Schapiro noticed in Cézanne's practice of modulation, especially in his still lifes, this self-disciplining motive that allowed him to transcend the "objectness" of painting. This transcendence was described earlier as the presence of the world in a situation: Both the situation and the world are raised to a poetic level by the indwelling of consciousness.

> The objects chosen for still-life painting—the table with food and drink, the vessels, the musical instruments, the pipe and tobacco, the articles of costume, the books, tools, playing cards, *objets d'art*, flowers, skull, etc.—belong to specific fields of value: the private, the domestic, the gustatory, the convivial, the artistic, the vocation and avocation, decorative and sumptuous, and—

less often—in a negative mood, objects offered to meditation as symbols of vanity, mementos of the ephemeral and death.[49]

To paint a still life is thus to "suggest a kind of world-view,"[50] a reality steeped in an understanding of the "value" and significance of the modes of dwelling in the world; the objects in a still-life painting, he notes, represent not only this dwelt-in world but also the richness and multiplicity of the modes of being-in.

The still life, Schapiro goes on to say,

> consists of objects that, whether artificial or natural, are subordinate to man as elements of use, manipulation and enjoyment; these objects are smaller than ourselves, within arm's reach, and owe their presence and place to a human action or purpose. They convey man's sense of power over things in making or utilizing them; they are instruments as well as products of his skills, his thoughts and appetites. . . . They are the themes *par excellence* of an empirical standpoint wherein our knowledge of proximate objects, and especially of the instrumental, is the model or ground of all knowledge.[51]

Schapiro was very obviously referring here to the Heideggerian description of the unity of the being of "things" and the act of existence.[52] As Schapiro clarified, each instrumental "thing" that bears within the still life the aesthetic value of living creatively

> comes to stand then for a sober objectivity, and an artist who struggles to attain that posture after having renounced a habitual impulsiveness or fantasy, can adopt the still-life as a calming or redemptive modest task, a means of self-discipline and concentration; it signifies to him the commitment to the given, the simple and dispassionate—the impersonal universe of matter.[53]

The impersonal universe of matter is built on those abstractions that Cézanne used in the practice of modulation in an effort to control and limit his emotional projections. The material entities, the familiar things, contained and exhibited the artist's temperament, now made to speak dispassionately through their logically concentrated structures.

Consequently, in this still life we come to see things from the inside and the outside, "in" the coalescence of time and space. The pedestal of the compotier is parallel to the picture plane, as is the stem of the wine glass, yet Cézanne also displayed the inside of the bowl of the compotier and the interior rim of the goblet. It is as if a shift in our point of view had made possible the apprehension of this space from different angles of vision in a fractured time. But even in such apparent distortions, the "logic" of modulation protects the continuity, the indivisibility of the space through the interpenetrating rhythms of the colored brushstrokes. Instead of experiencing the objects as distorted, the space as divided, and the narratively projected time as fragmented, the modulated medium delivers the expanse and diversity of *duration* as it extends in space and qualitatively changes in time.

Thus these new kinds of distortion were not accidents of the unconscious, nor were they physiognomic scars charged with repressed emotion; they were the manifest intentions of a painter who had found a way to paint duration by concentrating on *controlling* patterns so that they expressed a dynamic schema of integrated relations (in purposeful abstractions and in meaningful equivalents) and also presented the arrested evolution of an enduring event. In conclusion, by opening out the interiors of his still-life objects, Cézanne effaced the hard distinctions between inside and outside; by drawing the oscillating ellipses of the rims with multiple contours, he blurred the exact boundary between the object and the space surrounding it. Thus, within the "halo" of outlining, a shape emerged from, and at the same time merged with, the spatial envelope in which it was in flux. As Merleau-Ponty noted:

> It is Cézanne's genius that when the overall composition of the picture is seen globally, perspectival distortions are no longer visible in their own right but rather contribute, as they do in natural vision, to the impression of an emerging or development of an object in the act of appearing, organizing itself before our eyes.[54]

Cézanne's "lived objects," which radiate their reality, were not *constructed* but were grasped in the process of forming themselves within the indivisible whole of the modulated space. As T. E. Hulme so succinctly put it: the space is shown "ripening,"[55] or, as Cézanne himself said, it is "germinating."[56]

Modulation can thus be summarized as an organizational apparatus that orders the medium into integrated plastic images. At this stage in Cézanne's development, the triumph of the plastic image over the symbolic image, as a more logical signifier of the artistic temperament, represented the triumph of abstraction over the false empathy of distorted appearances. In his efforts to put into practice condensation, his second technique of invention of plastic imagery, he continued his researches into the abstract properties of "logical" synthesis; but he was now searching for permanent and stable (ideal) patterns that could stand as the overall, synthetic "keynotes" of his designs.

Condensation

Cézanne began to paint alongside Camille Pissarro as early as 1872 and, upon receiving Pissarro's advice to paint objects as solid forms of geometrical configuration, the young Aixois added to his experiments in the patterning of *taches colorées* concurrent investigations into the signifying functions of patterns built purely on ideal linear forms. Whether Pissarro consistently practiced his own advice and can be thus given credit as a precursor of Cézanne's practice of this particular technique is highly questionable. Cézanne's own sustained application of geometric condensation is not easy to follow either, although he advised other painters to practice it and continued to speak of it until the 1900s. What is certain is that he repeatedly told other painters

> Tout dans la nature se modéle la sphère, le cône et le cylindre. Il faut s'apprendre à peindre sur ces figures simples, on pourra ensuite faire tout ce qu'on voudra.[57]

Clearly, his experiments with linear form helped Cézanne discover an additional aesthetic language that he used to supplement his language of color relations. The "apples," he found, could be condensed into spheres with repeated curves to gather and contain their solidity while insinuating the interpenetrability of their contours with the surrounding spatial "envelope." Mont Sainte-Victoire, he found, could be made into a pyramid; the ascending diagonals could be made to converge at three points to stabilize the form, bind its parameters, and, at the same time, extend its massiveness upward, forward, and backward in space.

In the example of a view of Mont Sainte-Victoire of 1895–1900, the pyramid is modeled with a sharp contour that suggests its solidity and its boundaries; however, in the empty space contiguous with an edge of the mountain, there is a visible streak of turpentine forming an angular pattern that follows the line of the mountain/pyramid and determines its boundaries by subtracting from, and dissolving, its extension. The streak itself is condensed into a pyramidal shape and is bounded by clouds on one axis and by the overlapping limb of a foreground tree on the other. This apparently negative element, a sign announcing the empty space of the sky, opposes to the solidity of the "mountain" the same geometrical configuration, the pyramid, into which the mountain's shape was condensed. Hence the pyramidal shape, as a sign for both the sky and its displacement—the mountain—connects the two as metonymic links within the total structure of the painting.

As correlates, the solid mountain and the inverted pyramidal sky reveal an essential form of the enduring continuity of matter. As the links within a plastic image, they relate space to *duration* not through absent equivalents, as in the *Maison du Pendu* and *Still Life with Compotier*, but by revealing the interpenetrability of matter and memory within the patterning of the canvas itself. The tensions in this work—and there are very significant tensions in all of Cézanne's "realized" works—do not embody implied emotions (as in the *Maison du Pendu*) or implied formative activity (as in the *Still Life with Compotier*); they are instead an obvious presence made possible by, to use Bergsonian terms, the convergence of a dynamic schema (projected forces and intentions) with a corporeal schema (telescoping images and perspectives). In this convergence, the line of the solid *figures simples* snaps, and the resulting layers then fall into place together like those of a tectonic fold. Whether straight or curved, horizontal or vertical, parallel or converging, the folding line manifests an essential possibility of natural evolution by condensing into it the forces signified by an ideal pattern—the turpentine/paint contour of our example. In ideal patterns of this sort, whose meaning involves the encounter of chance and intuition, artistic activity reaches into the lived world and maps out its "extensity," substituting it in the canvas for the perspectival space of mechanical optics. The apparent distortions in the essential lines of condensation thus present a spatio-temporal concentration of matter in the *passage* of the pictorial fabric. It is safe to say that Cézanne's condensation acquires its full meaning when conceptualized as Bergsonian concentration.

Through condensation, Cézanne *found* patterns that were certainly more abstract than the visual/tactile *taches* of modulation. The condensed stereometric *figures simples* reduced matter not just to *surfaces*, as in modulation, but to pure lines that could be "captured." But in fact the formal syntheses achieved in the process of modulating and condensing a painting could lead only to a form of "realization" that Cézanne often called a mere *toile* or an *étude*, not to what he finally considered a "completed" or fully "realized" painting. Nevertheless it should be repeated that, as techniques, modulation and condensation brought forth, through the tenacity of the artist's experimental fervor, types of harmonic schemata to be used as specifically aesthetic signs.

The experiments discussed here took place during the "darkest" time in Cézanne's spiritual and artistic education, 1880–95, which found him struggling with dependency on his father, polemical disputes with friends, and the economic worries of having a family in secret; in spite of all of this, his experiments were directed at a comprehension, theoretical as well as practical, of harmonies almost musical in character. Only through the disclosure of the full range of abstract signs or, what is the same, basic pictorial figures for harmony could the painter hope to signify aesthetic, as opposed to psychologically conventional or repressed, emotions and to give birth to ever more refined affective essences and make them a precise vehicle of purely aesthetic values.

Roger Fry praised the experimentation of this period of Cézanne's development and described the plastic images created in it with the term *significant form.*

> There is a whole series of still-lifes—most of which are little known—devoted to studies of skulls, sometimes a single skull, sometimes three or four together. It is needless to say that for Cézanne a skull was merely a complicated variation upon the sphere. By this time he had definitely abjured all suggestion of

poetical or dramatic allusion; he had arrived at what was to be his most characteristic conception, namely, that the deepest emotions could only exude, like a perfume—it is his own image—from form considered in its pure essence and without reference to associated ideas.[58]

The expression *significant form* is used by Fry to point to his theoretical recognition of conscious aesthetic syntheses that would transcend the incurable associationism of symbolist and abstract images. In syntheses such as these, the autonomy and spirituality of the symbolist image would be preserved not in vague and ambiguous abstractions but in precise self-signifying form. Fry noticed that after Cézanne this type of significant form was the correlate of a new "type of emotion," an "aesthetic emotion" that "exudes" in the act of artistic creation.

But emotional, aesthetic essences were not enough to guarantee or support an uncontested acceptance of the existence of syntheses created by a reflective and purposeful (i.e., free) activity; such "essences," in their contingency, would be still attached to the contingencies of natural evolution. By the same token, the self-signifying character of plastic images as signs would be merely formal and empty, a condition that Ribot had clearly noticed in superior linguistic abstractions. It was this contingency and the associationism of the corresponding inventive syntheses that Cézanne was struggling against in his tenacious experiments; he was guided in his search by a belief in images that might "realize" the carnal substance, the endurance and value of *forms of life*. If associational images are primarily the metonymic sedimentations of habit and the gains of resourceful invention, the practical contexts within which additional— truly synthetic, hence reflective—metaphoric exchanges with other images or parts of images could occur are very limited and inflexible. Metaphoric equivalents within plastic images can only be, as indicated earlier, either false or merely implied. Cézanne's insistent commitment to a search for a "harmony of harmonics" showed a preunderstanding on his part of the possibility of images that would reflectively combine metonymy and metaphor, that is, of images in which *multiple* metaphoric transfer of elements taken from many different practical and semantic contexts would point to the operative presence of a free creative activity that was attentive to the call of purpose and value. If plastic images always bring the world down to a situation, the reflective images Cézanne was looking for always placed a situation spatiotemporally *in* a world. As will be explained later, the fixation of the structure and style of the dwelt-in world determined Cézanne's final technique of "realization of motifs," which were no longer "found" but "invented" through this technique. Consequently, his "significant forms"—the "contemplative" and "visionary" images of the late period—transcended the formal meaning as signs, even superior affective signs, that Fry, and all formalist associationism before and after him, attributed to art; they were indeed symbols of the uniqueness and worth of the artwork when it results from the intensity of an aesthetic existence.

The Motif

Cézanne's letters from his period of experimentation with modulation and condensation and also from the time of the great series that was to follow are full of remarks about how difficult he found the attainment of realization of "motifs" and how the motif constantly eluded him in his research. He never pointed to any of his paintings to declare that he had, in it, finally achieved full realization of a motif. The already discussed duplication of the pyramidal pattern in one of the paintings of Mont Sainte-Victoire did indicate that the triangle could be used as a motif that successfully united all of the syntactical references (solid/void, rock/sky) so important in the painting, within a precise attribute of its essential form. But he never declared with full satisfaction that he had reached the end of a final quest to *realiser le motif,* that he had definitively and consistently advanced from discovering motifs to "inventing" or realizing them.

In a conversation in 1896 with Joachim Gasquet, Cézanne revealed the influence of actual poetic models on his own attempts to realize a motif. He spoke to his friend of his great admiration for a particular descriptive passage "painted" by Honoré Balzac in his novel *La peau de chagrin* (*The Wild Asses' Skin*) of 1831. In one passage, which Cézanne felt to be a realized motif, Balzac described a still life in an interior domestic scene animated by evocative references to an exterior landscape.

(La nappe) blanche comme une couche de neige fraîchement tombée et sur laquelle s'élevaient symétriquement les couverts couronnés de petits pains blonds.[59]

Citing this passage, Cézanne confesses:

Toute ma jeunesse, j'ai voulu peindre ça, cette nappe de neige fraîche. . . . Je sais maintenant qu'il ne faut vouloir peindre que 's'élevaient symétriquement les couverts' et 'de petits pains blonds.' Si je peins 'couronnés' je suis foutu. . . . Comprenez-vous? Et si vraiment j'equilibre et je nuance mes couverts et mes pains comme sur nature, soyez sûr que les couronnés, le neige, et tout le tremblement y seront.[60]

Although he was aware of the possibility of painting "couronnés" as an impressionist would, that is, as a part of his rendition of the blond rolls and the wintery snowdrifts of this interior/exterior landscape synthesis, Cézanne realized that he must focus not on the identification and completion of this impression but instead on a new articulation of his medium and on specific methods that would transcend and modify the means of formal construction of signs for an impression; he was seeking to express *comme sur nature* a more intimate and complex synthesis of these signs with the signs of his long-term lived involvement with the scene. Balance and shading, he said, would be the way to achieve the part-to-whole and whole-to-part harmonies in the ordering of his painting. Actually to paint "crowned" would be as inadequate for his present purposes as to "paint the sun" simply by painting the sign for it, as Monet did. To represent scientifically the rolls and the place settings and not make intentional use of their potential metaphoric correlatives, "snow," and "crowns," would be to simplify and discredit the role of the synthesizing consciousness, its "trembling" *(tremblement)* as the motivator of the signs.

A motif, then, was an abstract metonymic pattern animated by vital metaphoric equivalences and thus converted, beyond its readability as a formal structure, into a nonformal sign, an announcement, of the lived world and the existential concerns created by the painter. Therefore it constituted a means to share in his living and creating: it was the pervasive influence of "crowned" on the interpenetration of the "golden rolls" and the "snowdrifts;" it was the design that the "landscape" selects when it "thinks itself" and "becomes conscious" through the painter; it is the absorption of abstract signs into empathetic means of sharing in poetic living. "With the motif," Cézanne explained to Gasquet,

> ce que j'essaie de vous traduire est plus mystérieux, s'enchevêtre aux racines mêmes de l'être, à la source impalpable des sensations. Mais, c'est cela même, je crois, qui constitue le tempérament.[61]

The motif was, then, the crystallizing of the mysterious sources of natural signs together with the actualization of one's aesthetic "temperament."

THE PERIOD OF SERIALIZATION (1890–1906):
Contemplative Images: *Realisation du Motif*

Evident in Cézanne's works from the experimental period was the intentional utilization of the plastic image to achieve and display pictorial harmony. This focus on harmony in the syntactical relations (modulation and condensation) was expanded in the early 1890s into a study of harmonic qualities in general through an ingenious analysis of the full range of reflective possibilities of certain subjects so that they would attain full expression not in a single painting but in an entire series.

The series initiated at this time, the meditative still lifes of the 1890s and the *Mont Sainte-Victoire, Bathers*, and *Cardplayers*, eventually resulted in "realized motifs" that reflectively exhibited the qualitative continuity of Cézanne's experience within the associations and dissociations in those series. His progress in this respect was marked by the gathering together and *systematizing* of repetitions and combinations of perceptions and memories. Unlike the plastic images, the series constituted more than an *écriture* of painterly signs, since, within the diversity of their freely changing patterns, the sedimented "realizable motifs" became the underlying and permanent *parole* of the aesthetic and existential aspirations of Cézanne's motivating temperament.

As *écriture*, the new series collected together, in a montagelike fashion, various episodes of viewing and remembering, in which the painter assembled, disassembled, and reassembled new patterns of formal harmony to express the full range of possible extensions of experience that could harmoniously grow out of each episodic situation. In fact, the late renditions of Mont Sainte-Victoire are very different in style and scope from interpretations of this theme Cézanne had been making from the 1880s, yet the memory of the early examples is preserved in the late ones and encompassed in their deeper and stricter systematization of formal and nonformal elements. Pictorial situations were thus shown as capable of revealing increasingly broader contexts of active indwelling and, in the end, the world as a determinate structure or style of being-in. In this respect, realization clearly meant "poetic indwelling," as Heidegger, following Hölderlin, has called it, a formula that Heidegger made even more precise in stating that the revelation, the truth of the world, is actualized, "comes to pass," in authentic works of art.[62]

Each episode, in its connections with the rest, reveals a "lived world," so the montage of the episodes of the series becomes more than an association of abstract images, more than the interactive experiencing of colors, spaces, textures, and moods in a plastic rhythm. But how can the viewer grasp this *surplus of meaning* in each episode and in the series itself? The clarification of this issue requires a careful analysis of three factors implicated in the significance of this surplus. The first of these is the character of the "lived world" and the manner in which a situation or situations are subsumed under such a world; the second factor is the order in which the surplus of meaning must be found: the whole always preceding the parts in the continuity of the episodes; the third is the identification of the instruments or signs of that continuity.

The main difference between the still lifes that exemplified the technique of modulation and the more ambitious treatment of landscapes and figures in the series of the last decade was not the relative thematic importance of the latter as opposed to the restricted thematic character of the former; as already indicated, there was also and most notably in this context a profound change in the relationship between world and situation. In the "plastic" treatment of themes, the world background remained implied as a horizon that was many steps removed from the circumstantial subject of the painting; in the new approach the pictorial situation was expanded to include its worldly horizon not only in the serial ordering of the multiple renditions but in each one of these renditions by virtue of their very obvious place in the series.

The proof of this difference in approach will be given in explaining the nature of the *continuity* between world and situation in the discussion of the other two components of the surplus of meaning of these paintings. What must be emphasized now is that the change in the world/situation relationship is metaphysically motivated by a change, within the experience of the painter, in the relationship of consciousness, whether perceiving or creative, to world. That change will appear most clearly if the type of contemplation in which Cézanne was engaged in these latter works is explained in its peculiar and quite original meaning. Of the late series of still lifes, Schapiro remarked:

> They [the objects in these still lifes] are never set as for a meal; the fruit is rarely if ever cut or peeled, the scattering of the still-life and the random spread and fall of the linen in irregular folds imply a still unordered world. The fruit, I have observed, while no longer in nature, is not yet fully a part of human life. Suspended between nature and use, it exists as if *for contemplation alone.*[63]

The notion of contemplation here invoked by this critic is quite traditional in its Platonist roots, and, in accordance with this perspective, it fully separates subject from world, making room for the contemplator in a realm "suspended between nature and use." This formula betrays a certain confusion between the philosophical tradition and Heidegger, the first represented by the term *nature* and the second by *use*, as applied to the interpretation of Cézanne. Probably Schapiro did not wish to appeal here to a metaphysically spiritual reality as the site of contemplation, but the characterization of art making and the art object as "suspended" inevitably leads to this conclusion.

Cézanne's efforts, witnessed by his description of Balzac's table, to immerse his creative activity in the signs that manifest it and in the objects that result from it should clearly discourage any separation of contemplation from action and from things—even things that appear to have been abandoned to "be" on their own. But if action and contemplation are not separable, does this mean that consciousness, with its synthesizing activity, must be placed back within the world as a part of it? Such an interpretation would point to a romantic, overwhelmingly pantheistic fervor more appropriate perhaps of a Constable "pastoral" scene with the immense cloud-filled sky toward which the uninhabited and impersonal landscape below is reverently lifted.

An accurate description of the place of the perceiving and creative consciousness in the late paintings of Cézanne should demonstrate his truly modernist inspiration, his independent discovery and artistic amplification of theoretical positions also held by Bergson and later elaborated by Heidegger and especially by Merleau-Ponty. For Cézanne, as for all the great modernist artists and philosophers, the place of consciousness was not outside the world, "suspended" in contemplation, because for him, as for them, contemplation was not separable from creative action; still, this union of the two was not the inexorable process of a universal spirit but the reflective and poetic striving of artistic existence.

Another great modernist artist, the poet Rainer Maria Rilke, used the image of the pyramid to exhibit with total explicitness the new and unique positioning of consciousness poetically in the world.

> To me it seems more and more as though our customary consciousness lives on the tip of a pyramid whose base within us (and in a certain way beneath us) widens out so fully that the farther we find ourselves able to descend into it, the more generally we appear to be merged into those things that, independent of time and space, are given in our earthly, in the widest sense worldly, existence.[64]

The independence from time and space that the poet speaks of does not separate either things or consciousness from the world; instead it places them at the edge of the world, on the tip of the pyramid that marks that edge and orients space and time toward the intensity and concentration of "worldly existence." Such positioning of consciousness is consistent, as I have repeatedly indicated, with Bergson's own ideas about consciousness and spatiotemporal "extensity," but also with Heidegger's placing of existence, as dwelling and residing, "alongside" the world. In his later writings, Heidegger inserted poetic dwelling even more precisely in the line of convergence of the four world horizons: earth and sky, mortal and immortal life.[65]

A contemplation that is inseparable from action, especially from such a sustained action as creative or poetic indwelling, still needs to be conceptualized in opposition to traditionally distancing, panoramic, and even imaginative (in the romantic sense) vision. In the new sense, contemplation must be taken to mean the ranging of an inventive activity, and of the complex and free acts that constitute it, over its component experiences (work, rest, celebration, conviviality) and its component acts (locomotion, exertion, manipulation, circumspection, anticipation, recollection).

The surplus of meaning in the contemplative images of the late series of Cézanne can thus be strictly correlated with the active ranging of an inventive experience, a ranging that delivers together with its immediately focused object(s) all the possible objects, and their correlated perspectives, that were intended in component actions. And, of course, the new sense of contemplation is totally congruous with the intensities of the multiple views of Mont Sainte-Victoire, with the implied effort spent in reaching every viewing point and the tranquility achieved after arriving, with the viewer's involvement in the instantaneous temporality of a flashing partial perspective and in the interminable geological time that it took to form the whole.

What is most important in the linkage of all of these active perspectives of Mont Sainte-Victoire is the conspicuous precedence of the whole—not just the total scope of each view, but the whole series—over the parts. This precedence determines the perceptual and creative continuity in the relation of world to situation and the consequent inclusion of the meaning of the world in the overall meaning of the series, of every painting, and of every part of each painting. That inclusion, it should be remembered, constitutes what was indicated above as the second component of a noticeable surplus of meaning.

The first and overwhelming impression of the precedence of the whole over the parts originates, as one should expect, from thematic rather than formal aspects in the richest and most complete episodes of the series, for example *Mont Sainte-Victoire Seen from Les Lauves* of 1904–6 in the Kunstmuseum Basel. In this example, the presence and precedence of the world is made manifest by relations among themes rather than by the significance of individual themes;

the relations relevant in this context are precisely those established by Heidegger as constitutive of a world. They are as evident in this example as in the ones that Heidegger uses to demonstrate the role of the work of art in gathering these relations into its rhythmic tensions.[66] In the painting, the relation of earth and sky is fully manifested by the outline of the mountain. The mountain makes the earth forces bulge in its contour, and at the same time, since it is a determinate and visible form that arrests the movement of those forces, it makes them disappear within its single presence and its majestic ordering of the surrounding landscape. The sky in its relationship to the earth is not represented in the particular portion of the canvas reserved for it; that portion has in its shapes and coloration a remarkable similarity and affinity with the appearance of the earthly plane. It should not be hard to perceive, in view of the above similarity, that the sky is evidenced above all by a light and coloration diffused throughout the entire scene that contains and connects the light and tone of the different hours of the day and seasons of the year. Color *diffusion* here is different from the *distribution* typical of modulation; the latter is constructed from part to whole, therefore by predominantly formal effects and considerations, while in *Mont Sainte-Victoire* it is reflectively organized by virtue of thematic considerations that, as connected with the world ensemble, proceed from the whole toward its parts.

In the contrast and tension between earth and sky, a framework is created for the intervention of another rhythm, the rhythm of time, whether complete, indicating ripeness, mortality, and destiny, or incomplete, indicating immortality and transcendence. This is the rhythm of the interaction of human beings with the "angel" (the "spirit of the place" or *genius loci*) and with a mysterious ruling transcendence that must be met with a peace-instilling blend of resignation and joy. These last two moods are actualized in, respectively, the density and the vibrancy of the painting. Thematically, then, the world is signified in the spatiotemporal compass of the work by an intricate network of relations that depend on each other and, as will be seen presently, on the consistent identity of formal elements to acquire their individual meaning.

It must be reiterated, to conclude the analysis of the precedence of the whole over the parts in these series, that such precedence was the main reason why the new approach to painting they introduced bypassed representation even though it resulted in what might be considered a traditional subject matter. These pictorial exercises did not intend to create a fictional world or a world of subjective emotion or meaning, but to mark, as Bergson would put it, the eventful convergence of earthly contingency with intelligible form, the felicitous completion of evolution by past, present, and future history. In that convergence and completion lies the ambitious significance of some of the greatest works of modernism: The realm of art sets itself up here as the one endeavor, among the many interests and fields of culture, that can locate, and bring to presence in works, hallowed circumstances in the history of the inhabited world (and, as will soon be seen, in the history of persons) in which such momentous events can and do come to pass. Things in these series are therefore not totally at rest in a "suspended" life, but, under the contemplative promptings of the artist, they visibly yield their individuality and disorder to the hope and expectation for a barely dawning harmony of harmonies.

Beside the precedence of whole over parts, there is further proof of the surplus of meaning in the amazing late series of *Mont Sainte-Victoire*. This proof is afforded by elements that at first sight might appear to be formal, yet through further analysis reveal themselves as part of the content, the thematic as well as the figural (metaphoric) content. Their role indeed is to transform the already analyzed metonymic continuity of whole to parts into a *metaphoric identity of whole and part*. Among these elements, three of the most prominent will now be discussed: arbitrary complementary color pairings, constructive brushstrokes, and compositional use of exposed areas of canvas. In order to constitute proof of a surplus of meaning, these elements must be carried over from one episode to another in the later examples of the series, including for the purposes of this discussion the already cited *Mont Sainte-Victoire Seen from Les Lauves*, (V 1529), Kunstmuseum, Basel, and *Mont Sainte-Victoire*, (V798), Philadelphia Museum of Art (figure 3). Both are dated 1902–6.

In earlier paintings of Mont Sainte-Victoire, color is modulated in accordance with the technique proper of plastic images. In *Mont Sainte-Victoire* (V454, 1885–87, National Gallery of London), for example, contrasting adjacent blends of warm and cool colors are metonymically used to abstract the component impressions from their "realistic" settings in search of a harmonious pattern with a unique emotional significance. As indicated earlier, this pattern is at the same time concrete and essential, circumstantial—even suited to the "atmosphere" of Provence—and predominantly formal. The restriction of the pattern to the finding and expression of such emotional particularity was, it should be remembered, a principal aim of the painter at the plastic stage.

In contrast to this early example, in both of the late paintings just cited the painter severely limited his palette to complementary pairings—specifically, blue/orange and green/red. This "arbitrary" distribution accomplished the opposite of what is indicated by the term *arbitrary*. To be sure, the colors are not denotative of bare sensations; they are not even correlatives of a uniquely invented emotion. What might be considered an arbitrary sign is in fact *natural*: Indeed, the emotion actualized in these colors is not adventitious; it is a *fundamental mood* not "found" by a subject but, in Heidegger's definition, a mood in which a subject finds itself preconceptually and therefore necessarily.[67]

The severity of this new discipline of color converts form into content, not a "formal" (as in the plastic patterns) but an empathetic content in which the creator/perceiver establishes his identity with his world (nature, community) and also with himself. The identity of content brings about an already noticed diffusion (fusion and dissolution) of the plurality of colors. From the perspective of a single fundamental mood, there is really only a unity, not a plurality, of color diffused throughout the canvas. In animating the series by remaining identical through its metonymic differences, Cézanne's revised palette became the first of the metaphoric components of the mature style; color had ceased to be a part of the atmosphere, whether physical or psychological, and had become, as indicated earlier, a "realization of the motif" of lived time.

Regarding the use of specific brushstrokes, a considerable change takes place also in the mature series and in particular in the three late examples analyzed above. In contrast with the underlying geometrical figures and the splitting and multiplication of boundaries that were typical of condensation, in the new style strong linear configurations are absorbed into the shape of the strokes themselves; significantly, the wedge-shaped strokes exclusively used in the composition of each of the three landscapes match the peculiar contour of the mountain, and they also translate its corporeality into their three-dimensional texture.

The identical strokes, in their persistence in each painting and from one episode to another, constitute a metaphorical element added upon the traces of the basic metonymic structures that have been so forcefully displaced in the new style. In their metaphorical role, the strokes do not act as a mere formal device: Instead of lines of *passage,* they constitute a *facture,* the marks of human effort that bring into the scene the active presence of the painter and of the human beings that inhabit the world of the painting. The effort of the artist is represented by the imprints of the strokes themselves, the effort of other human beings by the paths built by the strokes into the landscape to show both the labor of living in that environment and the history of the human choices enacted in those trails. The signs of the surplus of meaning in the series and in every one of its units are thus metonymies and metaphors, formal and related to content; the transition from each to another of these devices is reflective rather than associational, in that the lived world and its complex relations are always implicated in such transitions. In the case of the wedge-shaped brushstroke the formal transition from metonymy to metaphor is motivated in the identical contours of the stroke and of the mountain; regarding content this transition is made possible by the coincidence of the world with the fabric of serviceable paths and with the constructive efforts they signify. As Heidegger has made clear, there is no lived world without paths that circumscribe it and without an encounter of choice and destiny in those paths.

> World is never an object that stands before us and can be seen. World is the ever-nonobjective to which we are subject as long as the paths of birth and death, blessing and curse keep us transported into Being. . . . The world is the self-disclosing openness of the broad paths of the simple and essential decisions in the destiny of an historical people.[68]

The motif Heidegger's words point to, and the brushwork Cézanne "realizes" in *Mont Sainte-Victoire,* can now be identified as "lived space," the "extensity" Bergson discovered as correlated with the active-creative conception of human experience and one of the meanings of the term *world* in Heidegger.

The third of the form/content elements that signify the surplus of meaning in the mature series, and specifically in *Mont Sainte-Victoire*, is the role of the exposed canvas in the composition. In all three of the late examples of the series, exposed areas of canvas of different sizes, but always relatively small, are left open in the intervals between some of the brushstrokes. Like the other signs of the surplus of meaning in these paintings, the exposed canvas appears initially to be purely formal; it is indeed a modification or displacement of other formal signs considered above (i.e., color pairings and constructive brushwork). A good indication of their ultimately nonformal character is the fact that they are not adventitious but *invented*, and therefore not truly arbitrary but *natural*, insofar as they actualize, realize, a motif. In the symbolist and plastic paintings, exposed canvas might have been included in "incomplete," or "nonrealized" works; the role of this device can be shown to be totally different in the later examples. This difference in roles can bring together the significance of the new kind of realization, the "realization of the motif," and the character of the metaphoric exchange that makes it possible. The exposed canvas cannot be a representational sign; it neither connotes nor is correlated with a sensation, it is therefore not *about* anything. In order to find out its precise function, it will be necessary to establish first what it stands for and in what way is it exchangeable with what it replaces. The exchange itself can give us a clue as to the identity of the mysterious metaphoric counterpart of the canvas: A portion of the material of the painting has become a part of the world of the work and it stands there *representing itself* as a direct sign of the materiality, the earthly condition of art. The specificity of this function can be substantiated by the fact that these three paintings contain exposed canvas and yet are primary examples of what the master considered as "realized motifs." The canvas must therefore stand for itself and not in the place of any sensations or subjective impressions. It has indeed been indicated that when it does stand for them, as in the empty space corresponding to the hands in the portrait of Vollard, some sensations are at least evoked, and in their absence the work is considered to fall under the category of the "unrealized."

The preceding argument allows for the conclusion that the materiality actualized in, no longer represented or causally connected with, Cézanne's contemplative paintings is a major part, the earth, of the motif of the world the new style realizes. Heidegger has forcefully described a parallel interdependence of earth and world:

> [T]he relation between world and earth does not wither away into the empty unity of opposites unconcerned with one another. The world, in resting upon the earth, strives to surmount it. As self-opening it cannot endure anything closed. The earth, however, as sheltering and concealing, tends always to draw the world into itself and keep it there.[69]

The interpenetrations of sign and signified, of form and content, and of the metaphoric counterparts that supplement the basic associational and representational metonymies, reach in the contemplative series the highest possible level of identity. The four dimensions of the lived world are indeed *actualized* in their signs, and so is the activity of reflective constitution that Bergson called (artistic) "intuition." The unity or interpenetration of all these factors is, in the end, the surplus of meaning the viewer is invited to discover gradually in the new, serial form of artistic "contemplation." This profound, empathetic interpenetration substitutes itself finally for the mechanisms of abstraction and the arbitrariness of the signs introduced in associationalist images. Contemplative interpenetration and empathy do indeed abolish representationalism in a way that symbolist and plastic associationism could never have matched.

Contemplative empathy placed Cézanne in the site of his "homecoming" as an artist. To corroborate and further clarify the meaning and the modernist character of the contemplative image created by Cézanne, it would be helpful to compare it with a rigorous description of the structure and development of such images contained in a poem of Wallace Stevens, "The Poem That Took the Place of a Mountain," that might very well have been inspired by Cézanne's paintings of Mont Sainte-Victoire.

> There it was, word for word,
> The poem that took that place of a mountain.
> He breathed its oxygen,
> Even when the book lay turned in the dust of his table.
>
> It reminded him how he had needed
> A place to go to in his own direction,

How he had recomposed the pines,
Shifted the rocks and picked his way among clouds,

For the outlook that would be right,
Where he would be complete in an unexplained completion:

The exact rock where his inexactnesses
Would discover, at last, the view toward which they had edged,

Where he could lie and, gazing down at the sea,
Recognize his unique and solitary home.[70]

The title of this composition points in its remarkable wording to the ultimate metaphoric and reflective nature of the contemplative image: The metaphoric substitution is directly presented by the words "took the place," which at the same time explain the exchange of two terms and point to the place, the lived space, to be opened and occupied by the poem and the mountain. The title line is repeated in the second verse and the makeup of the two metaphoric terms is established with the expression "word by word," which could ambiguously apply to either of them, indicating the fact that they are both composed of signs, some pictorial and some literary.

The next couplet refers to the lived, extended character of the action—and rest—of the poet in the making of the poem, of the placing of it in the world, and of the slow, dust-gathering process of the opening and outlining of a world on the part of the poem. The creator breathes the oxygen of this world, lives in it, even before it is created. The third couplet calls the reader's attention to the reflective temporality of contemplation; the first line of the poem with its allusion to a time past, both in the conclusive meaning and in the tense of "There it was," already suggested at the beginning in the laboring artist standing at a terminal point of view that is reinforced by the "It reminded him" and the "he had needed" of the later lines. This standing marks the direction of reflective time. Yet creation is narrated in all its vicissitudes in its own temporality that proceeds from past to future. At the initial moment of his need the poet longs for a place, the place of identity, that is not static but is instead connected with creative and reflective time through the expression "to go to in his own direction"; this direction is indeed already known in the terminal stance but also preunderstood along the way.

The narrative character of the process of creation and its basic constituting metonymies are next explained in the recomposition of the pines, the shifting of the rocks—a shifting that takes place within the stance of the viewer and within the contingency of nature—and ultimately in the repeated choices of the wanderer picking his way "among clouds." The end of this exploring already seen from the "initial" reflective moment is the outlook that "would be" right. This end is called "completion"; and the reader could infer that, like Cézanne, Stevens is describing modernist completion, "realization," because this terminal point exists by itself—unexplained, and also in the process and in the artist—where it would be explained.

In the next-to-last couplet, the metaphorical exchange of poem for mountain has already taken place, and the result is the union of the two in the "exact rock," the essential identity that contains all the metonymies, "the inexactnesses" of the way. The view that is provided at the top of this mountain is the landscape of the world from its "edge," a landscape that could be completed only by the placing of the poem in the place of the mountain. In the last couplet the poet reaches the goal of his contemplative efforts: He "lies" and "recognizes" the sea, the limit of the world, and the world itself as his "home," "unique and solitary" or totally his own. The familiarity of this home is predicated on vision: The poet sees more than the sea and the totality of the world; in the fixity of the world's margins and trails the poet sees everything, both within a final perspective and within the limited perspectives of his wandering. It must be pointed out, to conclude this textual *explication* of the poem, that the couplets replicate, in their formal structure, the transformation of metonymies into metaphors that has been noticed in the other aspects of the poem and in the paintings; the opposition of the semantic elements of the first lines to those of the second is metonymic in the early couplets, metaphoric in the late ones.

The conclusion of Stevens's poem confirms that poetic indwelling is indeed the "homecoming," the conversion of the world into a "region" and a "home" by the poet (artist), that Heidegger made the subject of one of his best aesthetic essays.[71] This conversion depends on the fully grounded (reflective) establishment of the metaphoric sign of which the mountain has been a paradigm throughout the universal history of poetry. The mountain is the summit and the limit of the world and also the point of highest visibility, the end as well as the beginning of all reflective circumspection. It is thus a preeminent object and the standpoint of the subject; but even though the mountain seems to be a natural sameness, a natural sign, it is so only *for* a free-ranging—creative—activity that is prior to subject and object and is the place of their identity, just as it is the place of the identity of mountains. Within free-ranging poetic indwelling and *for* it, events and situations can acquire a practical, emotional, and existential sameness in spite of their inherent differences and the arbitrariness of their separation from their surroundings. That practical, emotional, and existential sameness is the ground of metaphor and, *as realized, it is metaphor.*

Metaphoric figuration is contemplative in that it sets forth visibility within the free ranging of activity: the visibility of things as well as the always implicit visibility of the world. Things are visible in the world, and conversely the world is visible in things; that which is visible for a poetic action is the familiar—as opposed to what is desired, needed, or simply used. Thus where there is a home, there is always a world; where there is empathy, there is sight, contemplation. The painter, the poet, and the philosopher capture and make explicit in these insights the core of the modernist message: the absorption of metonymy into metaphor, of abstraction into empathy, and of tactility into visuality.

Visionary Imagery: *Realisation du Motif*

Visionary images were defined, in Bergsonian terms, in chapter 1 as "the blending of many ideas. . . . The strangest dreams, in which two images overlie one another."[72] In the contemplative images the corporeal schema of interaction with the environment was still predominant, hence their visual nature was very clear; the new images are called "visionary" because, in contrast with that visual character, they are formed, at the imaginative level, with fragments of actions, perceptions, emotions, and linguistic equivalents that compose what Bergson called a "dynamic schema." In contemplation, active seeing controls the conceptual identities that are established within a world; in visionary imagination, a "blending of many ideas" controls what is ultimately visible or hidden in what is seen. These features of the

visionary will determine the ensuing considerations about the different types of hidden images in Cézanne and about the *collage* structure that distinguishes these images from contemplative *montage*.

There are two types of hidden images in Cézanne's oeuvre. In
the first type, the hidden image becomes present because of the vagueness or abstractness of a painterly element: A jagged line that is almost "abstract" in its nonreferential qualities might appear as the
profile of Mont Sainte-Victoire *and/or* of the painter himself; the
color modulation of an "apple" might suggest the blush of the ripening fruit and/or of a human face; a flowing line might transcend
planimetric restrictions and unite the relaxed limbs of a reclining
bather with the roots from a tree in the background. Thus the ambiguity or abstractness of the painterly element yields the dual reference by acting as a *shifting mechanism* so that the line translates from
one image to another and the colors contribute to embody first one
and then the other form, disclosing both images concurrently and
implying that their relationship is one of contiguity in space, time,
pattern, or sequence.

Substitution through similarity of form is accompanied here
by continuous passage, metaphor by metonymy. The face of the
mountain and the face of the painter share the same jagged line, and
the cheeks of the apple and of a human have in common the twin
rosy circles of a blush. What remains important in these substitutions is that the complex formed by the two (or more) integrated
images is kinesthetically and synesthetically continuous and in it the
components share a certain perceptual copresence.

In this first type of hidden imagery, the duality of references
operates usually within only parts of the total painting, within details of single objects—mountains, clouds, pools of water, fruit, drapery folds—and often these metonymic-metaphoric shifts not only
are supported by the perceptual activities that shift the painterly elements but also are reinforced by verbal signifiers, like puns and emotive signifiers such as personifications. The "face" of a mountain,
"cheeks" of an apple, "limbs" of a tree, "face" of a clock, "mouth" of
a shell appear in Cézanne's paintings as images that shift from the
inanimate vehicles of the signs to their comparable human equivalents. Perhaps because of the subordinate detailing that constitutes
the motivation of this first type of hidden imagery, its examples have
been frequently considered unconscious or subconscious "condensa-

tions" (in a psychoanalytic sense)[73] in which one component of the image represses the other while it continues to present it in connotation. The psychologically "visionary," the hallucinatory, character of these kinesthesias and synesthesias and their associated repression of certain emotional complexes are not as important, however, as is establishing their "visionary" (in the Bergsonian sense), that is, their *poetic*, character in order to account for their intensity and duration, their reflectiveness and stability, as pictorial *parole*, in Cézanne.

There are thus some hidden images in his early, and of course his late, styles that properly fall under the category that is now being defined and analyzed as "visionary." They are indeed examples of the first type of hidden imagery discussed above. It must be kept in mind that, in the "symbolist" and "plastic" stages, these first instances of the "visionary" are subordinated to the metonymic effects that were predominant in those stages, and they remained almost unrecognizable from the false and absent metaphors with which metonymies were associated by the painter at the time. Their presence within those stages can only be explained as the emergence of an additional type of "found" motif: While developing a theory of figurational presentation, whether symbolic or plastic, Cézanne began to establish a limited repertory of personified hidden images that transcended pure realization of sensations and realization "on nature" by enhancing the narrative possibilities of the motifs he was discovering.

From the perceptual/imaginative identification of metonymic/iconic images in the "face" foreshadowed in the mountain range, in the clouds, in the folds of the drapery, and in the clock front, the master would eventually advance, perhaps because of the skills in the use and understanding of symbols developed in his contemplative paintings, to the realization of a second type of hidden imagery. His mixing, in the symbolist and plastic periods, of experimental vision and visionary vision may be considered *poetic* only in its transformation of figurative representation into a presentation by signs. The poetics of vision remains, however, still *prosaic* in the predominance of metonymic syntheses, still realistically *narrational* (indeed, this narrative has as a content the simple anecdotic contingencies of the impressionist perceptual image) and still *associational* in its dependence on references to parts of an object of ordinary vision for validation.[74]

To summarize the description of this first type of hidden visionary images and clarify their elementary poetic character, it must be said that they are the pictorial counterpart of the rhetorical *simile*, the simplest and most conventional form of the metaphor. In both the literary and the pictorial similes, there is comparison rather than sub-stitution: the two terms are present and they reinforce each other metonymically through their contiguity. In these images, the simi-larity of the two terms to be exchanged is limited to superficial quali-tative identity, while in the richer metaphors, as rediscovered by Cézanne in his later styles and by all modernist masters, the semantic contexts from which the two terms are extracted lie far apart; not only is there a greater measure of qualitative difference between the metaphoric equivalents, but their equivalence is fundamentally prac-tical, emotional, and existential, therefore aesthetic.

The second type of hidden visionary imagery also utilizes the shifting capabilities of the painterly elements—the specific formal devices of the new kind of shift will be discussed below; however, the relationship between the two or more images to be integrated is not a simple translation by similes but results from complex synecdo-ches in which each image stands practically, emotionally, or existen-tially for the whole. Indeed, these relations represent substitutions of whole-to-part or whole-to-whole that can only be understood as reflec-tive in a Bergsonian sense. These particular substitutions are, as was discussed in the previous section, also typical of contemplative im-ages; the difference between the contemplative and the visionary exchanges lies in the distinction between serial, contemplative *mon-tage* and visionary *collage* to be considered presently, but also in the fact that montage substitutes the whole of the lived world for its parts while collage substitutes the whole of an existential course for its own parts.

An important, though still transitional, example (it is both con-templative and visionary) of the second type of hidden visionary image is *The Large Bathers* in the Philadelphia Museum of Art (fig-ure 4). In describing this painting, it must be borne in mind from the start that its formal elements should not be first analytically dis-cerned as parts of a distinct whole. The whole here is a Bergsonian fusion of many ideas that would become trivialized perceptions if they were to be dissociated or connected merely as similes. The ap-propriate method of description to apply to the second type of vi-sionary images is that of phenomenological "imaginative variation," which requires an initial sense of the whole in transformation and a sense of the replication of the whole in the parts. Although it will ultimately come to rest in phenomenologically interpreted formal elements, such as shapes, color, or texture, that "replication" cannot arise at the formal level or else the "synthetic" composition and description of the painting will be reversed and betrayed.

The enigma of the interpretation lies, then, in the discovery of the identity of the "blending of ideas," the whole in transformation, that is the realized motif of this painting. But how is it possible to locate this theme if a descriptive passage from part to whole is methodologically precluded? To solve both of these difficulties, the methodological and the thematic, it will be necessary to concentrate on the signs of the transition or exchange from one image to another that have been previously labeled as "shifters." They will lead to the shifting whole without forcing the interpreter to rely on naïvely representational parts of a naïvely representational whole; the interpreter should not assume that the optical shift has already taken place in the painting and then accept the interpretation of it as confirmed by the multiplicity of prior images, but—as Bergson and Cézanne would want it—should let sight poetically conform to the suggestions of a conceptual "dynamic schema."

It is in the nature of the shifter to be both abstract, that is, not placeable within any common sense object or theme, and also ambiguous, that is, formally capable of belonging, as a quality, to more than one interpreted object or theme. In *The Large Bathers* (figure 4) the most conspicuous shifters are the homogeneous texture of the surfaces, the abstract and arbitrary colors, and the vagueness and indefiniteness of the figures; each one of them reinforces the others and thus all three act in unison. Concerning the surfaces, it should be noticed that even though the arrangement of the composition might suggest a conventional separation and distinction of objects or parts of objects in both the "apparent" (landscape) and the "hidden" (face) images, the uniform treatment of the picture plane with homogeneous brushstrokes confines the objects and the images themselves within a solid juxtaposition, a unique kind of closed configuration. The colors are designed to strengthen the general uniformity suggested by all the shifters; the palette is largely limited to complements, blue and orange, which produce an intimate rather than naturalistic atmosphere, whose only translucency is suggested by tonal changes that contribute to the transformation of one image into another.

The vagueness and indefiniteness of the shapes of objects works at the formal level and in the dissociation of the images at the level of content. Formally the vagueness and indefiniteness of shapes mix with the other shifters and reinforce the solidity and uniformity of the pictorial whole. Regarding content, these almost equivocal shapes ("trees," "human bodies," "water," "sky," "face in the sky") carry the burden of the shift by having a different identity in each dissociated image while blending with each other and appearing as an independent and unique phenomenon during the exchange.

The preceding description of the elements in transformation permits now the identification of the ambiguous whole or realized motif. It is itself a reality that shifts and in so doing produces both community and plurality, intimacy and shame; it is the *sexual body* and its life, pervasive as a theme yet divided into the realms of nature and society and, within each, anonymous as a universal force and manifested also in an unique face that may gather for each human being, and for the painter in particular, a history of personal erotic memories. As this shifting theme is dissociated into images, it becomes possible to separate from it the phenomena (nudes in a childhood landscape, face of Mme. Cézanne) that may have been seen naively, without any regard for the shifting theme and process, as the terms of a simple metaphoric exchange; those images should not be qualified in any particular order as "primary" and "secondary," because they are hidden not in each other but in the changing motif. The critics who have recognized the existence of multiple images in *The Large Bathers*[75] have generally perceived them as analytic components of a simile and thus have identified them as trivial episodes in a naïve chronological or psychoanalytic history of the painter, not as the embodiment of his aesthetic/existential cares.

Attention to the central, shifting motif rather than to the dissociated images as the originating point of the interpretation leads directly to the joint consideration of the temporal and metaphoric character of the shift in this second type of visionary images. The specific temporality of their shift reveals a certain simultaneity of the terminal images, not with each other—they are not metonymically contiguous—but with the slowly changing motif. This simultaneity contrasts with the serial succession of contemplative images that still preserve a certain metonymic continuity. Thus, the metaphoric exchange in the late visionary images requires a total replacement and absence of at least one of the terms; in *The Large Bathers*, both terminal images are replaced by, and hidden in, the shift itself.

The conversion of metonymically contiguous images into multiple metaphoric images that simultaneously transform and disappear into each other was to become a characteristic device of cubism. As a pictorial and sculptural technique it received the name *collage* and became a sign of the rupture of modernism with the simpler analytic abstraction and symbolist empathy of the transitional years. The definitions and discussions of collage by contemporary and subsequent critics exhibited a perception on their part of the efforts of cubist artists to transcend the linearity and relative superficiality of associations by contiguity and similarity. Collage was presented by their initiators as an extraction of things or parts of things from their natural contexts and their incorporation into the artwork as an assemblage; through this process their nature and significance as components of the world was put into question. In fact, the autonomy of the artwork as an object separable from the world, if only by virtue of its unique meaning, was also questioned; as a consequence, all aesthetically achieved meaning and identity was made to depend in many modernist and postmodernist trends not upon the encounter of chance and creative existence but upon the incidental accumulation of things and upon the formal possibilities of analyzing and deciphering—that is, *reading*—that accumulation.

In *The Futurist Moment*, Marjorie Perloff gave careful attention to the invention of the collage in its historical and critical settings. Within these settings she was able to focus on the "fitting together of parts and pieces" typical of collage structures, and on the equally typical conflicting emphases on "explicit and deliberate presentation of the heterogeneous" and on "the integration of the diverse combinatory constituents."[76] This conflict of emphases was attributed by Perloff, following Gregory Ulmer, to the conceptual overlap between collage and montage: "'Collage' is the transfer of materials from one context to another, 'montage' is the 'dissemination' of these borrowings through the new setting."[77] Underlying the partial coincidence and differentiation between collage and montage is a deeper separation of the two that arises from the connection of collage with space and montage with time relationships. The difficulty in integrating the metonymic/metaphoric with the spatial/temporal aspects of these definitions needs to be clarified in order to arrive at a less confusing understanding of collage and montage and also of the peculiar phenomenon that has been characterized as "collage" in Cézanne's late work.

The confusion between montage and collage originates from their initial association with literature, the art of time, and painting and sculpture, the arts of space, respectively. In fact, montage arose specifically from film practices that were, if anything, anti-literary. The key to the differentiation must therefore be found by assuming that both devices are spatiotemporal, an assumption that was fully explored by modernist painters and sculptors while modernist writers renewed their symbolization of temporality through the use of techniques borrowed from the new forms of presentation of the visual image.[78] With this assumption in mind, differences between collage and montage will appear as differences of spatiotemporal organization in works of art, whether verbal or plastic. If proper attention is paid to the example of film, as well as to the way in which onomatopoetic and alliterative sounds work, it will be possible to infer that montage is predicated on the function of short-term memory that is connected with basic and habitual actions and unites static images in an extended or specious present; collage, on the other hand, uses long-term, reflective memory, which is connected with many different existential contexts and creative purposes and reaches for a "blend" of images to present the whole of a conscious life before its parts can crystallize in static presentations.

Clearly, this conception of collage would apply only to the best instances of it produced by Picasso, Braque, or Boccioni; these instances involve a blending or fusion of images that transcend the presentation of occasional poetic moods or moments and attempt to reflect the continuity of the creative life and its blending, in a precarious but concentrated whole, with ordinary life and with the natural world. The more impressionistic collages, such as Carrá's *Demonstration for Intervention in the War* (1914, Collection Gianni Mattioli, Milan) or Marinetti's poetic performances of *Zang Tumb Tuuum*, either were superficial accumulations of metonymies and visual or onomatopoetic similes, or else they were meant to approach short-term memory montage effects. The grammar and syntax of accumulation of elements in these latter examples involve simple strings of causally connected successions and similarities without any reflective interpenetration of the metonymies and the metaphors. The simple juxtaposition of these devices was severely criticized in London and Petersburg;[79] in response to this trivial associationism, the modernist masters all attempted in various ways to create higher imaginative syntheses. Their complex poetic/artistic inventions were as aesthetically successful as they were revolutionary; unfortunately the theoretical clarification of these higher syntheses was and continues to be based on associationism because of a general neglect of the Bergsonian theories of conscious synthesis that many of them either duplicated in creative terms or understood and appropriated.

The position as a master that Cézanne enjoyed among the leading modernists originated precisely from the complex character of his contemplative and visionary images, which have been defined in the present study as reflective combinations of the metonymic and the metaphoric and which parallel the precedence of intuition and action over simple memory in Bergson. The contemplative images of the philosopher and the painter display, in their serial references, a corporeal schema of the world as a home that approaches the precision and immediacy of short memory. Yet these images remain under the control of a concentrated and indistinct intuition of the ongoing creative life that is eventually dissociated into practical actions and perceptions. Contemplation, as Bergson and Cézanne understood it, is thus the origin of the spatiotemporal unity of montage, and can be called "montage" in a preeminent sense.

The visionary image originated also in both masters from the indistinct, intermediary intuition of life; but in these images, the intuition of the qualitative unity of life, instead of undergoing dissociation by application to the practical sphere, was superimposed on the dreamy, uninterrupted continuity of vital impressions. The ambiguous visionary image thus shared in the concreteness of this "stream" by preserving its original intuitive indistinctness and mixing it with a curious variety of detail; through the blending of details and ambiguity, the specificity of short memory was submerged in the qualitative memory of the whole of life. Thus Cézanne's visionary collages generally displayed an ambiguous image of the transformation process to be dissociated into its metaphoric interpretations, while the best of the cubist collages still relied on the dissociated images to lead the viewers to a purely imaginative reconstruction of the transformation process. In the cubists, the "materials of the imagination"[80] brought their own worldly contexts into the composition.

The total context of the composition (the life and the life-world of the maker) lacked here its own materials; these had to be supplied by the imagination, hence the disembodied unreality of these collages. In the visionary collages of Cézanne, the materials of the total image were a synthesis of elements borrowed partly from the world of things—this was even clearer in the exposure of canvas in contemplative montages—partly from conscious action, from affectivity and from attention to life. These mixed materials were present in the context of the shifting totality, hence the presence of the motif was embodied or *realized* in them. For this reason, Cézanne's approach to collage has been considered in this study the most fundamental of the two, even though the cubist approach is better known and commonly considered the most basic and typical.

In this new understanding, the visionary image, the "collage of metaphoric diversities" defined in the first chapter, appears clearly as a realized motif rather than a trick of the imagination founded on purely arbitrary signs. The further understanding of this type of image prompts then a reconsideration of the metaphoric shifters within *The Large Bathers* as (natural) signs *of the shifting motif* rather than of the transformation of one image into another or of the motif into dissociated images. In the earlier consideration of the shifters, colors and surfaces were seen as producing an intimacy of space, an absorption of natural extension, including the viewer's surroundings, into the virtual but confining limits of the painting. In the new understanding, color must be seen as the sign of the qualitative, rather than the extensional, significance of change. The changing motif is not signified by a change of the spatial distribution of colors, a change, for instance, from exterior to interior, or from discontinuous to continuous space. Color tonalities and color differences interpenetrate: There is blue in the bodies and ochers in the sky and water; there are different tonalities of blue and ocher unfolding everywhere without any marked discontinuity in each extended application of either color. This peculiar coloration could be described as a fusion, different from the diffusion of the *Mont Sainte-Victoire* series in that its various intensities constitute a sign of qualitative change rather than of any change in the physical disposition or in the measurable time of objects.

Thus the temporality signified by the mysterious spatiality and coloration becomes also an enigma in *The Large Bathers*. What is presented in it is clearly not a physical moment or accumulation of moments; but neither is it a psychological time that would be linked through allegorical similes to psychical situations such as ecstasy or to psychical states such as spiritual adolescence or decline. Indeed, the accumulation of physical time was signified through its own specific signs in the *Mont Sainte-Victoire* series; and of course any use of allegory would be excluded from a realized motif. The possibility of a signification of eternity must also be excluded, because the metaphorical signifier of eternity would be a moment of plenitude, such as the noon hour or twilight. The lived temporality of the *Bathers* is thus neither in nor outside of any specifiable time; in its concreteness it would seem to point without alternative to Bergsonian *duration*.

The equivocal character of all the bodily shapes, the third shifter in the preceding interpretation, must also acquire a new significance when connected with the ambiguity of the shifting motif. The shapes in this context should not be interpreted but should be allowed to function in their qualitative role, which only a complete psycho-physiological response can reveal; their quality is undoubtedly comic, and it is manifested by that mixture of shock and surmise that ends in a smile of recognition. In his essay *Le Rire*, published in 1900, Bergson gave an explanation of the "grotesque" as a sign of an incomplete penetration of matter by life that leaves partially animated bodies in a condition that exhibits at the same time the rigid automatism of the machine and the numbness of the somnambulist. This condition was exploited often in modernist art, especially in cubism, to evidence in an ironic vein the unexpected life that the materials of an artwork acquire in their artistic setting.[81]

In *The Large Bathers* Cézanne introduced the grotesque into the work to make the painting a primal scene of instruction, part recognition and part *discovery* of a similar state of enervation. In Bergson's description this state lies between gravity and grace:

> [O]ur imagination . . . sees the effort of a soul which is shaping matter, a soul which is infinitely supple and perpetually in motion subject to no laws of gravitation. This soul imparts a portion of its winged lightness to the body it animates: the immateriality which thus passes into matter is what is called gracefulness. Matter, however, is obstinate and resists. . . . It would . . . immobilize the intelligently varied movements of the body in stupidly contracted grooves, stereotype in permanent grimaces

the fleeting expressions of the face. . . . Where matter thus succeeds in dulling the outward life of the soul, in petrifying its movements and thwarting its gracefulness, it achieves, at the expense of the body, an effect that is comic.[82]

The grotesque is thus in its very nature the *direct manifestation* of the shifting motif throughout the painting.

In a parallel treatment of the theme of the bathers, "A Lot of People Bathing in a Stream," Wallace Stevens insisted on the comic character of the naked body that announces the vicissitudes of eroticism:

We bathed . . .
And in these comic colors dangled down,
Like their particular characters, addicts
To blotches, angular anonymids
Gulping for shape among the reeds. . . .

. . . floating without a head
And naked, or almost so, into the grotesque
Of being naked, or almost so, in a world
Of nakedness.[83]

The animated signs of the shifting motif do not allow any longer the naming of it, as was done before, with a generic name or title: the sexual body and its life. The motif, as a unique state of qualitative intensity, requires a full description that will present it in its realized condition in the painting. For a brief formula that condenses the pictorial significant form, one may recur to the intuitive accuracy of Kierkegaard and speak of the realized shifting motif of *The Large Bathers* as "the sensuous-erotic in its immediate stages."[84] But condensed formulas will not suffice to present the motif in its sensuous presence; it is necessary to follow Kierkegaard beyond his initial naming of it and translate this presence more fully into words using the poetic resources that he summoned to recreate within literature the musical creation of the theme by Mozart.

Kierkegaard discussed the realization of the sensuous erotic in three significational contexts, each contributing in its own way to the essence of the motif and to its realization. These contexts were the cultural-historical ground of the realization, its medium, and, most important of all, the structure and "stages" of the existential experience itself. The issue of the cultural ground for the realization of the sensuous erotic contains an art-historical and a personal dimension insofar as the artist contributed through his creative life to the clarification and recreation of art-historical (poetic) themes that molded and modified his personal religious, ethical, and ethnic beliefs and habits. The sensuous erotic was for Kierkegaard a form of experience that involved a confrontation of body and spirit and a delimitation and exclusion of the former by the latter. In Kierkegaard's reflective view, delimitation of an experiential realm was not possible without a certain exclusion and repression of it; thus he pointed out that every aspect of the sensuous was included in Greco-Roman culture within the total complex of the beautiful personality, the indissoluble unity of pleasure and virtue that characterized the realm of the soul in classical ethics and art. Classical culture lacked also a sense of freedom from destiny that would permit the embodiment of an experiential attitude by an ethical hero or protagonist. Eros, the principle of love, does not fall in love; he only controls love in nature and society. The appearance of the sensuous erotic, its realization as a unique kind of freedom with specific opportunities for sin and salvation, took place when Christianity brought about a more precise delimitation of the realm of the spirit, of its demands and perversions.

Kierkegaard's considerations apply to the reemergence of the aesthetic-erotic personality in the romantic period; in order to make them relevant to Cézanne, they must be adapted to the specific dimensions of the recovery of spirituality by modernism. For the modernist artist, Christianity had already begun to pass over into the territory of myths occupied by previous cultural forms. Modernism was, in a sense, a nostalgia for all the mythological aspects (classical, Northern, Celtic, medieval) of the Western tradition and an attempt to transfer them to the culture-making powers of art. Art now had to become ironic, less serious than it was in aristocratic and bourgeois societies, but also more serious, since it saw itself as a form of life capable not only of preserving the old but of creating new myths to go along with new forms of reason.

Cézanne participated in this cultural-artistic predicament with a mixture of ideological conservatism and artistic radicalism. His art may have some ironic aspects attached to the various innovations of his technique and to the motifs themselves he was trying to create. The persistence and solitude of his theoretical and practical efforts indicate, however, that beyond the narrow struggle for artistic originality he saw—humbly but very clearly and with genial stubbornness—the magnitude of the consequences of his achievements, whether thematic or technical, for the spirit of his time.

The pictorial realization of the sensuous erotic in *The Large Bathers* was therefore, for Cézanne the painter and the man, a dialogue with the tradition of nude painting, a reaffirmation of the erotic quality of human existence in a mechanical age, and a mature reckoning with levels of experience he had practically denied or fragmentarily affirmed in his relations with women. As Kierkegaard recognized, the artist, through visionary concentration, becomes the protagonist of the realization of a spiritual state that would be lost in the confusion of individual and social everyday existence. For Cézanne the person, the qualitative intensities of the erotic, of its resistance against and rise toward spiritual intensities, could come to pass only in the struggle of Cézanne the artist with emotional and existential mediocrity and with the opacity and limitations of expressive media and expressive signs.

Kierkegaard indicated that the appropriate medium for the sensuous erotic, if it is to be presented in its immediacy, is music:

> In the erotic-sensuous genius, music has its absolute object. It is not of course intended to say by this that music cannot express other things, but this is its proper object. In the same way the art of sculpture is also capable of producing much else than human beauty, and yet this is its absolute object; painting can express much else than the beauty which is celestially glorified, and yet this is its absolute object.[85]

In this context, the philosopher is following rules for the presentation of subject matter by means of specific signs that had remained stable since Lessing. In early aesthetic theory, natural signs such as shape, color, and texture were said to present abstract subject matter in painting, sculpture, and architecture; arbitrary signs such as words were assigned to the presentation of concrete states of affairs and states of mind. Painting could thus present the concrete, but only if it had been first articulated in words in the same way as was done in the theater. Music, finally, gravitated between the plastic and the literary arts, because it presented abstract subject matter by means of signs that shared in the natural and the arbitrary.

These conventions had dominated the distinction and separation of the various arts and had also established a strict association between reason and sensibility, with the former always controlling the latter for the purposes of moral education. As was demonstrated in chapter 1, at the end of the nineteenth century a total transformation in the understanding of signs and of their participation in the formation of images changed the traditional connection of visual signs with abstract, and of auditory signs with concrete, subject matter. Combinations of signs, including visual and auditory ones, were now seen as capable of representing different degrees of abstraction, depending on the richness or selectivity of the materials of the image, and different degrees of concreteness, depending on the synthetic individuation of the subject matter within the *lived* experience that constituted its context. This conversion of the representational role of sensation into a new role as presentational sign anticipated in aesthetics the philosophical emergence of a complex associationism and of reflective theories of synthetic experience and expression. With the possibility of constructing associational or reflective images by using different signs without any limitation, the traditional distinctions among the arts broke down and the merging of several forms of art within the confines of any one of them became prevalent in modernism.

An equally important effect of the new role of signs in art was the elimination of the control of intellectual or moral subject matter over the means and the media of experience and expression. The dissociation of sensibility and intellect denounced by modernist aestheticians was removed from the arts. On the one hand, the senses were credited with having their own intelligence; on the other hand, the materials of the sign could reach high levels of dematerialization and became as animated as the human body and very intimate extensions of it.

The incorporation of signs into images and the intuitive/reflective merging of sensibility and intellect in Cézanne have been followed in this chapter as they gradually led to the conversion of metonymic signs into metaphoric signs within the contemplative and visionary images. The conclusion and coronation of these processes can be understood to be Cézanne's ability to present a typically abstract subject matter—the sensuous erotic—in an immediate, truly sensuous embodiment without appealing to the musical sign. But it is also possible to discern in Cézanne's visionary *Large Bathers* a crystallizing of the image with a degree of concreteness that could not be achieved within the musical medium.

The difference between the abstractness of the musical image and the concreteness of the visionary can now be explained as a difference in narrativity that can be produced by the dissociation of an experiential motif—an indistinct intuition—into its component images. This dissociation can only lead in music to a highly conventional isolation and identification of the stages of an emotion expressed by tempo and, ultimately, by the logic that articulates the movements of a composition. Cézanne's *Large Bathers* and *Cardplayers* constitute masterful demonstrations of the achievement of narrativity in painting through the dissociation of shifting motifs that embody the entire life of the creator. This dissociation originated from an indistinct image—a shifting motif—that contained metonymies sedimented through a high concentration of action and intuition; it ended in a colorful and emotionally charged articulation of perceptions, memories, and dreams.

All of these considerations on medium and subject matter explain the overwhelming presence of visionary paintings like *The Large Bathers* and *The Cardplayers* as well as their enormous impact on the history of sensibility and the history of communication. An impact such as this has been imitated, trivialized, and disseminated in artistic education and experimentation, in the arts of propaganda, and in the use of the media. It cannot be truly duplicated without a share in the existential commitment and the ability of a Cézanne to realize motifs.

The realization of the sensuous-erotic motif in *The Large Bathers* involves the same possibilities of analysis into stages as those described by Kierkegaard; but this analysis must be carried out with the caution recommended by the philosopher:

> [T]he expression "stage" . . .must not be insisted upon as implying that each stage existed independently, the one wholly separate from the other. I might, perhaps, more pertinently have used the word "metamorphosis." The different stages taken

together constitute the immediate stage. . . . Above all, however, one must avoid considering them as different degrees of consciousness, since even the last stage has not yet arrived at consciousness; I have always to do only with the immediate [sensuous-erotic] in its sheer immediacy.[86]

Kierkegaard did not permit the interpreter of the sensuous-erotic motif to consider the images into which it could be dissociated as previous to the motif itself, nor did he allow that the interpretation be carried out from an analytic level of consciousness higher than the one inherent in the existential condition of eroticism.

The philosopher separated the stages by appealing to three different musical images in Mozart. The first, represented by the musical expressions of Cherubino in *The Marriage of Figaro*, shows a state of desire in which its object is beginning to emerge although it has not yet found its embodiment. The image of this state is therefore still immersed in a metamorphosis:

> The sensuous awakens, not yet to movement, but to a hushed tranquility; not to joy and gladness, but to a deep melancholy. Desire is not yet awake, it is only a gloomy foreboding. In desire there is always present the object of desire, which arises out of it and manifests itself in a bewildering half-light of dawn. This relation obtains for the sensuous: by clouds and mists it is kept at a distance; by being reflected in these it is brought nearer. . . . The desire is quiet desire, the longing quiet longing, the ecstasy quiet ecstasy, wherein the object of desire is dawning, and is so near that it is within the desire. The object of desire hovers over the desire, sinks down in it, still without this movement happening through desire's own power to attract.[87]

If this first stage would manifest desire as dreaming, the second will present it as seeking. Kierkegaard recurs to the musical figure of Papageno in *The Magic Flute* to dissociate the second stage from its intuitive qualitative ground:

> Desire is directed toward the object, it is also moved within itself, the heart beats soundly and joyously, the objects swiftly vanish and reappear; but still before every disappearance is a

present enjoyment. . . . Only momentarily is a deeper desire suspected, but this suspicion is forgotten. In Papageno the desire aims at discoveries. This craving for discovery is the throbbing in it, is its sprightliness. It does not find the precise object of this search, but it discovers the manifold, as it seeks therein the object it would discover. Desire is thus awakened, but it is not yet qualified as desire.[88]

The third stage, the end and resolution of the metamorphosis of the erotic, should be desire itself. In its links to its own metamorphosis, however, desire is a qualitative intensity that cannot be petrified in a stage; it must present itself like the other stages as a manifestation of a whole life (Bergson's *concentration*, Heidegger's *concern*):

The first stage desired the one ideally, the second stage desired the particular under the qualification of the manifold; the third stage is a synthesis of these two. Desire has its absolute object in the particular, it desires the particular absolutely. . . . Hence, desire in this stage is absolutely sound, victorious, triumphant, irresistible and daemonic. . . . such is Don Juan's life. There is a dread in him, but this dread is his energy. . . . Don Juan's life is not despair; but it is the whole power of sensuousness, which is born in dread, and Don Juan himself is this dread, but this dread is precisely the daemonic joy of life.[89]

Kierkegaard's reading of Mozart was made possible by a narrative dissociation of the sensuous-erotic motif that was, in spite of its sensuousness, more literary than Cézanne's pictorial rendition. By means of the visionary image, the painter achieved a narrativity that is partly contained in the signs of the metamorphosis of the motif—the whole of the painting when it is read as a collage—and partly in the various possibilities of its dissociation into multiple images. The signs of the shifting motif—color interpenetration, temporality as duration, and the comic—lead to an awareness of narrativity, not as a formal device that would introduce literary subject matter but as the presentation of eroticism in an empathetic realization that opens up the entire life of the viewer as it opened the entire life of the painter.

Concerning the possibilities of dissociation of the motif into images, Cézanne gave us enough clues to look for the first stage in the charged multiplicity of value of all the sensory signs that places the viewer immediately in the plane of the dream. The viewer is led to the second stage by the multiplication of bodies as signs of objects to be recognized and enjoyed. This is the moment of seeing as pleasure. The third stage of the erotic emerges in *The Large Bathers* as the moment of reading: the conquering and reconquering of the object in the faceless bodies and in the elusive face in the sky.[90] This dissociation of signifiers is concrete enough and explicit enough in this painting to reveal the mystery of Cézanne's narrative interpretations of his own erotic life through the fighting of the three erotic stages for prevalence and presence within the shifting motif. The motif is rich enough in qualitative intensity to contain all of its—Cézanne's—existential dissociations; it is also enigmatic enough in its narrativity to hide which of the stages of the erotic prevailed in the indistinct image of the painter's life. Perhaps he himself did not know, or thought it not worth knowing.

DEATH AND NON-FIGURATION
Cézanne's Ultimate Synthesis

How can the signifying (semiotic) condition and thematic nature of the object of art be characterized in view of the changes introduced by modernism? In answering this question we will retrace the course of this investigation and summarize the profound modifications of the artistic image and its function introduced by the events that were considered in the developmental analysis of the theory of images and of Cézanne's images in the previous chapters. Because one of the main themes that grew out of this analysis was the altered status of the relation of object and subject, that is, the progressive disappearance of the representational function of art in modernism, it must be understood that our question concerns both the object—the content, subject matter—*of* the work and the work itself as an object in the world. The concepts of abstraction, expressionism, nonfigurative art, nonreferential art, and other concepts commonly used in current aesthetic theory and art history to characterize the nature and condition of the object in the forty-year period of transformation are inadequate, because they lack the complexity necessary to describe changes that were as multiple as they were diverse.

However profound and significant partial expressive and technical modifications of the art object may have been during the first

145

three quarters of the nineteenth century, the nature of this object, and its relations to the subject—artist, public—must be characterized by the use of the term *traditional* to express both the role of the signs, natural and arbitrary, that embody art and the *sense and reference* of those signs. Implicit in the use of the term *traditional* is the assumption that the romantic conception of the art object as *symbol* did not substantially alter the imitative or mimetic function that had been originally entrusted to it by Platonism and did not completely do away with the use of allegories in the constitution of the sense and reference of the romantic symbol.

The traditional art object, whether classical, baroque or romantic, had as its sense—if this term is understood as the organization of content or meaning—a physical, a human, or a spiritual form. This form was translated into the sensuous realm of images by rules of analogy between concepts and percepts—allegorical decorum—that presented a metaphysical object either in opposition to the deficiencies of a sensory thing or as prefigured in its qualities. In both these modes of participation, one involving negative analogy and the other positive analogy, the metaphysical object or content was absent from the sensory image, yet it was seen as capable of filling a certain intentional void that was found in, and contributed to the significance of, the latter.

The reference of the traditional artistic object to its image was established, thus, by the relation of mimesis or imitation, which was understood to be natural (the art object is constituted by direct perceptual signs) in the visual arts and arbitrary or conventional (the art object is constituted by interpretative signs) in the verbal. However, in traditional philosophy, poetry, and literature, even arbitrary or conventional imitation was, in the end, natural; indeed, in accordance with the philosophical tradition, all *forms of significance* or structured signs are connected with metaphysical *forms of being* through allegorical images—conceptual paradigms, narrative schemata, or visionary personifications—that make explicit the transcendental function of ideal forms as the *final causes or purposes* of all existence. Thus the analogy produced by traditional imitation in art and literature was at bottom more causal than poetic, more metonymic than metaphoric, and of course this fact made all art ancillary to intellectual and moral knowledge or wisdom.

The network of relations of sense and reference connecting image and ideal, or metaphysical, reality traditionally constituted the art object as object or, in the categories of the literary arts, as a "topic"; in semiotic terms, these relations motivated the signs that embody the work. Motivation appeared already as *realization*, as the joint effect of sense and reference that indicated for every object the degree of reality that it enjoyed through imitation and the fictional character—complement of unreality—added on to it by the corresponding remoteness or distance from the highest levels of reality. In traditional art, the object—the realized motif as a union of sensory form and ideal form or content—was thus the product not of sensory but of *metaphysical* imitation (participation), and this participation always involved a placement of the work (object) of art on the highest levels of reality.

At the end of the nineteenth century, the romantic symbol underwent a profound change that was already implicit in the workings of the notion of alienation within the philosophical systems (especially Hegelian thought) that gave conceptual status to the new idea of the symbolic. In poetry and art, and eventually in all forms of culture and expression, the symbol came to stand for an embodiment of enhanced or *displaced* psychic activity that, in art, was said to be first a denial (sublation or *Aufhebung*) of common affective responses to reality and then a sedimentation of emotion charged with displaced vital, economic, social, or sexual energies or "instincts." It should be emphasized that this displacement, however differently it came to be understood, was the equivalent of the traditional absence of the metaphysical object from the image and *would replace the function of imitation by converting sensations into signs in all subsequent art movements.* The "metaphysics" of the symbolist movement gathered within itself a variety of attitudes, some spiritualist, some simply oriented toward the cultural sciences, in which the symbol became the stand-in and the repository of acts and intentions that could not be mechanistically explained and yet had a place within the realm of life and especially within the human world.

The sense or meaning of the object in artistic or literary symbolism was (or was the effect of) a metonymically displaced activity or tendency, while its reference was established by the relation of correspondence or equivalence between that absent activity and the structure of the signs that embody it. When the correspondence or equivalence was determined by empathetic or vital correlation and the content of the artistic object was, as indicated above, a displaced form of life or energy, the interpretation of the art object would be simply a reading of the metonymic displacements of life or energy through *traces* of those displacements that might have been left in the structured synthesis of the embodying signs (such was the eventual direction taken by Freud and his followers).

In this mode of understanding, interpretation always had to overcome the arbitrary character of the substitution of the structure of the signifiers for the series of metonymic displacements that it was taken to signify. But since the structural synthesis of the signifiers was the only repository of that metonymic activity and its displacements, the object formed by them, in particular the art object, could be considered a motivated sign only after a reading by its creator or by qualified interpreters. Before such a reading the sign that ascribed equivalence to sensory structure and conscious history would be totally contingent and hence totally ambiguous. When seen in this light, the symbolist movement must be characterized as the theoretical matrix of all the "hermeneutics of suspicion" or hermeneutics of alienation that would subsequently define culture as a gathering of the various provinces of displaced meaning and art as one—perhaps even the most important—of these provinces.

The activity of creating signs can be isolated as an independent moment within every form of psychic activity and the resulting conscious syntheses. Positivist psychologists, linguists, and ethnologists, and their neo-Kantian counterparts at the turn of the century, began isolating this activity and defining all its manifestations as language; they also emphasized the *conventionality* of the sign-making activity in its relation to other human activities, whether the transforming of food, the making of tools, the decorative crafts, or the rituals of social coexistence, to the point of making the equivalences of all those activities, and of parts of them and of their contexts, pure objects of instinct, chance, or play. (Neo-Kantians would mitigate this fragmentation of culture by advocating the primacy of the category of relation and introducing total paradigms or relational models that marked the design of the human world and linked the various provinces of signs.)[1] Linguistic objects were constructed, but also deconstructed, by reading or interpretation; reading in such a generalized and fluid creation of signs was, from its very start, abstraction from the stream of sensory life.

In the plastic arts, as in all other cultural provinces linguistically understood, the resulting abstract objects had as their field of reference the linguistic or forming activity itself, not the vital or environmental contexts engaged by the senses, though in impressionism and analytic cubism reference to "natural" reality still had a cursory role. The sense of objects, including the art object, within this abstracting tendency was constituted by purely formal patterns that may, at the end of playful experimentation, be seen as recovering and arresting the unique plasticity and aliveness of a sensory rhythm. To supplement such fluidity and conventionality in cultural objects, advocates of abstraction appealed eventually to the power of nonhuman or superhuman agencies, including language itself, or to political domination and emancipation, and even to libidinal energies conceptualized as "instincts." In this appeal they joined, and still continue to join, the fundamental attitudes of symbolism in defining meaning as the conventional mixing and matching of displaced energies and not as the unique effect of extraordinary concentration and freedom (à la Bergson, Cézanne, and modernist masters).

These changes in the understanding of the art object have led, and continue to lead, to adaptations in and reconsiderations of the method of art history. From its inception this discipline has relied on a combination of *description* (and documentation as an instrument of fixation of the art object) with *explanation* (interpretation), as a means of determining the nature and value of that object. After the neo-Kantian systematization of these terms, "iconography" was understood as gathering the various descriptive procedures, and "iconology" as gathering the conceptual and explanatory procedures. Initially the grounding of explanation associated with iconology was the metaphysical doctrine of imitation that was suited to the subject matter of classical and romantic art, but as the conception of the object changed and the artworks themselves evolved in their techniques and subject matter with the impressionists and their successors, both description and explanation evolved as well.

In nonrepresentational art, description has had to rely increasingly on very complex examinations of technique and much less so on identification of sources and of factual and literary subject matter. On the other hand, explanation has had to contend with the transformation of the sensory object into a semiotic object and as a result has abandoned the metaphysical justification through imitation and has largely become a clarification of the significance, and the various roles, of abstraction and an extension of the symbolist procedures of interpretation of displaced energy. Contemporary art history does now often depend on social theory, whether Marxist, structuralist, or critical, on psychoanalysis, and on the mainly linguistic procedures of deconstruction and media simulation to establish the meaning—sense plus reference—and the place in the world of art objects, especially of those created in and after the late nineteenth century (these procedures are, however, increasingly being applied to earlier works and styles).

In all of these techniques, the explicit or implicit appeal to an absolute foundation, whether linguistic or social, as common to all cultural phenomena, including art, has led to a determination of artistic form *by contents other than aesthetic* and to the consequent reduction of aesthetic criteria of justification and evaluation to criteria firmly situated in fields other than art. The conjunction of technical iconography with symbolic explanation through abstraction and displacement has therefore produced an almost complete abandonment of iconology; the formation or development of icons or images out of aesthetic and psychological procedures *with their own distinct and autonomous roots in some existential interests and intentions* has been sorely neglected. With this neglect, art's contribution to culture tends to become secondary and to be subordinated to other individual and social aims, some revolutionary, some therapeutical. The creative subject, one of the most productive embodiments of responsibility and personal life that art has to offer to culture, has thus come to suffer the same total eclipse that has overshadowed subjectivity in other fields.

In the present investigation, a study of the various types of image—symbolist, plastic, contemplative, and visionary—and the conceptual justification of them (the iconology of Cézanne's works) in conjunction with the description of the technical methods of production and identification of these different images (the iconography of his paintings) have produced a distinct line of interpretation that is specifically applicable to the master as a modernist. There are clearly symbolist and abstract or plastic images in Cézanne that were explained in chapter 4 as the work of displaced emotions and semiotic abstraction; but there are undoubtedly other images, identified in this study as contemplative and visionary, that can be best understood by a hermeneutical method based on the aesthetics of Bergson, Heidegger (Kierkegaard), and Merleau-Ponty. Contemplative and visionary images are indeed the most important and characteristic of the master and the ones that contributed most to produce a core of inventive concepts and techniques that distinguish those works of modernism that are now generally considered classical from other works and techniques that should be seen as primarily experimental.

Even though this is current practice, the sense and reference of these new (now classical) images of Cézanne should not be separated from each other by a linguistic and/or causal interpretation; indeed, sense and reference are totally fused in the reflective syntheses of montage, for contemplative images, and of collage, for visionary images. Contemplative images place the artist, and of course the viewer, always already in the world.[2] Creative and active concentration in the work make that *unity of subject and world come to pass in the form of aesthetic and existential truth*. Visionary images in turn present the aesthetic and existential struggle for *unification of the course of life*, of the artist as well as the viewer, *as completed in the work*. Thus these images are in no way fictional or even vitally playful; the realization of the motif is always a motivation of reality, an actualization of "truth *in* painting."

An interpretation of modernism that grants such a central role to contemplative and visionary images and their intervention upon reality is a necessary and valuable contribution to the understanding of this period and movement. It adds a center to prevalent conceptions of modernism that are badly in need of it. In these conceptions, modernism was constituted by a tension and struggle between the extremes of romantic, organic symbolism, with its continuation in the symbolist movement and in some "high modernist" masters, and the abstraction and linguistic "indeterminacy"[3] of the experimental avant-garde, which are said to have originated in cubism and futurism and to have led directly to postmodern artistic forms and performances. In these interpretations that rely exclusively, whether knowingly or unknowingly, on *associationist* theories of the image, and ignore *reflective* images as an alternative means of understanding modernist art, there cannot be an aesthetic middle ground and reconciliation of empathy and abstraction, the tactile and the visual, the metonymic and the metaphoric. When reflective images are removed from the conceptual core of modernism, its most distinctive expressive instruments disappear, and the movement itself breaks down as an independent art-historical phenomenon: On the one hand, its symbolist component is absorbed by its romantic and traditional antecedents; on the other hand, the abstract and "indeterminate" component fades into a postmodernist pluralism that, because of its rejection of a distinct modernism, is itself deprived of roots and of a hermeneutical line of sight.[4]

A reflective theory of the image and the discernment of the corresponding (contemplative and visionary) categories of images in Cézanne would not prove sufficient on its own to serve as a ground for a general theory of modernism. Nevertheless it may prove to be more than an adequate beginning for such a theory because of the wide acknowledgment of the innovations and scope of the master's art on the part of representatives of all the extremes of modernism. Preliminary explorations of other modernist artists such as Henri Matisse,[5] Paul Klee, Marcel Duchamp, and even of postmodernists like Robert Rauschenberg and Jasper Johns, as well as of modernist and postmodernist writers such as Gertrude Stein, Wallace Stevens, Jean Genet, Samuel Beckett, and John Ashbery, have shown the presence of reflective images in their works and the value of using such images in interpreting them.

This final chapter of this investigation of the poetics of painting in Cézanne is devoted to a study of *The Cardplayers* as a visionary image. The study of this image will encompass the iconographic and iconological sources of the partial images of the players and of the skull that are intertwined in the compositional structure of the painting; inevitably, in its preliminary stages, the examination of these roots and sources will employ iconographic and iconological perspectives that are more pertinent to the study of the isolated images and therefore will present the motif not as a metaphor but merely as a simile, the first type of visionary image that was discussed in chapter 4 as contained in Cézanne's oeuvre. It should be understood that this mode of presentation is all that the traditional, and in the end associationist, reach of iconography and iconology could achieve. It should follow from previous remarks on these methods, and on Cézanne's unique development and realization of collage as a visionary shifting motif, that the preliminary stages of this analysis of *The Cardplayers* will serve only to sort out *the materials of the imagination* (first the pictorial, then the narrative, and then the psychological or affective) that are fused and dissolved in the ultimate shifting motif of the painting. The final stage of the analysis will proceed to the study of the formal signs and the existential meaning of the visionary motif itself.

THE PICTORIAL MATERIALS OF THE IMAGINATION:
Analytic Components and Antecedents of
the Shifting Motif of *The Cardplayers*

There are five major canvases of cardplaying scenes in Cézanne, but because none of the oil canvases are signed, the dating of the series is difficult. The series is generally listed as having been painted between 1890 and 1899.[6] Three of these oils have two figures, one has four figures, and the remainder have five; therefore they are usually referred to as "Group A," the four- and five-figure compositions, and "Group B," the two-figure groups. Vollard, Venturi, Badt, Gowing, and Reff[7] all agree that Group A preceded Group B; that is, the earlier canvases contain the most figures and are larger.[8]

In both paintings of Group A three men are shown at a table playing cards. In the one located in the Barnes Foundation (V560), a man smoking a pipe leans against the back wall of the room to the left with his arms crossed; a small child looks over the shoulder of the central cardplayer. The table is aligned parallel to the surface plane and has a drawer that opens toward the viewer. The two cardplayers, opposite each other, lean forward with outstretched arms that form centrally converging diagonals. The pose of the man in the center further establishes the diagonal configuration: His legs and arms counter the illusory convergence. He is hatless and appears younger than his companions, and his position, parallel to the viewer's space, serves to further set him off from them. The setting is the most detailed in this version; its wall holds a pipe rack with four pipes, a framed painting, and a shelf with a two-toned pot. A large billowing drapery fills in the space to the right. The folds of the drapery are repeated, at least in their volumetric lines, in the coat of the cardplayer seated in front of it.

In the second painting of Group A (V559 in the Metropolitan Museum), the child has been eliminated, as have the wall shelf and

painting. The same V shapes of converging and countering diagonals, the billowing drapery, and richly folded coat are present. The
hatless cardplayer has been replaced with a hatted, bearded cardplayer
who resembles Cézanne; the artist has inserted himself as a smoking
onlooker. He stands with detached curiosity in the background of
this hauntingly self-reflective composition.

The compositions of the Group B paintings are all similar to,
but decidedly different from, those of Group A. They all contain
two figures who sit across a table from each other; the third player
and the onlookers in these versions have been eliminated. The coun-
tenances and clothing of the two players have also been altered: The
smoker is now seated on the left side of the table, and the more
rotund, heavily draped player of the Group A paintings has been
replaced with a younger, mustachioed man with lanky limbs. (Cézanne
does not have a walk-on part in these paintings.) The paraphernalia
on the table—stacks of cards, a pipe—has also been deleted from the
Group B paintings, and a lone wine bottle stands at the back of the
table, visible through the card-holding hands of the players. The
table in the paintings of Group B does not have a drawer; thus the
convex references of the Group A paintings are lost. The decorations
and spatial organization of the room in which the game takes place
are cast in deep shadows and create the illusion of receding planes
that appear to converge in an obscure rectangular background that
could be either a window, a mirror, or a painting of a landscape.

The earliest of the Group B paintings is thought to be the Pellerin
version (V556; figure 5); the next in the chronology is the Courtauld
version (V558); and the final in the series is the Orsay version (figure 6). The Orsay version has the same basic format as the Pellerin
painting, but it exhibits more precise linear rhythms and strictly bal-
anced relationships between recessional planes and quadrants and
between objects and their surrounding spaces. In passing from the
conception of the works in Group A to the Pellerin version (figure
5), Cézanne seems to have arrived at the arrangement showing two
figures at a table in a concave space. In the reworkings of the initial
composition, the painter appears to have been making slight alterations and progressing through various arrangements, linear configurations, color "moods," and viewing alignments, while searching for
and inventing the shifting motif that, as will be presently explained,
blends the cardplayers with the skull.

By changing the angle of inclination of the arms, the shapes of the knees, and even the relative position of the lines of the two hats, Cézanne "foreshadows" the image of the skull in the cardplaying scene. The angle of the outstretched arms of the gamesters is his most obvious device for discovery and invention. Through the five versions, the poses of the arms have been altered to finally attain a strictly angled pose that forms the cheekbones of the skull. The line for the gap of the nose is created by the reflecting glint on the wine bottle, which Cézanne has been moving around in the previous two paintings to determine its ideal placement. The gaping eye sockets are produced by two voids in space created by the V-shaped disposi-tions of the cardplayers' arms, which have been growing in size and textural intensity in the progression of the paintings from Group B. An allusion to teeth is supported by the four rectangularly shaped knees under the table. In the Pellerin version (figure 5), the table edge is closer to the canvas edge and thus the knees are not given a very prominent view, but in the "next" painting, the Courtauld ver-sion, Cézanne substitutes a rounded knee joint that repeats the curves of the elbows. The allusion to teeth is most visible in the Orsay version (figure 6) as the knees line up like the four front teeth of a skeletal smile.

In this culminating work, Cézanne blends the playing figures and the skull and forecloses any interpretation of the visionary motif as a mere simile or optical illusion. For the moment, how-ever, the alternation of the multiple readings may be kept at this elementary level and the viewer will thus be led to the apprehen-sion of the skull, in its function as material of the imagination, mainly as a secondary image subordinate to the scene of cardplay-ing. It should be noted, however, that the process of perceptual identification of the skull allows for both images to be seen either consecutively, if the partial images are brought into focus before the entire shifting motif, or simultaneously, if they constitute it. The ordering of the apprehension of the lines, colors, and space as signs produces the various images; the two visual formulas can be either separated by the viewer with quick alternations of attention, or fused, as Bergson would suggest, with slow and insis-tent transitions that would make the skull transparently visible through the scene of the play, and vice versa.

Cézanne's careful formulation of different arrangements of the same signifiers—lines, colors—to express different signifieds—the gamesters and the skull, on the one hand, and their fusion, on the other—indicates that the attainment of realization of the motif does not necessarily require an obvious and overt connecting reference, but may, as Baudelaire instructs, gain evocative power by suggestion or indirect reference "comme de longs échos qui de loin se confondent / Dans une ténébreuse et profonde unité."[9]

As materials of the painter's imagination, suggested images, "hidden" like Cézanne's skull in the visual field of a work of art, have numerous and famous precedents in the history of painting. In the *French Ambassadors* by Hans Holbein the Younger (Cézanne most likely never saw the painting itself), the distorted anamorphic skull disruptively placed beneath the "painted" portraits constitutes a visual puzzle so difficult to read that the viewer is compelled to conform to its spatial peculiarities rather than to the norms of common human perception. Its oblique laterality stands in marked contrast to the sharply focused icons of church and state prominent in the scene above it; the distorted angle of viewing results in the illusion that the skull is indeed grinning to mock the feigned dignity of the two figures above it.[10]

Another work with curious distortions and "hidden" imagery that informs its meaning was visible to Cézanne during its exhibition in Paris in 1899,[11] that important date for the timing of the Orsay version (figure 6). The enigmatic *Spinners* by Diego Velázquez presents a confusing series of posed groups that are not spatially unifiable.[12] In this painting, weavers in a tapestry factory have a vision of an ancient legend connected with their craft. The vision, which takes shape in an anteroom in the background of the composition, is of the story of Arachne, that mortal weaver who challenged Minerva to a contest, only to be punished by the goddess for her hubris by being metamorphosed into a spider and damned to weave for all eternity.

The scene, as dramatized in this work of Velázquez, shows the tense moment before her transformation when Arachne is receiving the judgment of the immortal one. The story, taken from the *Ovide moralisé*,[13] is an appropriate subject for the *Spinners;* it is not only introduced into the painting as an "offstage" vision, but it also is illustrated by the inclusion of tiny spiders "hidden" in the corners of the spinning room, busily weaving their own webs. Although virtually invisible, the spiders not only reinforce the complexities of the subject matter of the painting but also complete the "chain" of *correspondances* or equivalents (Arachne-spider-working-class seamstresses in their dim surroundings) presented for the allegorical purposes of the painting.

Less allegorical in its intention is Vincent van Gogh's *Sunflowers*, in which the "eye" of the flower contains the vague shape of a human eye.[14] Again, what appears to be a still life with its inherent warning against *vanitas* eerily transcends its spatial and temporal limitations and acknowledges the viewer—in this case by actually looking out with an engaging eye—and extends his or her consciousness into the subject matter.[15] The punning quality of van Gogh's hidden imagery is indicative of his symbolist leanings.

Cézanne was also attracted to the symbolist intent of this kind of moralizing punning imagery, which he developed in several paintings. In *Uncle Dominic* (V77) he ironically poses his uncle as a Dominican monk (which he was not), and in *The Artist's Father* (V91) the pattern of the print type and the sharp white edges of a newspaper are repeated in the patterned modulation of the face of the father holding the newspaper.[16] This picture is invested with ambiguous feelings of identification on the part of Cézanne with Zola, who in order to earn his living was forced to write for the conservative newspaper *L'Événement*. The portrait is also imbued with latent recrimination toward the father, whose links with conservatism and exploitation are established through the metonymic displacement of the print pattern from the page to the parental face. These two early works do not contain shifting motifs comparable to those of *The Cardplayers* or *The Large Bathers* but are more like the first type of visionary image discussed in chapter 4 in which salient parts of a painting are given an ambiguous significance consistent with the potent feelings to which they are bound.

There are two other paintings that, much like van Gogh's blinking sunflower, contain the hidden image of a skull, not as a shifting motif but as a simile. In a study of Eugène Delacroix's *Roses and Hortensias*, Cézanne included the secondary image of a skull in the solid and void structuring of his own drawing of the bouquet set against its background space. Cézanne owned the Delacroix painting;[17] he studied it frequently, and his drawings of it exhibit a high degree of experimentation in condensation and modulation. The angles of the growth of the leaves of the flowers and the empty spaces between them create two parallel voids for the empty eye sockets of the skull, while the branching stalks of the plants resemble the hanging hinge of the jaw joint, and the canopy-like dome of the flower blooms forms the roundness of the cranium. In a conversation with Maurice Denis in 1906,[18] Cézanne stated that he had found ("discovered") in the *Hortensias* the same "motif" that he had noticed in Veronese's *Supper at Emmaus;* this common motif was constituted by the similar positioning of converging diagonal lines that organize the structure of the works into vertical, horizontal, and planimetric thirds together with the contrast between solid areas and empty spaces that he had so well formulated in his drawings of the *Hortensias.* He must have elaborated the motif of the skull in his copies after the *Hortensias,* but his own studies after the Veronese are incomplete sketches and do not reveal the hidden skull image. However, while Veronese's *Supper at Emmaus* most likely influenced Cézanne in his experiments with the motif for the *Cardplayers* series, its influence is to be related to the iconography of cardplaying rather than as an example of hidden imagery.

Paolo Veronese was greatly admired by Cézanne, who made numerous copies of *The Supper at Emmaus* of 1560 and also advised others to study it.[19] In this large oil painting, Cleophas and his companion are shown sitting across from each other at a table that is parallel to the surface plane, as in Cézanne's paintings. The two disciples reach forward, and their outstretched arms create the same converging orthogonal focus that Cézanne employed, but in the Veronese, Christ sits behind the table in the position Cézanne chose for the placement of his own self-portrait in *The Cardplayers* (V559 in the Metropolitan Museum).

Although there are two other *Supper at Emmaus* paintings (one by Rembrandt and another by Titian) in the Louvre that we might examine for compositional similarities with *The Cardplayers,* it is not necessary to do so. This very brief analysis of the affinities of Cézanne's series with the Veronese painting points to the possibility that Cézanne might have substituted himself for Christ and the skull for the bread.

Another painting with a skull image is a work of Cézanne's own devising. The *Chateau Noir* (V667) represents an infamous house in which purportedly alchemical experiments were held and that was nicknamed by the local townspeople the "chateau du diable." Cézanne presented it as a skull-like structure, colored with a bleached-bones hue and detailed with window openings that resemble the apertures of a skull. Thus to the "house of the devil" Cézanne assigns the legendary emblem of Satan.[20]

However, the skull does not always carry a demonic reference as in the *Chateau Noir;* Cézanne utilized many of its other meanings in his still lifes and also in some paintings of human figures. As a memento mori, the skull is included in many still lifes that could be classified within the category of the *vanitas* theme. *Still Life with Skull* (V61) is a good example of Cézanne's illustration of the *vanitas* (emptiness) of earthly things. Included with a faded rose, an open book, and a consumed candlestick, all of which refer to the passing of time, is the skull as an earthly emblem of the mortal life. The skull is also included in Cézanne's repertory as an object of meditation for the human mind.[21] In *Boy with Skull* (V679), Cézanne's son is posed in a meditative stance as if lost in his own thoughts. The inclusion of the skull with such a meditative pose recalls the classical portrayals of certain martyrs, such as the hermit saints Jerome and Anthony, Francis of Assisi, and the penitential Mary Magdalene, in which the skull is included as an emblem of triumph over sin and death and also as an emblem of supernatural wisdom.

The substitution, by Cézanne, of his son in this role is probably an identification of his own self and, significantly, of the son with a martyred and redeeming victim.[22] Other paintings that insist on this theme, the *Repentant Magdalene* and the *Temptation of St. Anthony,* repeat this brooding pose. In Cézanne's notebooks there are sketches of two other brooding figures, Eugène Delacroix's *Sardanapalus* and *Michelangelo*; and Cézanne makes use of a pose similar to that given to Michelangelo in two of his own renditions of the *Smoker* (V686, V688). The model for the smoker in those canvases is the same man, a local gardener, as was used for the final *Cardplayers.*[23] Saints, martyred kings, bouquets of cut flowers, artistic geniuses, an Aixois man and his own son support, then, the full range of emblematic and symbolic associations of the skull (in the first visionary mode) that justify its consideration as pictorial material for, and as part of the overall shifting motif in, the *Cardplayers.*

THE NARRATIVE MATERIALS OF THE IMAGINATION:
Scenes of Cardplaying and Card Fables
as Sources of Emplotment

Sources for the narrative subject matter of *The Cardplayers* series can be identified as more-direct precedents in numerous treatments by other artists of the actual subject of cardplaying. These sources, while never completely appropriated by Cézanne for his own use, do contribute certain iconological complexities to the discovery and invention of the cardplaying/skull motif. The most frequently cited source for the series is an oil painting, *The Cardplayers,* from the Musée Granet in Aix-en-Provence, attributed to the seventeenth-century painter Mathieu Le Nain and dated 1633–40. Its location in Cézanne's hometown has perhaps suggested it as an obvious precedent.[24]

As one of the anticlassical painters of the seventeenth century, the younger brother of the better-known Louis was often classified among the Caravaggisti, and indeed this painting is in many ways a synthesis of several of Caravaggio's works. It contains the same three-figure composition of Caravaggio's *Cardsharps,* and the moralizing anecdote of "immaturity being outsmarted by worldly experience" is the common subject, as in both the naïve young soldier is shown being tricked by two older and conspiring opponents.[25] Mathieu Le Nain also borrowed the tenseness in eye contact and gestures from Caravaggio's *Fortune Teller* as he shows the gamester with the winning ace (like the alluring gypsy girl in the Caravaggio) look "out" of the painting and into the imaginary space of the viewer as if to involve us in his treachery. The intense beam of light, which passes like a diagonal wave through the composition, repeating the path of the eye beams, is also Caravaggesque and adds to the tense drama of the situation. We know that Cézanne saw and admired the painting by Mathieu Le Nain because he took Émile Bernard to the museum, pointed to the Le Nain, and exclaimed "That is how I would like to paint!"[26] The numerous authors that cite the M. Le Nain as the main source both of Cézanne's interest in the subject matter and of the composition of *The Cardplayers* disregard the point in the wording of his remarks to Bernard. Cézanne admired "how" Le Nain painted, not "what," and when he used stylistic traits of the Caravaggisti within his own strict method he altered their traditional significance.

The compositions of the *Cardplayers* series have the same shallow, stagelike setting parallel to the picture plane as Mathieu Le Nain's work. In both the Le Nain and the Cézannes, a horizontal is established by the table, and the table further serves to break up the space of the composition into receding planes. This spatial arrangement is consistent in all of the above paintings, even though Cézanne diminishes the number of figures in Group B. The specific "stages of life," youth and maturity, represented by the two players in the M. Le Nain are also present in the three paintings of the Group B series: An older man clenching a pipe in his mouth opposes a man who, though of similar features, has fewer heavy facial lines and thus appears to be younger. The older cardplayer exposes his cards to the viewer's scrutiny; their values are not distinguishable and, in contrast with the Le Nain, there is no gesture or indication of someone having won or lost; instead they are shown "in the act of playing."

Cézanne's cardplayers, immovable and silent, look only at their array of cards, not at each other, with frozen glances that might embody some psychological aspects of cardplaying. No action or relationship is assigned to the players other than their involvement in the game; even in the Group A works, the three at play and the onlooker(s) are silent and still. In the painting of Group A at the Metropolitan Museum, the one in which Cézanne inserted his self-portrait, Cézanne's own position is that of the mediator in the M. Le Nain (or the spy of Caravaggio's *Cardsharps*). As mentioned earlier, in the "next" painting of the series, the Pellerin version (figure 5), Cézanne replaced this self-portrait and inserted a wine bottle instead.

The bottle, murky in color and almost blending into the space around it, accentuates the spatial void prominent in the center of the canvas and in all paintings of the Group B series; this void, dark and full of shadows, has grown in size so that it has become a true presence in the paintings. By the "end" of the series, in the Orsay version (figure 6), these murky colors appear to have pushed the players almost to the edges of the canvas.

The use of the contrast of light and shadows as both a concealing and an illuminating device, the planimetric separation that allows for both concave and convex references, and the tense relationships between objects and their surrounding space, are all consistent with the composition of the Le Nain. But Cézanne saw many more scenes of cardplaying and gaming in his many tours of the Louvre and other museums, and like a *bricoleur* he picked up many compositional devices from other paintings he had seen and incorporated them in his search for the fully realized motif in the *Cardplayers* series. These imaginative details[27] (that is truly what they were to Cézanne—compositional devices, spatial tricks that he could try in his experiments) can be ultimately considered as narrative, for it was pictorial reflection on his life, on social relations, and on his conscious/unconscious emotional investment of local objects that gave specific significance to his recollections from the Louvre and from his studies.

Other paintings considered by Cézanne scholars as possible thematic sources for the series include David Teniers's *Tavern Interior*[28] and Jean-Baptiste-Siméon Chardin's *Castle of Cards*.[29] Although the Teniers presents many details of a tavern interior, complete with dog, untidy children, and cluttered floors, its focus is a table around which sit three cardplayers. The two who sit opposite each other are again allegories of Youth and Maturity, and they too have those exactly aligned poses with repetitive sharp angles for knees and elbows that Cézanne chose as a means to represent the strictly facing arrangement of cardplayers.

Though very different in form and content from other paintings of the cardplaying genre, the Chardin does resemble a watercolor of the 1890s by Cézanne ("Study for *The Cardplayers*").[30] In the Chardin, a young boy sits at a table and constructs a house of cards; the light strikes his bent arm and illumines the expression of concentration on his face. Deep shadows surround him and appear to pass in and out of the card house, thus serving to obscure the identity of the setting. In this watercolor Cézanne does not appropriate formal details from any of these compositional elements; he simply borrows the pose and the active concentration of Chardin's sitter to set the mood for his own motif.

Two other paintings, not in the Louvre but known to Cézanne, can also be counted as thematic sources.[31] Gustave Caillebotte's *Game of Bezique*, of 1880 (now in a private collection in Paris), was exhibited in April 1882 in the Impressionists' Exhibition in Paris, which Cézanne attended.[32] It is a contemporary scene of inveterate gamesters seated at their familiar table, playing cards and smoking. The other painting, Ernest Meissonier's *Cardplayers* of 1860–63 (Metropolitan Museum) was known to Cézanne, who copied the pose of one of its figures in his contemporaneous (1860–62) drawing *Cabaret Scene*.[33] In this drawing, Cézanne captured the shared mood of the participants, their reciprocal involvement in the play, with one man anticipating a good hand and another already drinking to it.

The subject of cardplaying was also treated in lithographs and engravings that appeared in the popular publications to which Cézanne subscribed. Cézanne greatly admired the lithographs of Honoré Daumier and adorned his studio with clippings of these caricatures from newspapers.[34] Although it is not known whether Cézanne possessed three of the lithographs that treat the subject of cardplaying and were printed in the French newspaper *Le Charivari*, these do have affinities with his two- and three-figure compositions.[35]

"Je suis le plus grand ennemi des factions" (*Le Charivari*, 29 November 1841) shows a member of Louis Philippe's Republican Guard watching two other figures drowsily playing cards. The poses of the cardplayers, the position of the table, and the inclusion, though off-center, of a wine bottle are similar to the elements of Cézanne's series. "Parisiens qui ne seront jamais placés sous la surveillance" (*Le Charivari*, 25 August 1847) shows three bourgeois playing checkers, unaware of the drastic changes to be effected by the forthcoming 1848 revolution.[36] The same narrative suggestions (that life as a game encompasses all the turns of destiny) can be found in a caricature appearing in the 13 July 1854 *Le Charivari* entitled "Comment . . . le Russe à tous les abouts," which is a comment on European politics at the time of the Crimean War humorously expressed by the exaggeration of hats and headgear.

Although there are many similarities in the basic formats of Daumier's lithographs and Cézanne's paintings, the expressive roles assigned to the figures in the latter attempt to show verism without being a commentary on popular customs. Daumier's figures are active, mannered, and sourly comic. The content of his works is expressed in the gestures, clothing, and facial expression of his actors. Cézanne must have noticed this, and he was reported to have said that what he admired in Daumier's scenes was "the expressiveness of his figures."[37] Cézanne's cardplayers, although intensely expressive, are silent, unmoving, both remote and close by, not unlike the familiar objects and settings of his paintings.

The "direct" sources we have examined, paintings and lithographs of the same subject, though usually the backbone of the iconographer's craft, have been used in this context mainly to provide chance examples of similarities in format and content. Taken together, they should serve best in providing a generalization of the mood and commonplaces of the genre of cardplaying scenes. For more narrative materials of the imagination, we must now turn to indirect "sources."

As already mentioned, Cézanne frequently clipped illustrations from newspapers and hung them in his studio; we know from Vollard[38] that he also often placed together in a group several magazine photographs of flowers to serve as a model for a still life because the many weeks of realization often extended past the bloom's natural life and the ephemerality of anything natural constituted such torment to him. Not only did he often paint a picture of a picture—magazine print—but he would even change the emphasis of its theme or use only a section of the original as a sort of synecdochic allusion.

He was perhaps inspired to do this by certain "cartoons" that appeared in the popular press and presented optical illusions yielding different images that depended on the spatial focus taken by the viewer. A well-known example is the vase/profile illusion in which the relationship of white to black is viewed as a figure/ground "trick." When one takes precedence over the other, one sees either the outlines of a pedestal vase or two human profiles evident in the same lines.[39] An optical illusion of this sort, though clever in its perceptual magic, is also a linguistic trick. The vase becomes a face, its English rhyming partner, by one small alteration: the substitution of one sound or phoneme for another. The most clever of these optical illusions almost always rely on a literary device of this sort—a figure of speech, or a pun—to create ambiguity as a theme. A French postcard of the 1890s is a case in point.

This postcard, *The Bachelor,*[40] is also of a black-and-white image that will yield two different pictures depending on how it is visually ordered by the viewer. Instead of being based on a figure/ground trick, like the face/vase image, the card relies on the ordering of the parts to the whole image. When one looks at the white areas as a series of unconnected parts, a variety of reclining and standing female nudes emerges, but when one looks at the white area as one large integrated spatial area, the image of a man's profile with bristling mustache and prominent nose emerges. The pun intended is, of course, sexual: The bachelor is composed of female nudes; he is filled with the female nudes he so desires, but he can never possess them because they are not physically contemporaneous with him.

This postcard is not a true *optical* illusion, as is the face/vase image, because it relies on the subtle nuances of painterly details such as shadows. It shows a primary image followed by a secondary image, and its title, *The Bachelor*, suggests that the image of the male profile must have prominence over the secondary image, the nudes; therefore, the secondary image is "hidden" or "disguised" in order to delay its disclosure until the bachelor's profile has appeared. In this particular sequence, the disguising factor is incompleteness: some of the nudes are themselves only parts of a female body, only those parts that are consistent with the lines and planes of the bachelor's facial features. Indeed, they are composed of a minimum of details to be barely recognizable and to give just enough credence to the viewer's suspicions that the enigma is an intended one. The enigma is "read" as a whole, an integrated image, however, before it dissolves into its ironic parts.

Another ironic optical trick of the same type as *The Bachelor* is a picture that includes a skull motif as the secondary image and also makes use of the *vanitas* theme. However, in *All Is Vanity*, a comic reference to the worthlessness of earthly existence is juxtaposed with the ephemerality of feminine beauty. In this image, printed often in the French press and in popular periodicals, there is a young woman *en déshabillé* who looks into her vanity mirror. Her bare back is presented to the viewer and her face is shown in a quarter-turned profile; but the mirror reflects a full view of her face and of her exposed bosom. She reaches toward a line of cosmetic and perfume *flacons* that will not preserve her youth.

The image is richly detailed, with much emphasis paid to contrasts of light and shadow, and the grouping of the lady with her vanity mirror "floats" within an undefined shadowed space. The shift from the obvious image to that of the skull occurs in these shadowed areas. If given prominence over the shadowed details of the individual objects (bottles, chair, *chignon*), the vastness of the white area of the mirror against the dark space of the background assumes the form of the cranium and unites with the other white or lighter areas to form the skeletal structure; the *flacons* become teeth, the skirt becomes the jaw, and the lady's head and its reflected image in the "mirror" changed into the empty eyes of the skull.

In *All Is Vanity* the youthful beauty is metonymically followed by her eventual diminished, shriveled form; where once there existed a beautiful face and its reflection, now there exists only the emptiness of the eye sockets in the image of death. Her vainness, her ephemeral beauty and youth are swallowed up by the empty holes of the skull. Her fleshiness, her glistening eyes, and her hair disappear and anonymous bones take their place. The difference between baroque and romantic *vanitas* and these popular-culture images is the comic, almost Chaplinesque, use of the print medium to support the illusion.

This use of the print as a tool of black comedy is already perceivable in Goya's *Melancholy* (P32) in the Prado: a beautiful girl is compared with a negative and morbid image of death in which the two images, and the function of the print itself in multiplying and trivializing images, are paradigmatically connected with the presence of a mirror. A becurled and beruffled *maja* gazes at a mirror, and instead of her own reflection she sees a snake coiled around a scythe. The classical morality fable is transformed here by aesthetic pessimism into the sarcastic familiarization of the shocking made possible by modern media.

As a part of a sequence of allegorical images, however, Goya's *Melancholy* represents one of the proverbial temperaments of earthly humans. In other paintings in the series,[41] Goya also suggests a metamorphosis: A sanguine gallant sees a monkey reflected in the mirror; a choleric constable sees a scratching cat, a phlegmatic student, a frog. But as in the illusion *All Is Vanity,* Goya has illustrated the *vanitas* theme through a filmic fade-in, a transposition of real feminine beauty and the icon of death.

Cézanne's uses of the skull also take advantage of the allegorical significance of the theme of *vanitas* as a narrative function, but in the end Cézanne transforms it. As will be discussed in the concluding analysis, the overall shifting motif of Cézanne unites the separable images of the game and the skull to produce a modern allegory that surpasses, in its experiential qualities, all of its precedents in the history of painting. The possible associations of fortune with death result in a much more rich and complex narrative than the traditional *vanitas* and memento mori subjects or than Goya's comic transposition of Beauty and Death. While exploiting the fortune/death associations, Cézanne has also recreated various personas (Ugolino, Hercules—see the next section—and perhaps also Michelangelo and

Delacroix, as well as the proverbial small town *rentier* of late-nineteenth-century literature and painting). As substitutes for various aspects of the life of the painter, *the narrative possibilities of these characters enhance the multiplicity and the drama of the shifting motif of The Cardplayers*. His reference to cardplaying as the locus of all the meanings of fortune, if iconologically quite specific and narrow, spans therefore a large range of narrative developments that combines structural ambiguity and biographical concreteness in a manner typical of Bergson's visionary images.

For Cézanne, cardplaying was both a very modern activity (note the contemporizing of his painting by the attire of his models) and a timeless reference to idleness and greed, evil and chance. It carried the simple meaning of gambling and also specific allusions to certain forms of card games, such as the tarot and more unusual fortune-telling cards, with their different "plots," and to other forms of cards, such as *leger-de-main* cards, which were themselves decorated with optical illusions and hidden imagery, of which a most important recurring figure was the skull.

The French deck of cards[42] contains fifty-two cards of four suits that symbolize the four "powers" of life and thus the ways of fortune: the *piqué* (spade) as a sword stands for military might, the *coeur* (heart) for romance, the *carreau* (diamond) for wealth, and the *trèfle* (club or baton) for political power. The high cards in each suit symbolize a hierarchy of authority: the king has the most worth; next, the queen; and the knave or knight, though of lesser influence, is still admitted to the named cards. The remainder of the suit's values are measured in quantity; thus, ten *carreaux* is worth more than only two, just as the actual possession of the gems also measures wealth. To win, the player must possess cards of greater quantitative worth than the opponent by holding a more powerful position through these markers of privilege and possession. Betting precedes the viewing of the cards and is based on intuitions of luckiness; the winning of the bet signifies success, the attainment of wealth, and the favor of fortune.

The four-suit card deck outlined above was not the only card game commonly played in the taverns and public halls. Although the suit deck of French cards dates from the fourteenth century, an even older form of card playing, fortune-telling cards, which was also popular and associated with vice, remained unchanged through the nineteenth century. With the tarot cards, one did not match the value of a dealt hand with an opponent's, but instead played a game of "cosmic adventure" in which by the selection of cards the future disposition of the world was revealed and within it the possibilities contained in one's present lot.[43] Therefore, by playing the tarot one attained knowledge that could be gainfully stored for future decisions; thus the opponent in the game of the tarot was oneself—or more precisely, the future of the self and the secret order of the cosmos.

The tarot card deck is composed of the lesser arcana and the greater arcana, known as trumps. The symbolic journey that the seventy-eight cards of the deck represent is one in which a hero (the imagery is masculine) undergoes trials, surpasses obstacles, matures, and eventually attains Wisdom. The setting of this journey shifts in the progression from the physical to the spiritual world, and the stages along the way are represented by allegorical figures that define the dangers and goals of each progressive episode. The turning point in the adventure is trump 12, "The Hanged Man" *(Le Pendu),* in which the hero is hung upside down from a gibbet, which alters for him the physical order of the world. This reversal of his viewpoint institutes, as a new setting, a spiritual realm, and an alternative characterization; he will now exercise his wisdom rather than his strength. In this new characterization he is thus assigned a new set of allegorical adventures. While hanging upside down, the hero undergoes a change from a state of vice, which falls from him in his reversed position, to a state of virtue, symbolized by the halo that now encircles his head. The next card in the progression is the unnamed card of death *(La Mort)* which represents the physical demise of the hero and his elevation to a fully spiritual state. *La Mort* marks another beginning, the start of a virtuous life that leaves behind the former life of vice and the purgative life of the hanging man; this blessed condition represents the integration of body and soul, youth and maturity, activity and meditation.

In trump 11 the hero had wrestled with a raging lion and discovered that it was only his own shadow; and after passing from the physical state to that of a shadowed existence, the "hanged man" starts a metamorphosis in which, like a chrysalis, he awaits his new form. Attained via trump 12, the new form is made permanent in 13 by *La Mort.* As the arabic number 12, *Le Pendu* signifies the continuity of his transitional form with the dualities of his former existence. The passage to a third dimension is similarly symbolized by the thirteenth trump.

The gibbet in "The Hanged Man" is sometimes depicted as being a living branch from the Tree of Life or a shriveled representation of a crucified Christian or an executed heretic. But this hanging of a sacrificial victim from a tree is also a feature of many other religious cults. It is found in the Icelandic sagas, in which the Norse god Odin hanged himself from the World Ash Tree, awaiting the inspiration of the mystic runes; and in certain Sumerian rites, in which the hanging in effigy of the god Attis on a pine tree, which symbolized the source of life and the *mater* of earthly existence, led to the restoration of his vitality.[44] In the tarot, the scythe-bearing skeleton of trump 13 cuts the "hanged man" from the scaffolding and liberates him completely from the bondage of his past. Thus death, in the tarot arcana, is not an evil force, but a connection between the past and the future, an instrument of continuity that unifies time and spiritual selves.

Le Pendu, in the tarot imagery, is therefore a hero, an adventurer with a shadowed past who attains nobility of character by valiantly overcoming a state of division predicated on some kind of dilemma. *Le Pendu* represents a psychic fusion of the past with the awaited future. The trials of the "hanged man" are not over upon his attaining his status as *le pendu*; they are about to proceed to a different level of spiritual or moral difficulty in which his newly acquired status as hero will be a requisite. Cézanne identified with the struggles of the "hanged man," who is for him "everyman," striving amidst the adversities of life; *Le Pendu* was for him a deeply personal self-image with which he shared many coincidences.

Cézanne's nickname came to be "Le Pendu," an epithet he acquired after the exhibition, at the 1889 Paris World's Fair, of his painting *Maison du Pendu*.[45] This painting presents, as subject matter, nothing more than a house of a man who has hanged himself, positioned at the intersection of a forked road. Without mythological, historical, or "academically" allegorical references, the painting was highly controversial. It was criticized for having no subject matter other than that of "drunkard" houses and for a reprehensible technique of applying paint with "a trowel."[47] However, the other young impressionists recognized in it their own goal of rendering *ce qu'il se sent* and praised this newcomer by honoring him with the *nom de pinceau* of his realized "impression" in the painting.

Le pendu as a tarot hero was not the only motif appropriated by Cézanne from cardplaying. Another popular form of cards, "transformation cards,"[47] became popular in the eighteenth century and continued in popularity in the nineteenth century. In these cards, the imagery of the tarot card deck converged with that of the suit card deck, and the suit cards were filled in with a humorous composition that connected the emblems of the suit. For instance, a card with a *piqué* could be transformed into a caricatured face with prominent jowls and jutting chin, and the *cinq des piqués* into a tea party of grotesque matrons clucking beneath their voluminous bonnets. The image most often borrowed from the tarot for the pastime of filling in transformation cards was the skull taken from trump 13, *La Mort*. All suit cards could be easily transformed into a skull and used as morbid caricatures of human subjects, but the king face card was most often embellished with this reference to death.[48] The converging of the face of the king with that of death led the way for another kind of transformation cards also popular in the nineteenth century. In *leger-de-main* cards the imagery is illusionistically placed so that it transformed as the position of viewing was changed.[49] A smiling face, when shifted, revealed a frowning face; a portrait of a beautiful woman transformed into that of a witch. When viewed from one angle, the hat of the beautiful maiden framed her tresses; when the viewing angle was reversed, the flower adorning the hat transformed into a hair-sprouting wart on a prominent chin. The identification of opposites, death and the king, smiles and frowns, beauty and ugliness, in these cards was in keeping with the various narratives associated with cardplaying and the character roles assigned to live the adventure of bodily birth and death, culminating in spiritual transcendence.

THE AFFECTIVE MATERIALS:
The Ugolino Drawing and Other Biographical Images as Indistinct Elements of the Motif in *The Cardplayers*

The shifting motif of *The Cardplayers* is not simply apparent as an active, intuitive (memory), and expressive (language) presence that fuses the explicit images, the players themselves, and the skull with one another in the Orsay painting (figure 6); it can also be said that it is repressed in a psychoanalytic sense. It is repressed both as a theme that has been reenacted and worked through in scattered pictorial treatments and as a terrifying and self-destructive emotion that has been dissolved into a multiplicity of other emotions and that has finally lost its sting in the mixture. The repressed and unbound[50] feelings displaced through the various associations of the skull can be tracked down, beginning with an examination of one of Cézanne's early drawings, where it retains its original violence. Cézanne's drawing (figure 7) will be analyzed, first in its most poignant and violent emotive significance, by reference to its original literary force in Dante's narrative of Ugolino in the *Inferno*, then in its relation to the subsequent stages of its dissociation as a motif, and finally in its transformation as a therapeutic exercise.

This prototype of the *Cardplayers* series was drafted when Paul Cézanne was only nineteen years old and sent in a letter (17 January 1859) to his friend, Émile Zola.[51] This drawing (figure 7) illustrates the story of Count Ugolino from Dante's *Inferno*: Five figures sit around a table on which is posed a skull; two of the figures have the same forward leaning positions of the cardplayers in the final version of the series in the Musée D'Orsay (figure 6).

Having recently decided to abandon painting and take up a career in law, as demanded by his father, the young Cézanne expressed in this letter (also included in figure 7) to his sympathetic friend the grief and boredom he experienced at his clerk's desk— expressed it in a manner that was both simple in its straightforward melodrama and also very intense and telling in its rhetoric. Clearly the Ugolino drawing was meant to illustrate his own tragic situation at this crucial stage in his life, but this drawing was also to have unusual significance in the future of Cézanne, who after a token attempt at his father's chosen career was to return eventually to painting and who, contrary to his father's predictions, emerged as one of the masters of French painting. The composition of this early drawing reemerged within the format of some of his still lifes, and finally, without losing any of its violent and therapeutic implications, in one of the most ambitious series of his later style, *The Cardplayers* of the 1890s. The polysemy, or plural meaning, of fortune and death at work in this early letter must have been a constant source of ideas on form and content for Cézanne in all stages of his life and art.

The story of Count Ugolino is told in Dante Alighieri's *Commedia* in the cantos 32 and 33 of the *Inferno*.[52] In the poem, Dante (the pilgrim) and his guide Virgil come upon Ugolino with his enemy Count Ruggieri, each devouring the other's skull but tormented by unsatiated appetites. They have become for each other (for their hunger and their hatred) a constantly renewed food source that they can never seem to completely exhaust. Seeing the shocked countenance of Dante, Ugolino stops his gnawing long enough to tell his story. The story he tells is rich in sensorial effects, dreams, and historic and symbolic references. The beginning of his story is without preamble and incomprehensible to anyone who does not know the events of his downfall; nonetheless, he opens his tale with the final chapter of his earthly life: He and his children are in the tower of hunger, sentenced by Ruggieri to starve to death. Ugolino has had a dream foretelling their death and after relating the dream to his offspring he watches them slowly and excruciatingly die.

Ugolino's sin, insatiable craving for power, is transformed into the cause of his and his progeny's death by starvation, and finally of his own eternal punishment, an everlasting physical hunger. Like the rest of the tales in Dante's *Commedia*, the story is composed around a central theme from which is generated a general mood built on similes, metaphors, and visions. The prevailing theme in Ugolino's tale is hunger, or *fame* (which in Italian is linked by punning with *fama*, power and renown). The theme finds expression first in Ugolino's dream, the setting of which is a hunting party and which recounts the visions of the "sharp fangs"[53] of the hounds and the tearing of the flesh of the hunted. Ugolino's dream in the tower is echoed by the children's nightmares, a motif that is insisted on when they call out for bread upon waking. Their calls are overheard by Ugolino, and he "turn(s) to stone"[54] in his torment. The bread/stone comparison is perhaps a reference to the story of Satan's temptation of Christ by proposing that he change a stone into bread to satisfy his own hunger. But for Ugolino the stone provides no sustenance. After two days, counted by the rising and setting of the sun, Ugolino stifles his cries of suffering by biting his hand; his children, mistaking the gesture as an involuntary hunger reflex, offer themselves to him as food. This offer echoes many other tales of filial sacrifice, such as Saturn devouring his children (even the stone as a counter-image to food is repeated), and the words of Ugolino's children imitate Isaac's speech to Abraham as he lay upon the altar ("Father . . . thou didst clothe us with this wretched flesh . . .").[55]

Overcome by hunger, the children "drop one by one"[56] before Ugolino's disbelieving eyes; one reneges and accuses his father in a speech reminiscent of the Seven Words of Christ on the cross ("My father, why does thou not help me?").[57] Grieving and blinded by hunger, Ugolino crawls around the corners of his cell, calling the names of his dead offspring; finally, driven mad by the gnawing *fame*, he eats of their flesh. This cannibalism[58] that furthers the theme of hunger is merely implied in Dante's poem. It is, however, consistent with the historical facts and rumors of Ugolino's treacherous life. Driven by a desire or hunger for power, the historical Ugolino manipulated his friends, enemies, and family to preserve his political position. As a Guelph, he ruthlessly persecuted the Ghibellines; when his position in the Guelph cause weakened, he betrayed them and joined the Ghibellines. Later, when his integrity was in question, he promoted a grandson to his own post of leadership; but then the grandson rebuked him and Ugolino arranged for his assassination. His was a life of criminal intrigue with which Dante was well acquainted, and the poet treats him as an incarnation of immoderate desire for earthly power with no respect for the perils of eternity or for the inevitable encounter with the most powerful of enemies, death.

Having finished his gruesome tale, Ugolino returns to his interminable meal and keeps gnawing at the skull of his earthly jailer. Insatiable *fame*, whether for power or fame, was his earthly sin, and insatiable *fame* becomes his eternal punishment. Skull locked to skull, Ugolino and his opponent reenact the excesses of their earthly passion without any possibility of resolution. Unable to consume each other totally, they remain unreleased from the circle of torment; unable to satisfy their hunger, they must give in to the constant urge.

As the primary image in the Ugolino cantos, the skull has a twofold purpose: It represents the undying ghost of Ugolino, who tells his story to the pilgrim; and, as a horrid image of gnawed, tortured bones, it is also a graphic image of death, the other face of the pursuit of fortune and fame. The skull is all that remains of Ugolino's earthly existence, of his historical life. Together with his infernal torture, the skull constitutes the primary motif of the extrahistorical life of Ugolino, that is, of his fame as an allegorical type of insatiable craving.

Cézanne included in his drawing (figure 7) a "dialogue" in which he assigned speeches to Dante, Virgil, Ugolino, an eldest son, a second son, a third son, and a grandchild; these speeches bring to life the figures in the drawing. A wooden door to the left opens and frames the two "pilgrims" with cloaks, peaked hats, and beards. One of the pilgrims points into the room at a table with two men sitting across from each other. Behind the table are three smaller male figures, the children, and on the table itself is an ewer containing a skull.

In the dialogue,[59] Dante asks, "Dis-moi, mon cher, que grignotent-ils là?" Virgil answers: "C'est un crâne, parbleu!" Dante replies: "Mon Dieu, c'est effroyable! mais pourquoi rongent-ils ce cerveau détestable?" and Virgil responds "Écoute, et tu sauras cela." This dialogue appears under the portion of the drawing that contains the pilgrims posed at the open door. Separated by a line, which follows the door's edge, the rest of the dialogue appears under the part of the drawing in which the table is situated. The father admonishes his offspring, "Mangez à belles dents ce mortel inhumain qui nous a si longtemps fait souffrir de la faim." The eldest son answers "Mangeons!" and the second son states, "Moi, j'ai bien faim, donne cette oreille." The grandchild requests "A moi cet oeil." "A moi les dents," the eldest son adds. The father urges, "Hé-Hé [Provençal for "gently, gently"], si vous mangez d'une façon pareille que nous restera-t-il pour demain, mes enfants?"

It must be stressed here that Cézanne's interpretation of Dante's two cantos is not an illustration of the story of Dante's sinner, of the setting in the ninth circle of hell, or of the events in the narrative. In his recasting of the scene, the children participate in the eating of the enemy's skull, and the painter has taken further liberties with the story by deleting the presence of Ruggieri. This deletion cancels the reciprocity of the punisher and the punished that was so direct in Dante's scheme, but it is preserved in the semantic unity of the French words for "hunger" and "fame" (*faim, fame, fameux*) and in the insatiability of hunger that devours those who suffer from it. In Cézanne's drawing, as in Dante's narrative, insatiability stands for the eternity of unbound desire that, in punishment as well as in redemption, unites the extremes of total attachment and total despair, hence the sarcasm with which Cézanne pointed to Ugolino's admonishment to his children to save some food for tomorrow's hunger. At a time in which the painter struggled with his desire for eternal fame, parental advice had forced him to renounce his craving in favor of tomorrow's needs. Cézanne narrated his fable in colloquial turns of phrase and with realistic detail, and this transfer from the archetypical to the familiar helped him, as it helped Dante, to intensify his own and the reader's involvement in the contagious, resentful mood of the story.

There were two major translations into French of Dante's *Commedia* in the first half of the nineteenth century that were used in the public schools and were possible sources. The earliest of the three, and the one that became the prototype for those that followed, was a translation from the Italian into French verse, done by Antonio Déschamps in 1824, of "the twenty best cantos" from the *Inferno, Purgatorio,* and *Paradiso.*[60] The major portion of these twenty cantos came from the *Inferno* and included the story of Ugolino. Déschamps preferred cantos that described elaborate settings, had a melodramatic climax, or had characters who were substantial enough to be exaggerated and developed into heroes or antiheroes.

Among the cantos that he chose, the two that narrate Ugolino's story undoubtedly met all of his requirements: a creaking tower, a dramatic death scene, and a pitiful protagonist. It had in common with the other selections the persistence of fate/death as the antagonist and cause of the victims' downfall (in the *Commedia* they are not victims but only sinners). For every one line of Dante's poem, Déschamps embroidered the meaning into an average of three lines, and the resulting text had, as one literary historian said, all the makings of a romantic opera. Déschamps converted his victims, heroes, and antiheroes into emblems of human nature (Lust, Paternity, Purity) and their situations or predicaments into melodramatic confrontations with personified forces. Francesca da Rimini became emblematic of lust, Ugolino of immoderation. Thus the original structure and content of Dante's poem as an allegory that is also a narrative of repentance was altered by Déschamps and converted into a theatrical interaction of prototypes.

The second translation into French of the *Commedia* that Cézanne could have known and that was also used as an authorized classroom text was by Pier-Angelo Fiorentino and appeared in 1840.[61] Like Déschamps's, this prose translation was of selected cantos, but, unlike his predecessor, Fiorentino tended to reduce the "wordiness" of the Italian by deleting "extraneous" descriptions. Nevertheless this translation also presents the characters of the *Commedia* not as repentant sinners but as symbols of the constant victimization of mortals by fate.

A more direct source of inspiration for Cézanne, in his rendition of Ugolino's story, might have also been the novels and poems of Victor Hugo, which were often concerned with themes taken from the *Commedia*. Hugo's *La Légende de siècles* of 1859 contains a poem, "La vision de Dante," in which the "prisoners" of the Inferno rise up and accuse their tormentors—the judges who had passed moral judgment on them, the generals who gave them orders, the popes, parents, and so on—of being the causes of their downfall.[62] In his clever plot, Hugo reversed the redemptive allegory in Dante's poem so that repentance was replaced by revenge. Also, the symbolic structure of the translations of Déschamps and Fiorentino was reversed and the hero/antihero roles were overturned. Thus, in "La vision de Dante" Ugolino becomes the victim of the power-hungry Ruggieri, and his story turns into the tale of the sufferings of a victim. Ugolino materializes as a pitiful specter before the fat and well-fed Ruggieri and condemns him for his own moral weaknesses.

Cézanne's drawing of Ugolino also presents an avenging character who offers Ruggieri's head to his children. Influenced by the romantic conversion of the historic *and* symbolic characters of Dante's *Inferno* into emblematic images of human shortcomings and instability intensified by tireless fate, Cézanne achieved a mechanical identification with an ideal human being tormented by passion and turned into a pawn of events. And like his other nineteenth-century sources, Cézanne also took liberties with the "extraneous" details of the story in his illustration.

The father and children are united in a plot of vengeful action against an enemy who is represented by the skull in the drawing (figure 7). They are not shown eating the skull, only conversing about it. Cézanne intensifies the melodrama of his interpretation by the mood of the dialogue. The pilgrims' conversation sets the mood as one of disdain for what they are seeing when Dante exclaims, "C'est effroyable," and the horrible vision that they and the viewer see is ironically presented as a quiet family group at the dinner table. The family is not dining but preparing to dine and conversing about what they will eat. Their ritualistic stance and the recitation of repeated phrases are, in their allusion to the painter's decision to proceed with his artistic life, very much like the Hebrew seder in which father and children make a sacrificial offering in preparation for the exodus from bondage.[63]

The fateful aspect of the family scene is present only in the appearance of the skull, and as the outstretched limbs of the two seated figures direct the attention of the viewer to it, so do the words in the dialogue. The ironic inconsistency of moods in the drawing and dialogue is further intensified by the hyperbolic tone that Cézanne assumed in his poem/letter. Like Dante and Virgil, who stand to one side (in the drawing) and sententiously comment (in the dialogue) on the scene being enacted before them, Cézanne also used, in his poem/letter, a tone of detached judgment delivered with exclamatory excitement.

> J'ai résolu, mon cher, d'épouvanter ton coeur
> D'y jeter une énorme, une atroce frayeur
> Par l'aspect monstrueux de cet horrible drâme
> Bien fait pour émouvoir la plus dure des âmes.
> J'ai pensé que ton coeur sensible à ces maux-là
> S'écrierait: quel tableau merveilleux que voilà!
> J'ai pensé, qu'un grand cri d'horreur, de ta poitrine
> Sortirait, en voyant ce que seul imagine
> L'enfer, où le pécheur, mort dans l'impurité,
> Souffre terriblement durant l'éternité.[64]

Kurt Badt has analyzed the drawing and its accompanying words in light of a psychoanalytic approach that seeks to locate in Cézanne's conflicting roles the emotional impulses that charge the scene. According to Badt, although his poem is written to Zola, a "coeur sensible à ces maux-là," Cézanne also referred to an unacknowledged viewer/reader (Cézanne's father), "la plus dure des âmes," who is apparently not moved by the "horrible drâme." Badt emphasizes the similarities in the filial relationship of Ugolino to his sons and of Cézanne to his father. Both relationships exhibited, he finds, strained dependencies, conflicting desires, and unresolved dilemmas internalized by the painter into fantasies capable of reappearing and being acted out, as Cézanne says, "durant l'éternité."

In this psychoanalytic interpretation of the drawing,[65] the children surrounding the table are identified as Cézanne's future artworks, the children of his creative genius; Cézanne, in the role of Ugolino, devours the skull, the head of his father, "the very head which thought up the devilish plan" to turn young Paul into a lawyer and condemned him to "die of spiritual starvation."[66] The future art will be engendered out of hatred toward the father, and thus the drawing in its repressed meaning is an admission of the suffering implicit in the confused roles of the artist as son of his father and as father of his works (he hates his father because he loves his art, but inevitably hates the art because he loves his father). As Badt points out, the reenactment of the conflict in the drawing does not end in a constructive plan for the resolution of his difficulties.

Within the context of the biographical situation of 1859, the drawing, as Badt interprets it, changed completely the traditional meaning of the sin of Ugolino; the original suffering under the addictive power of a passion that, like gnawing guilt, could not be purged was now transformed by Cézanne into the suffering created by a double bind of love/hatred toward his father, a love/hatred that was itself inevitably permeated by guilt and the source of eternal damnation corresponding to ambition for eternal fame. The key to the transformation is the overdetermination of the skull, which stands, as it curiously stood in Dante, for both the devourer and the devoured, the loved and the hated object. An important element of the change of meaning of the story was the role that repression (irony) acquired in it as the repository of a passional impasse (love/hatred, each narcissistically crying for and reproving the other) that, like death, admits no resolution.

Badt's psychoanalytic reading of Cézanne's conversion of the story of Ugolino into the textual vehicle of a repressed and never-resolved double bind constitutes a step in the right direction. Indeed, this transformation is the most natural outcome of the possibilities of overdetermination that were contained in the symbol of the skull and constitutes an appropriate fixation of this symbol as a stand-in for the ambiguities of a love/hatred relation. Yet this important fixation remains episodic and tenuous in its exclusive connection with the oedipal struggle; it consequently restricts the very broad significance that a much richer symbolic nucleus (the double-bind/ death complex in which death is made the equivalent of every impossible and fatal choice) would come to have in Cézanne and in other modernists.

The confusion of roles and the overdetermination of the symbol of the skull in Cézanne's drawing are consistent with the split of the subject, into accused and accuser, suggested by Hugo; together they explain the *affective intensity and particularity* of the meaning of the image of the skull in Cézanne's memory and intuition. But in this psychoanalytic interpretation, as in other associational methods, the skull is dissociated from the theme of the series, the shifting motif of the last painting, and is assigned an exclusive explanatory function as the single key to the complex significance of all the aspects of the drawing. Because this drawing is interpreted in the present study as an *indistinct image or metaphorical nucleus* of the visionary shifting motif of *The Cardplayers*, the image of the skull will have to be fused with other images and other emotions that are collaged in that ultimate motif.

Another important complex of images that contributes to the expansion of the oedipal love/hatred/death motif into the more general double-bind/death motif is implied in Cézanne's insistent use of the myth of Hercules during the crisis years of 1858–59. In a letter to Zola dated on 7 December 1858 (therefore preceding by more than a month the drawing and poem of Ugolino) Cézanne included a poem that begins with the lines, "Hélas, j'ai pris du Droit la route tortueuse."[67] In the text of the letter there are several references to the Greek mythological character;[68] but the Hercules that Cézanne identifies with at this time is not the triumphant hero who was admitted to the society of the immortal gods and goddesses; it is instead the indecisive, naïve young mortal who must choose to attempt or not to attempt the heroic route that destiny is allowing, even forcing, him to choose. He is confronted with, and must decide between, two lives: an earthly life, represented by aimlessness and indistinction, or a life of active virtue (ἔργον) in which he will be tested and judged worthy of being granted immortality.

The story of Hercules at the crossroads was invented by the Greek Sophist Prodicus and related by Xenophon in the *Memorabilia* (2.1:22ff.)[69] It contains imaginative (tempting) descriptions of the two choices. The virtuous life is presented as a twisting, rocky path whose turns are not visible in advance. Trees block the path, water obstructs the passage, and in places the path is lost in weeds; but at the top of the rocky climb is a personified image of fame, waiting to apotheosize the virtuous one. The path of vice, ironically, is straight and wide and leads directly to a sunny pasture where dryads bathe in a calm pool and woodfolk sport and play cards.

Like Hercules when presented with the choice between mediocrity and distinction (both of which had, of course, different meanings for the artist and his father), Cézanne chose, for a time, the "virtuous" way demanded by parental authority. The demand itself was a law, and the vocation to which it led was the practice of law, a fact vented ironically by Cézanne as doubly, indeed triply, punitive since what appeared to be his choice was in fact the choice of another: "J'ai pris, n'est pas le mot, de prendre on m'a forcé!"[70]

Indications of the deep significance of the references to Hercules as signs of a double bind can be found in another unfinished poem included by Cézanne in the same letter.

> Hercule, un certain jour, dormait profondément
> Dans un bois, car le frais était bon, . . .
> Donc il dormait très fort. Une jeune dryade
> Passant tout près de lui.[71]

The details of this scene—Hercules is asleep, the setting is an agreeable place of escape, a young forest nymph comes close to him—point to the topic of temptation; and the fact that temptation marks the presence of a double bind is implied in the reason given by the artist for not finishing the poem: "But I perceive that I was about to say something stupid, so I hold my peace."[72] Cézanne obviously balked before the tangle of consequences on either side of the choice. The bourgeois life of the legal clerk was increasingly annoying and unacceptable to him; on the other hand, the artist's life seemed to be only a pursuit of radiant visions that always turned into smoke. Each of his choices was attractive only as an alternative to the other; considered by themselves, they were each deceptive; and their common deception was both desperately desired and deadly enervating—a death in life.

The paradoxical tempting and deceiving roles of art, so debilitating and disheartening to a young artist threatened and isolated by

the prosaic attitudes of those close to him, can be corroborated by a
very graphic description by Cézanne in a poem included in a subsequent letter to Zola, dated July 1859:

> Tu me diras peut-être: Ah! mon pauvre Cézanne,
> Quel démon féminin a démonté ton crâne?
> Toi que j'ai vu jadis marcher d'un pas égal,
> Ne faisant rien de bien, ne disant rien de mal?[73]

The artist freely associates his predicament (art as a double bind)
with the symbol of death by referring to himself as a skull—*crâne*—
tempted, "disconcerted," by a female devil; for some time—*jadis*—
he has been incapable of accomplishing anything good and of expressing his rage with harsh words.

> C'est ainsi qu'à mes yeux se présentent parfois
> Des êtres ravissants, aux angéliques voix,
> Durant le nuit. Mon cher, on dirait que l'aurore
> D'un éclat frais pur à l'envi les colore,
> Ils semblent me sourire et je leur tends la main.
> Mais j'ai beau m'approcher, ils s'envolent soudain,
> Ils montent dans le ciel, portés par le zéphyre
> Jetant un regard tendre et qui semble d'approcher,
> Mais, c'est en vain, en vain que je veux les toucher,
> Ils ne sont plus—déjà la gaze transparente
> Ne peint plus de leurs corps le forme ravissante.
> Mon rêve évanoui, vient la réalité
> Qui me trouve gisant, le coeur tout attristé,
> Et je vois devant moi se dresser un fantôme
> Horrible, monstrueux, c'est le DROIT qu'on le nomme.[74]

The pursuit of artistic forms is generally, but in particular under the circumstances in which Cézanne finds himself, a chase after
ethereal visions perhaps never to be possessed other than in momentary glimpses, enrapturing while they appear but totally depressing
when they vanish without any assurance of returning again. In
Cézanne's situation, when the beautiful forms of his visions escape
him, reality leaves him not just empty but "groaning . . . a phantom
arise(s), horrible, monstrous, it's LAW that it is called."
   Clearly, then, the symbolic significance of the skull as a sign of

deadly futility was displaced in these times of crisis from one text in which the double bind was initially fantasized (July 1858 letter and poems about the forced law career and the temptation of Hercules) to another in which the association of double binds with the skull was emotionally established in its oedipal significance (January 1859 letter and poem about Ugolino) and then to another that recapitulated the fusion of the skull with double binds in the context of the vocational impasse (July 1859 letter and poem about Cézanne's skull assailed by the forms of beauty and the specter of the law). In a Lacanian interpretation, *each of these texts stands separately for a different double bind, and together, as they are linked by repetition and by psychoanalytic reenactment, they become metaphorically exchangeable for the history of their displacement.*

There are other such displacements of the association of tempting but futile choices (fortune) with the skull (death) in the pictorial record of the master. An additional vehicle for the displacement of the same association, a copy of Delacroix's *Hortensias*, was introduced in the previous section among the pictorial materials for the final shifting motif of *The Cardplayers*. It will be discussed here as affective material because it supports the association of fortune (double binds) with the skull and it also highlights important erotic motivations partially submerged in the previous verbal and visual texts.

As indicated earlier, the design of the flowers in the copy of the still life gives way to an intrusive, disquieting apparition of a skull. The dual imagery in the *Hortensias* represents much more than a verbal-visual pun resulting from free association, for it involves, by association with the name of his wife, the circumstances of Cézanne's marriage as one more paralyzing choice. The painter met Hortense Ficquet in 1869 when she modeled for him; he had a son with her in 1872 and, after a relationship characterized by distance and neglect, married her in 1886, again under some pressure from his dying father, who strongly wished the painter to legitimize his son. She was clearly an insistent fantasy for Cézanne; he painted her twenty-eight times and drew her portrait at least fifty times. As discussed earlier, she has been identified as the face hidden, as a secondary image, in *The Large Bathers*. (figure 4).[75] In the *Hortensias*, whose date ca. 1900 significantly overlaps with *The Large Bathers*, it is not her portrait that emerges through the change in the meaning of the signs of the still life but the image of the skull; the skull is not composed of erotic details—eyes, nose, locks of hair—as *The Large Bathers* was; instead, it is defined by the absence of them. The empty eyes, cavernous nose, and shadowed jaw are the reverse of the fleshy, exuberant femininity inscribed in the landscape of *The Large Bathers*.

The juxtaposition of the two works shows, however, the same ambiguous feelings toward the yoke of erotic impulses, in its competition with the yoke of art, as the ones exposed by the oedipal crisis and the vocational crisis. *The Large Bathers* presents, as was seen in the previous chapter, the immediacy of the erotic drive, but it does so through the instrumentality of art, and thus it transfers to this medium the dialectical relations between desire and its object that can be perceived most clearly in Kierkegaard's "existential psychoanalysis" of eroticism. More fully than in any previous pictorial or poetic text of Cézanne's, erotic impulses can be characterized in this one as a fertile ground for the double binds so common in the painter's emotional depths. In a partially different vein, the *Hortensias* shockingly presents the eroticism toward Hortense as contaminated by the skull and its long association with double binds.

It must be reiterated at this juncture that the specific and complex network of associations connecting the oedipal crisis, eroticism, and artistic vocation with the fate/fortune symbol of double binds (death/the skull) has been closely analyzed above to explain the insistence on, and emotive intensity of, the image of the skull as a material of Cézanne's imagination. In fact these associations are not unique to Cézanne; they were poetically established in romanticism as the outcome of the clash between the aesthetic and the ethical definitions of human existence. This clash itself was the inevitable issue of the dualities and paradoxes (matter/spirit, body/soul, good/evil, time/eternity) built into the succeeding frameworks of Western metaphysics. Traditionally, poets and artists had translated, through the figurality of the aesthetic medium, the conceptual paradoxes into emotional ones; indeed this translation was, as earlier suggested, the work of decorum.

The aesthetics of the end of the nineteenth century represented both an exacerbation and a termination of that artistic/ontological predicament. Although this situation had many moments and representatives, it is possible to point to Baudelaire as its most complete catalyst and spokesman; the word *modern* had, in his use of it, this entire range of implications, covering the personal outlook, the frameworks of thought, and the form and content of art. The copresence of the symbolic markers "flowers" and "evil" within his most important title constituted a rallying call for totally new attitudes: Better *to dwell* in inevitable temptation and inevitable despair as the joint site of an existentially paradoxical condition than to go on deceiving ourselves by using metaphysical ideas as means and avenues of a purely imaginary escape![76]

This call, typical of transitional fin de siècle aesthetics, to dwell in the paradoxes of our condition and to accept its splintering consequences for aesthetic form and content, is precisely the challenge that Bergson and Cézanne, among other modernist thinkers, poets, and artists, attempted to meet and transcend. Indeed, the modernist attitude would endeavor to overcome both traditional metaphysics and the acceptance of its paradoxes as conceptual and existential double binds by at least two transitional generations (1848, 1870) of premodernists. Clearly, the main thinkers and artists of the modernist movement—Cézanne amongst them—shared with the transitional generations the experience of living with an abundance of double binds; but this initial sharing gave way in the new masters to a new hermeneutics of the Western tradition of thought and art, to a new and creative existential stance, and, certainly in the case of Bergson, to a direct actualization and awareness of the worldly basis and the possible outcomes of human freedom, neither one of which is grounded, in this philosophy, as they were in classical and modern metaphysics, on largely unjustified intellectual presuppositions.

An example of this overcoming by the modernists of the conceptual and artistic double binds of their predecessors can be gathered from the different interpretations of the erotic in Cézanne, as discussed in this chapter and in chapter 4. Although these interpretations derive their reflective justification from the metaphysics of desire within the Kierkegaardian framework (existential symbolism) and the Freudian framework (repressive symbolism), for the sake of brevity the ensuing discussion will focus primarily on personal issues. It should not go unnoticed that the two different methods used in the preceding examinations of the *Bathers* are suited to two quite different affective dispositions.

In this chapter, a repressive attitude, which is perceptible in the painting as one facet of the thematic significance of the dialectical progression of desire, has been examined psychoanalytically in order to connect the inclusion of the painter's wife in an apparently idyllic and monumental setting with her inclusion in an unsettling environment, the *Hortensias,* marked by the metonymic/metaphoric sign of double binds. By contrast, in the earlier description of the overall meaning of the *Bathers* as a fusion of the component images into the shifting, visionary motif of desire, that motif was understood to be an integration of the images themselves (Bergson) and also an integration and transcendence of the stages of desire (Kierkegaard). That reflective transcendence conveys not only a final reconciliation on the part of the painter with the constraining powers of eros but also an acceptance of their contributions to his creativity and to his liberation from an oppressive destiny. It must be reiterated here that this latter interpretation implied that Cézanne finally came to grips with eroticism and was able to signify it and live it *immediately*, in all its physical and spiritual vastness, without the duplicities and melodrama that distorted the emotive tone of his many symbolist paintings about this topic.

Such an understanding will shed considerable light on the *Large Bathers* (figure 4) as a notable instance of an aesthetic and existential treatment of the erotic by a great modernist master, a treatment that liberates the libido from its traditional lascivious connotations and also from its narcissistic (whether repressive or sublimating) significance in nontraditional aesthetics. The restoring and instituting efforts, the attempts to heal the imagination, on the part of all major modernists were indeed not limited to the erection of a new "mythology of eros" between the old uneasy relations of body and soul and the new symbolism of repressed and displaced energies. The further creation of a "mythology of modern death" was an equally important part of the modernist program of revision of the traditional metaphysical paradoxes and of their offshoots within the turn-of-the-century formalist, decadentist, and materialist attitudes and ideologies.

The interpretation and description of the final *Cardplayers* (figure 6) that follows is meant to be an example of the modernist mythology of death. The shifting visionary motif of the painting presents vast changes in the conceptualization and experiencing of death, changes that, although grounded in deeply personal transformations and maturation, Cézanne shared with the most acute and ambitious representatives of the new mentality in poetry and the other arts. Within this mentality, death is not to be looked at as the cessation of biological existence, as the cause of profound terror or resignation, as a moral experience, as an avenue for religious discipline in temporal life and salvation in the hereafter, nor as the symbol of an instinct, thanatos, that represents double binds as well as the desire for their resolution.

The originality of the sense of death incorporated in the visionary motif of Cézanne's masterpiece might be gathered from the preceding examination of its pictorial, narrative, and affective materials; in the last analysis, however, the conceptual and aesthetic core of this new sense of death transcended the sum of these materials. It will be necessary therefore to unveil it through a minute and accurate description of the overall motif of the painting. But the "mythology of modern death" embodied in it stood against both the long-established and the new perceptions and beliefs listed above, so it will be useful to preface Cézanne's pictorial rendering of that "mythology" with a phenomenological and poetic meditation on its fundamental features. This meditation will clarify and corroborate, by means of the words and insights of two great modernist prophets, Rainer Maria Rilke and Wallace Stevens, the reader's tentative discovery of the complex meaning of *The Cardplayers.*

EXCURSUS:
On the Mythology of Modern Death

In a letter he wrote a year before he died, Rainer Maria Rilke clarified for his Polish translator the profound experiences, existential as well as conceptual, that had led him to revise and reconstruct the Western sense of death both in accordance with his own poetic instincts and in light of very powerful philosophical and spiritual perceptions bred by the tense climate of the crisis years in which he lived.[77] He adamantly insisted in this letter, as he had in the transparent words of the *First Duino Elegy,* on the unity of life-and-death:

Affirmation of *life-AND-death* turns out to be one in the Elegies.
. . . We of the here-and-now are not for a moment satisfied in the world of time, nor are we bound in it; we are continually over-

flowing toward those who preceded us, toward our origin, and toward those who seemingly come after us. In that vast "open" world, all beings *are*—one cannot say "contemporaneous," for the very fact that time has ceased determines that they all *are*. Everywhere transcience is plunging into the depths of Being. . . . It is our task to imprint that temporary, perishable earth into ourselves so deeply, so painfully and passionately, that its essence can rise again, "invisibly," inside us. We are the bees of the invisible.[78]

This quotation gathers in one space all the elements and themes of the intense focusing *upon life* that was promoted at that time by the elevation and reactivation of the notion of "creative evolution" in the cultural sciences and in the arts with the consequent loss of ground by positivism. With this elevation and reactivation, creativity became the guide for a variety of experiential attitudes at the reflective and the practical (moral, poetic) levels. Those who shared in these attitudes abandoned the objectifying and dissecting tendencies of modern European thought in favor of flexible cognitive and practical approaches that were intended to keep human beings interpretatively in tune with the abundance of signs provided by the bountiful earth and used by them to structure and communicate a *total* sense of their environment and a *total* sense of possible and valuable forms of life. In this experiential climate, to live is to exist communicatively, and correct awareness or *truth* is attached not to axiomatic or empirical—rational—forms of cognition but only to those forms of experience that produce and support harmonious outlines of the world as lived-in and of the life project as lived.

As Rilke lucidly intimated, this communicative impulse of life is at the same time physical and spiritual and makes "transience" constantly flow into "the depths of Being," not into Nothingness. Being is "the Open" constantly enlarged and deepened by the contributions of creativity, especially of creative life. These contributions are safeguarded in life and by life and therefore do not die; the terror of silence attached to death is erased by the endurance and multiplication of these contributions. Thus forms of life speak by their endurance; they become words that rise "invisibly" in us and deliver the habits and memory of all previous life. The suggestive Rilkean formula "We are the bees of the invisible" is secretly redundant, since the "We are" in it would make no sense without the beelike gathering that is life itself and the "invisible" realm of the word to which life is constantly raised. Because it appropriates the mutability of quantitative and qualitative change and it grounds all forms of completion *and* incompletion, that invisible realm of the word that "we are" is spanned by the possibility both of time and of no-time. The word as time (word-in-time) is always in process, relative, incomplete, and deconstructible. The word as released for indefinite appropriation is intertemporal; it is "the angel" of the *Elegies* that exists both with the living and with the dead:

> Angels (they say) don't know whether it is the living
> they are moving among, or the dead. The eternal torrent
> whirls all ages along in it, through both realms
> forever, and their voices are drowned out in its thunderous
> roar.[79]

At the core of this "modern death" is precisely the overlap of all time and no-time, an overlap that is the conceptual and experiential equivalent of the possibility for every creative being to be as word constantly entering into death, yet to continue to live, and also for the word to be brought out of death, to be recreated as life by a living being. This might be the synthesis of all of Rilke's insights: that the overlap of all time and no-time extends the metaphoric sense of spiritual "simultaneity" to its fullness. When seen in its most distinctive clarity, this fullness presents a double face: the communion of all living beings, across time, *in* the intertemporal word and the ultimate intent of speech, the will to utter words-in-time, as always a yes to life *and* to death.

Although this synthesis began to inform his poetic word very early in his career and reached a programmatic formulation in the third part of *The Book of Hours*, "The Book of Poverty and Death," it was only during the often-interrupted composition of the *Elegies* and the (at times) distinct expectation that they might never reach completion as experience and speech that Rilke gradually came to understand the contributions of the word—the work of art—to the creativity of life or, what is the same thing, the thematic connection between his poetry and his life. In those years of uncertainty about his own work, Rilke came to adumbrate the theme of his poetry—

the "sayable"[80] in all poetry—as the total concentration of the will on the task of continuous conversion of life into word, that is, the *contemplative unification* of his lived world and the *visionary unification* of the course of his life. Thus the ultimate function of these two categories of images, which were described in their form and content through examples in the previous chapter, proved to be, in this existential context, the fullest realization of the conversion of life into art and thus a fulfillment of the newly discovered role of art as the most basic site and the prototypical form of creative evolution.

As Rilke persisted in the writing of the *Elegies* for over ten years and celebrated their long-delayed completion with the *Sonnets to Orpheus*, he reached full awareness of the sacrificial value of the song. Perhaps more than anyone else, he thus restores to art its obscurely intended function as the locus of passage into and out of the underworld; and he gently laid out for his contemporaries and successors, beyond the goals of survival, fame, or the will to power, the pure labors involved in the affirmation of life as inseparable henceforth from the affirmation of death.

> Prejudiced as we are against death, we do not manage to release it from all its distorted images. It is a *friend*, our deepest friend, perhaps the only one who can never be misled by our attitudes and vacillations—and this, you must understand, *not* in the sentimental-romantic sense of life's opposite, a denial of life: but our friend precisely when we most passionately, most vehemently, assent to being here, to living and working on earth, to Nature, to love. Life simultaneously says Yes and No. Death (I implore you to believe this!) is the true Yes-sayer. It says *only* Yes. In the presence of eternity.[81]

It is most remarkable that Rilke claimed to have gained clear access to this mythology of death through the influence of Cézanne; he stated on various occasions that he learned this lesson on death in Cézanne's work and again in his life, but most of all in the unique relation between the work and the life of the painter. In a letter of 21 October 1907, Rilke commented on the inability of the great artist to write about art, of his clumsiness when he was forced to explain *his art in words*. In reading Cézanne's correspondence to Émile Bernard, the poet seemed to have come face-to-face with the artist's proclivity to be trapped into double binds when confronted with choices they had not channeled through their art: "The sentences . . . balk and bristle, get knotted up . . . he drops them, beside himself with rage."[82] Yet Rilke could see none of these problems in the artist's infallible selection of colors and their messages, or in the assurance with which the work takes precedence over all other choices during Cézanne's advanced years. The poet might have summarized what he learned from Cézanne in some words of praise that witnessed to his own struggle to achieve the same unity of life and the poetic act: "Only a saint could be as united with his God as Cézanne was with his work."[83]

Rilke's remark on the antiromanticism of his own sense of death suggests, if only by implication, that the transformation of this fundamental experience might have been the key to the modernist overcoming of the organicist metaphysics of the spirit with its view of being as a power of force that constitutes itself in a necessarily productive or developmental way. Implicit in this organicist view of being (and in various ways in all metaphysics) was a sentimental attitude toward death as the enemy of life and the consequent need to absorb death in the inexorable progress of the universe toward wholeness, identity, and self-awareness in which no energy or form can ever be lost. The new apprehension of the word as a "form of life" released from the vital purposes of survival and regeneration and converted into the medium for the integration of qualitative change can be singled out as itself the key factor in the transformation of the sense of death.

What was characteristic of modernism in the field of ideas (besides the elimination of the subject/object separation) was precisely the abandonment of the attempt to produce a metaphysical proof of the emergence of one realm of being from another, the phasing out of the timeworn intellectual endeavor to make present the efficacy of being as *causal* and, most of all, the achievement of a clear sense of that efficacy as *creative and communicative*. This new way of ideas eventually found expression in very different but concurrent philosophical systems (those of Bergson, Husserl, Heidegger, and Wittgenstein); but because the manifestation of creativity and communication has its first—and in some ways its fullest—enactment in art, it was only in the evolution of the views on the image, and of the image itself, at the end of the nineteenth century that the passage from a causal to a phenomenological proof of the creative and communicative efficacy of being could be properly captured. The course of this concurrent evolution of the image *and* of the theories of the image was painstakingly charted in chapters 2 and 3 and need not be repeated here, but the interpretations carried out in this chapter, and still to be completed in the final reading of *The Cardplayers*, would be unjustified and vacuous without that foundation. What is possible to emphasize now, on the strength of that secure foundation but with a great deal more evidence, is that the connections among *creativity, death, and the word* were better understood, and of course much better displayed, by modernist artists—the custodians of the word as image—than by modernist philosophers. It should not be surprising, then, that the greatest among these artists, whether poets, painters, musicians, sculptors, architects, or practitioners of several arts, would share in the awareness of those connections as a major theme of their work. A brief survey of the poetry of Wallace Stevens should corroborate this claim.

One of the major difficulties in understanding Stevens is precisely the constant fluctuation between reticence and abruptness in his assertions; his rhetoric is always so polished that it is difficult to perceive when his reflective experiences are conclusive and when they are overly biased by an emotional charge that will be eventually neutralized in broader reconsiderations. This difficulty is the result of an acute perspectivism in the laying out of time relations, which is most clearly reflected in his considerable use of the image of the hours of the day and, most of all, of the seasons of the year; the seasons—Winter, Spring, Summer, and Fall—topically stand in his poetry for fundamental moods, for the ages of human beings, and for the perspectives on time and eternity that are opened from those situations. They also stand for specific modes of awareness, such as abstraction, ecstasy, and revelation, connected with sharply focused definitions of temporality and with different significance for the constitution of a course of life. Often, the image of a moment of the day or a season is even further complicated by a reversal of its significance as previously established through metaphoric connections among several of the above layers of meaning.[84]

The rhetoric of these perspectives is centered in different personifications of the poet, sometimes as a grave or a desperate stoic, sometimes as a "flippant" epicurean, sometimes, impossible as this may seem, as a skeptic transcendentalist, and sometimes as a Nietzschean lover of necessity and unity in change. It is important to record the coexistence and confusion of all these attitudes about time and death in a modernist such as Stevens because, within the overall agreement of the modernist movement in the ultimate aesthetic and existential understanding of these themes, Cézanne's struggle with these issues was closer to Stevens's fluctuations than to Rilke's Mozartian precocity and steady progress toward an orderly and profound systematization.

Nevertheless it is possible to point in Stevens's delineation of a "mythology of modern death" to an irreversible, however tentative and reluctant, growth of his *belief in a specific contribution of the word—of poetry—to creative evolution;* this belief is confused with others in the early poetry and finds a distinct expression in the middle years and a majestically transparent embodiment in the late work. The main obstacle to the above growth is the precariousness[85] of the poet's hope in the possibility that his word, his art, might be accepted and brought back to life by others whether in his lifetime or afterward.

The rising of the word from a mere desire of all nature to speak establishes the symbolism of the palm as word in an early poem, "Infanta Marina." "Somnambulisma" explains that the poet is driven by this desire to speak more than by any other:

> Without this bird that never settles, without
> Its generations that follow in their universe,
> The ocean, falling and falling on the hollow shore,
> Would be a geography of the dead.[86]

The purely evolutionary character of this drive toward order is modified almost from the start in Stevens by the poetic discovery of creative and qualitative features in the cosmic order; "The Idea of Order at Key West" manifests a sense of the power of the word to complete the world that will not change in his later work: "She was the single artificer of the world / In which she sang . . . the sea, / Whatever self it had, became the self / That was her song."[87] The relations of cosmic evolution to the senses of reality, time and death, were embodied in a powerful intuitive rhetoric in this early phase of the poet, but at this juncture they were still heavily indebted to classical, recent, and current sources; that intuitive rhetoric began to show enormous increments in originality and distinctness as it split in two directions in Stevens's middle years.

One of the directions of aesthetic feeling and thought that emerges then is connected with the epistemology of abstraction, the reduction to the "First Idea" of the world, and the focusing on visibility as a mode of persistent emotive and imaginative indwelling that breaks through the stereotypes of habitual perception. This stance had many unintegrated and in some respects antithetical components; it was naturalistic and narcissistic; it was traceable to the competing influences of Emerson, Nietzsche, and Santayana; it paralleled similar stances in the diverse symbolisms of Whitman and Mallarmé; and, as indicated earlier, it lacked innovative approaches to temporality.[88] The prevailing attitudes toward death within this first stance were the Lucretian absorption of death within the abundance of nature, the appeal to ecstasy as compensation for death and the embrace of the love of fate, all of which are conventional poetic topics. Both life and word were framed within this stance by one of the metaphysical antinomies prevalent in the premodernist generations: the transience of time into nothingness versus the survival of essential meanings only in thought. With an appropriate change of antecedents, this aesthetic and intellectual stance corresponded in Cézanne to the advanced symbolist and the plastic approaches to painting.

Against this first stance, a second one appeared in Stevens's middle years; in it, creative evolution, temporality, and death were combined under a decisively modernist convergence of life and the poetic word. This second stance was articulated through a wealth of contemplative and visionary images, the most brilliant, humble, and terse in the poet's corpus. The struggle of poetic creativity with the necessities and contingencies of nature and life can be shown in some intense poems of this period written both before and after "Notes toward a Supreme Fiction," by all accounts the watershed of Stevens's poetry.

"Extracts from Addresses to the Academy of Fine Ideas" adumbrates the unity of the place in which humans exist as "half earth, half mind" and the unity of time as the "troubles to produce the redeeming thought." The ecstatic identities between oneself and the lived earth give strength to the "belief in one's element, . . . the repeated sayings that / There is nothing more and that it is enough to believe." From such belief come "stanzas of final peace":

> Thence come the final chants, the chants
> Of the brooder seeking the acutest end
> Of speech: to pierce the heart's residuum
> And there to find music for a single line,
> Equal to memory, one line in which
> The vital music formulates the words.[89]

The last lines of this poem, "Behold the men in helmets . . . ," strongly suggest that a mature groping for final chants must bring about the replacement of the traditional views of death and immortality, which in spite of themselves perpetuate the paradoxes of evil. The poet is envisioned in these lines as a soldier willing to sacrifice himself (to be defeated) for a good cause.

The fusion of the word-in-time and the intertemporal word, the first destined to die in the contingency of its situation and the second destined to be shared by persons from all epochs, was first evident in Stevens in "Chocorua to its Neighbor": "To speak quietly at such a distance . . . and to be heard is to be large in space . . . to perceive men without reference to their form." The dead poet, the submerged intertemporal word, seems "Both substance and non-substance . . . fire from an underworld, / Of less degree than flame." Stevens wrestled with traditional images of the intertemporal word that are not suited to modernist intuitions:

> speak of this shadow as
> A human thing. It is an eminence,
> But of nothing, trash of sleep that will disappear
> With the special things of night, little by little,
> In day's constellation, and yet remain, yet be,
>
> . . . the common self, interior fons.
> And fond, the total man.[90]

In "Esthétique du Mal," however, the poet found an avenue for his belief in the intertemporal word by making it the other side of the poetic word that dies in time, "the soldier of time." The fusion of the two words was now placed by Stevens between "the insatiable bird," the appetite of the cosmos for integration or speech, and "the mountain of shadows," the poetic tradition, both of which move in circles and strive to transcend the fate of eternal return:

> The bird
> In the brightest landscape downwardly revolves
> Disdaining each astringent ripening, . . .
>
> A mountain in which no ease is ever found,
> Unless indifference to deeper death
> Is ease, stands in the dark, a shadow's hill,
> And there the soldier of time has deathless rest.
>
> Concentric circles of shadows, . . .
> Form mystical convolutions in the sleep
> Of time's red soldier deathless on his bed.

Transcendence could be then characterized as "the metaphysical changes that occur, / Merely in living as and where we live."[91]

The definitive sign for the intertemporal word, "the palm," reappeared in "Description without a Place" as a visionary image juxtaposed to a contemplative one.[92] Stevens was here his most modernist self, beyond the extremes of Eliot and Pound and very close to Rilke and Trakl in their understanding of the sacrifice, the "going under,"[93] of the word-in-time and of human beings that is necessary for intertemporal dialogue. In intense contemplation the locus of each poetic description expands toward the limits of the world:

> Dazzle yields to a clarity and we observe,
>
> And observing is completing and we are content,
> In a world that shrinks to an immediate whole,
>
> That we do not need to understand, complete
> Without secret arrangements of it in the mind.

The sign of the intertemporal word is hoisted in this world, which is "intenser than any actual life," and in the "much-mottled motion of blank time":

> A palm that rises up beyond the sea,
>
> A little different from reality:
> The difference that we make in what we see

And our memorials of that difference,
Sprinklings of bright particulars from the sky. . . .

It is wizened starlight growing young,
In which old stars are planets of morning, fresh

In the brilliantest descriptions of new day,
Before it comes, the just anticipation

Of the appropriate creatures, jubilant,
The forms that are attentive in thin air.[94]

In this vision of the intertemporal light, in which moments of many lives and also moments of one life are fused, Stevens surpassed the topical uses of morning and evening stars in the literary tradition and stood next to the modernist Rilke, who also spoke about the youthfulness and the oldness of the latent word.[95] Most importantly, in singing the realization of the unity of life as a word generously offered beyond death, Stevens surpassed also the romantic tradition that looked to self-realization in the song as a negation of death.[96] In the generosity of intertemporal dialogue, the poetic word became justified not as ecstasy but as word, and the poetic act acquired its worth through death, not as a negation of it. These points were driven home with utmost poignancy in "The River of Rivers in Connecticut," a poem in which the dying Stevens, like Cézanne in his final years, resolutely converted his life into word and generously anticipated the flow of his life into the river that does not flow:

Call it, once more, a river, an unnamed flowing,

Space-filled, reflecting the seasons, the folk-lore
Of each of the senses; call it again and again,
The river that flows nowhere, like a sea.[97]

There are four recurrent visionary images that parallel and recapitulate the growth of Stevens's belief in the efficacy of the poetic word: the giant, the skeleton, the mask, and the rock. They will be given special consideration here because of their close affinities with the skull motif in Cézanne as direct signs of the convergence of time, image, word, and death. It would be difficult to find better poetic descriptions of the shifting cardplayers/skull motif of Cézanne's *Cardplayers* than Stevens's piercing lines on his own related motifs. The interpenetration of these images in Stevens occurs in both perception and intuition; thus he gave us, as a collage or imaginative construct, an equivalent of the extensions of perception and of the unification of the artistic life in the visionary Cézanne.

Giant, skeleton, mask, and rock have enough perceptual *similarities* to be included as metaphors in a collage; the *diversities* of temporal allusion within each one, and from each to the others, invite and encourage bypassing of their naïve symbolism as similes in favor of their synthesis into a unified, if shifting, motif. As a complex visionary image, they stand, just like the moments of the day and the seasons, for different relations of parts and whole in personal and collective life and *for the different modalities of time flow* that these different relations create.

The perceptual similarities alone would be enough to identify the skeleton with the mask, the mountain, and the giant. A family resemblance runs through this set of objects; they all do not have all the pertinent features, yet each shares some important traits with the other participants. The skeleton, the rock, and the mask, for example, share rigidity of structure, while the rock or mountain shares with the giant the bulk created by accumulation of elements; the skeleton might share with the giant a strange and otherworldly aspect, while the skeleton (skull) and the mask might share a potential for animation.

In "A Postcard from the Volcano," bones are transformed into mask: "with our bones / We . . . left what still is / The look of things"; the mountain (rock) and the skeleton are intimately fused in "The Man with the Blue Guitar": "the mountains of one's land. . . . The flesh, the bone, the dirt, the stone." "Gigantomachia," a poem easily lost in Stevens's corpus, is a wonderful experiment in the constitution of a shifting metaphoric motif that includes dead soldiers, the giant, the mountain, and the mask:

Each man himself became a giant,
Tipped out with largeness, bearing the heavy
And the high, receiving out of others,
As from an inhuman elevation
And origin, an inhuman person,

A mask, a spirit, an accoutrement.
For soldiers, the new moon stretches twenty feet.

This motif, extraordinarily complex in the above elaboration, will be abstracted as "simple" and "single" in larger poems that complete the look of reality or offer blueprints for the unification of human lives. The strange and otherworldly giant appears in "Chocorua" as "a shell of dark blue glass, or ice, / Or air collected . . . a tree in the middle of / The night . . . luminous flesh / Or shapely fire." The giant, who as a mountain is inanimate, as a mask is, however, "fixed but for a slight / Illumination of movement as he breathe(s)"; the mask in "An Ordinary Evening in New Haven" becomes theatrically alive: "The venerable mask . . . occasionally speaks. . . . This should be tragedy's most moving face." [98]

In Stevens, the four images in their strangeness and otherworldliness are not ghostly or terrifying except for their mysteriousness and sacredness; they stand at the gate of open being and show qualitative turns in duration. Like all great modernist images, they delimit the reflective side of action, the extensional side of intuition, and, as words, they are placed on both sides of death. "Chocorua" is an incisive lesson in this multifaceted role of the image as mediator among the various dimensions of qualitative change. The cumulative word that "we" are breathes "in crystal-pointed change the whole / Experience of night" and it inhales "A freedom out of silver-shaping size, / Against the whole experience of day." Stevens asks persistently about the "force" that impels the growth of this giant, about the "desire" and "thinking" at its source. He responds that men want it to be "image . . . of their power, thought . . . beyond / Their form, beyond their life, yet of themselves." Perturbed by his own disbelief, the poet wrestles with contradictory formulas for the image as image: "It is like a thing of ether that exists"; as if to reassure himself, he repeats: "But it exists / It exists, it is visible, it is, it is." And, looking about for the most simple revelation of its being, he perceives it, in Bergsonian terms, as a new qualitative state of the world, "An innocence of the earth and no false sign."[99]

The Bergsonian Stevens sees qualitative change as extended through the metaphysical levels that reason imposes upon it: "It is not in the premise that reality / Is a solid. It may be a shade that traverses / A dust, a force that traverses a shade." Through this conceptual grid, different forms of time appear attached to cosmic change, contingent change, and creative change. "The Pure Good of Theory" presents the cosmic flow in which "Time is a horse . . . without a rider on a road at night." Human life with its concentration seems a slowing of cosmic time, "A retardation of its battering, / A horse grotesquely taut"; but cosmic time, topically, does not stop, it appears thus as the "hooded enemy" that makes all music "inimical" and only "preludes." "Description without Place" presents lived time in its dimensions and directions. History, as the "integrations of the past," is not "our affair, which is the affair / Of the possible." Human life is stretched out toward the future, the span of its projects, imperatives, and promises: "The future is description. . . . The categorical predicate, the arc." As lived time reaches toward a new level of concentration in the intertemporal work, as "men make themselves their speech," time begins to matter, the uniqueness of a lived life must stir, make itself "in sound. . . . Be alive with its own seemings."[100]

A beautifully strange poem, "This Solitude of Cataracts," fantasizes Stevens's roaming outside of cosmic time and lived time; from a flow that stands still "like a lake," he imagines looking back at the cosmic flow, walking beside it "under the buttonwoods, beneath a moon nailed fast." This fantasy recreates the strange temporality of the skull and of the mask brought about by human aspirations to exercise awareness from the other side of destruction, "To be a bronze man breathing under archaic lapis . . . his bronzen breath at the azury centre of time." Similarly, in "The Owl in the Sarcophagus," his friend Henry Church walks "living among the forms of thought . . . conceiving his passage as into a time / That of itself stood still." This perennial time is, however, seen here as the time of dialogue, "a meeting, an emerging in the light, / A dazzle of remembrance and of sight." A wonderful summary of all the conditions of intertemporal dialogue is given in the shifting motif of "Primitive Like an Orb," a motif that gathers, with a conviction equal to that of Rilke and Cézanne, the transparency of the image, the collaging of words and signs with the materials and colors of the earth, and the arrested motion and gigantic size of the accumulations of the mind:

> That's it. The lover writes, the believer hears,
> The poet mumbles and the painter sees,

Each one, his fated eccentricity,
As a part, but part, but tenacious particle,
Of the skeleton of the ether, the total
Of letters, prophecies, perceptions, clods
Of color, the giant of nothingness, each one
And the giant ever changing, living in change.[101]

CONCLUSION:
The Trump Card/Players

The preceding investigation on the mythology of modern death is meant not to compare Cézanne with Rilke and Stevens, even though influences of the painter can be found in the poets and all three clearly shared central topics. Neither is it intended as an interpretation of Cézanne through Rilke and Stevens; indeed, rather the opposite is true: The search for examples of the treatment of the topic of death in modernism was prompted in this study by a perception of profound differences in the images of death in the various periods of Cézanne's painting. The heart of this investigation is the complete turnabout in Cézanne's inspiration from the allegorical similes of the early stages to the visionary images of the late stages—images that embody a unity of life through various presentations of time and death. That decisive turnabout must be identified here with the aesthetic inception of modernism.

The purpose of the discussion of "modern death" has been twofold. First, in arriving at a clear view of the motif, it was necessary to bracket all possible preconceptions about death itself; these preconceptions, which in turn impose metaphysically one-sided time structures upon us, are very strong and well defined because they are rooted in religion, traditional art and literature, as well as popular culture.[102] Second, to have adequate access to a *visionary shifting motif* like that of *The Cardplayers*, it is helpful to trace, at the *iconological* level, the reflective, existential and aesthetic, as opposed to the traditional-mimetic and psychologistic-associational, reasons for forming icons in modernist literature that point to equivalent reasons in modernist art.

With this introduction the reader-viewer can now follow, and even anticipate, the forthcoming *iconographic* reading of *The Card-players* in a properly modernist spirit. It must be clarified in this context that, because sensations became signs in modernism, surface description had to transcend naïve perceptual accounts and become a *reading* of surface structure signs, in this case the signs of the shifting motif that precedes the dissociation of particular images, to be accompanied by an *interpretation* of the deep structure of that motif, in this case the unified sense of human life arising from a distinctively new fusion of time, death, and the word—the work of art.

This sense of the coming to pass of the unity of life *in, and as the visionary motif of, the work* has been suggested by the explanation of the intrinsic structure of visionary images; but an independent confirmation that would work intuitively for the painting itself would be very helpful as proof of this explanation. The difficulty encountered in the discovery of the shifting motif of *The Large Bathers* will also be encountered now in the surface description of *The Cardplayers*: Because the perception of the motif in terms of its signs must precede that of the images that may be dissociated from it, it is impossible to isolate the motif by an appeal to those images. To circumvent this difficulty, it will be necessary in what follows to duplicate the procedure adopted at the end of chapter 4, that is, the investigation of the surface signs of the shifting motif. However, because of the inherent ambiguity of shifting signs, that investigation by itself will prove to be thematically incomplete in *The Cardplayers*, as it was in *The Large Bathers*. To make it complete and convincing, it will be necessary here, as it was before, to return to the iconological level of interpretation and carry out at that level an analysis of aspects of the whole suggested in a tentative way by the tropes that motivate surface signs.

The preliminary naming of the motif pointed in *The Large Bathers* to "the sexual body." With that clue on hand, the analysis proceeded there to an elucidation of the contents of this image and discovered, through Kierkegaard, the imaginative components or phases that constitute the iconological depth of the theme and suggest the partial images to be dissociated from it: the personifications of Cherubino, Papageno, and Don Giovanni. The value of this Kierkegaardian interpretation arises from its insistence on the inseparability of the iconological components of a visionary theme; however, Kierkegaard's analysis was made possible through his conversion of the musical image into a literary one, with the consequent loss of the immediacy of the musical sign. The fusion of the iconological components of a visionary motif is, as was asserted then, more indissoluble in the modernist pictorial sign than it was in the musical, therefore it would be very hard to interpret the ambiguity of these pictorial signs and discover, *in its proper particularity and immediacy,* the thematic content to which they point.

Fortunately, as has been shown in Rilke and Stevens, the modernist visionary image can be produced in poetic words with a very high level of immediacy, and thus it is possible to appeal to it and to bring forth, without the artificiality and distortions of analysis, its iconological components and its experiential, affective, and psychological identity. The poetic dissociation of the visionary aspects of death in modernism has already been carried out in the preceding excursus, which yielded with all immediacy, in the overlap of the images of the giant, the skull, the mask, and the mountain, the unique overlap of time, death, and the work and the peculiar unity of life that this overlap creates. Thus, a third reason for that excursus and a further indication of its benefits can now be added in retrospect. The iconographic reading and interpretation will proceed therefore in a direct fashion; it can leave behind all the issues pertaining to the identification and justification of the iconological motif, and it is hoped that this motif will appear in its utmost immediacy, if the signs selected for its exhibition are favorable. All of these procedural considerations can be summed up by a reiteration of the inseparability of iconography from iconology and, within the former, of the different signs of the shifting motif. Considerations of one of the signs will quickly bring up its relations to all the others.

The most apparent sign of the shifting motif of *The Cardplayers* is the complexity and strangeness of its coloration. In the present study, color has been defined differently in the different phases of Cézanne. The symbolist phase was characterized by a color *dematerialization* that signified vague emotions imaginatively constructed in, or along with, the scene they qualify; colors combined with lines, volumes, and other signs to construct a charged perceptual image. In the plastic phase, color was *distributed*; the full spectrum was modulated to create fresh developments of color syntax, fresh harmonies that would uncover and thus realize new motifs of perception and emotion.

In the contemplative phase, color was *diffused;* complementary color pairings produced a harmony of harmonies, an empathetic mood that extended vision to the limits of a lived world while it unfolded and integrated the qualitative rhythms of lived time. In the first description of a visionary image, *The Large Bathers,* typical of the painter's last phase, color appears as a *fusion* or *interpenetration* of an arbitrary complementary pair, blue and orange. This interpenetration creates homogeneity and intimacy in space and dissolves all qualitative change, especially the emotional tonalities of the comic and the erotic, into pure duration.

In *The Cardplayers,* Cézanne transcended even that color fusion of other visionary images. A visionary image is realized as a motif but not in perceptions; it is, in a Bergsonian sense, a dynamic scheme or "the germ of a visual representation."[103] As a germ of representation, *The Cardplayers* offered peculiar problems regarding color that the painter had to confront in order to place his depicted theme at the intended level of conscious presentation, in this case the presentation of an object *as absent.* A careful examination of this painting will show that Cézanne intended to produce the colors of a pure image *in* a perceptual analogue.

In contrast with the color pairings of *The Large Bathers,* the painter's palette displays in *The Cardplayers* a progressive decolorization of a single color, the yellow that spreads from the brightest area of the painting, the convex shoulder of the younger player on the right. From this brightness, the saturation of the yellow diminishes, and darker and darker colors accumulate, as if turning around the convexity of the shoulder and back of the left player toward the darkness of the top left corner and the dark concavity bound by the arms and faces of both players. By regressing tonally from brightness toward complete obscurity without ever reaching it, the painter seems to be reducing all the colors in the scene to high and low values of the initially saturated yellow. In so doing, he has produced an unconventional color gamut based on yellow and thus different from the natural spectrum. This gamut stands in *The Cardplayers* for the coloration characteristic of a pure image—that is, a graduated scale in which every tone can have *multiple values and no actual perceptual value.* Indeed, the color gamut of a pure image can be translated into the natural spectrum of colors or into any other syntagmatic chain with conventionally assigned values.

The three white areas—the pipe, the displayed cards of the older player, and the collar of the younger—stand against the imaginary space of the scene; they act as reflecting elements that contrast with the animated translucency of the visionary color gamut. The isolated whites mark the precarious reality of the surface plane and point to a connection between the "extensity" of the tridimensional space and the active role of vision in a dynamic schema; the spheric depth of the painting is based on tensions between light and darkness and not on perspectival illusion. In this painting, visionary space is more real than the space of visual practice, and thus the tonal tensions connected with visionary constitution do not stand for allegorizations of natural or spiritual realities but signify the creative activity and the unified life in which it is contained. The shifting function of coloration is demonstrated by a circulation of tonalities from the basic yellow theme to the potentially dissociated images: The earthy and bony tones of the skull are applied to the cardplaying scene, while the colors of the self-gathering skull, an eddy of emerging and disappearing tones, are the signs bearing the emotions involved in the passage from life into word.

The "figures" of the painting—the players, the room, the local objects, and the skull—are the second formal shifter or set of signs of the visionary motif. As visionary images, these figures are *all* emergent perceptions, and thus their pictorial vehicles—the colors, the lines, the tensions, the space and, as will soon be seen, the temporal flow—are more thematic than they are. *The Cardplayers* would be misinterpreted if the viewer took figurative perception as a point of departure for reading or understanding or even viewing the scene; all the emerging objects must be seen through their constitutive signs, and these signs constantly interfere with the perceptual formation of isolated objects and return the viewer to the flow of life that runs through the vision.

What allows the interpreter to enter into that flow is precisely the thematic function of those signs; indeed, in that thematic function *the shifters constitute the motif as a poetic trope, a figure of the creative activity.* As emergent figurative perceptions, the isolated objects are not the support of allegorical similes; they should be bypassed until they are metonymically or synecdochically recovered as parts of the whole after dissociation. The viewer who is attentive to signs rather than sensations is gently led by them to seek and find the mystery of the whole and then recover its parts in their lived distance from each other and in the equivalence of each with the whole. The constitutive signs of the shifting motif are understood, then, as metaphoric family resemblances that hold together the evolving collage or vision of an entire life.

The joint experiencing of colors, space, and figures *in* the shifting motif forecloses any possible function of the lines as defining space; lines have been converted into the pure pictorial gestures that Hans-Georg Gadamer explained so well:

> These are not simply the gestures of individual human beings in a pictorially represented world. They are themselves pictorial gestures. Nor am I simply thinking of the gesturing human figures whose form can just be recognized here and there. The background against which they stand out and with which they are interwoven is itself no less a gesture in accordance with the principles of surface and color.[104]

These gestures or vital germs of speech cast the total shifting motif in the metaphor of a mask by alternating rigidity and animation in the linear configuration of every possible image to compose the "physiognomic" quality of the whole painting. That physiognomic quality is repeated in the condensed patterning of local objects, of the faces and bodies of the players, and of the fluctuating skull:

> There is almost nothing psychological involved [in these gestures] and little interpretation of subjective interiority. Almost everything is merely the interiority of the mask that masks nothing, the interiority of rapt attention wholly absorbed in the enigma of our existence.[105]

The intertwining of color, space, lines, and "figures" as signs of the shifting motif constantly directs the viewer of *The Cardplayers* toward time, the most active of all the shifters in the painting and the one that is closest to the unity of life that is the meaning of the overall motif. As Paul Ricoeur recently showed,[106] the temporality of cultural artifacts and particularly of the work of art must be approached as a synthesis of the time(s) manifested in the work with the temporal framework of the creation; Ricoeur calls these two aspects of creative temporality "narrated time" and "narrative time."

This distinction will be adapted here to the Bergsonian and modernist beliefs in which the time(s) of objects and images flow(s) out of different forms of concentration upon lived action that itself has its own modalities and spans of concentration.

Within these beliefs, narrated time and narrative time constantly flow into one another. The narrated time in Cézanne's masterpiece may thus be understood as the convergence and clash of the time flows of the dissociated images, while the narrative time can be perceived as the flow of the shifting motif in which the lives of the creator and the viewer take shape singly and together and break through the necessity of cycles and of continuous irreversible progress characteristic of the metaphysical images of time. Narrated time becomes, in this context, a recovery of the individual flows of partial spans of a life in their relation to the whole; narrative time is the fusion of all these spans in an underlying biographical flow that is endowed with unique qualitative concentration and duration and is open for sharing.

The shifting structures of the color, space, lines, and figures described above preclude the possibility of seeing the scene as an arrested moment in time, a momentary perception that expands imaginarily toward narrated past and future. The central motif and the partial images are, from their very emergence, both in motion and in process. What is seen is action, but the playing itself is just one part of the interplay of the emerging images in time; thus it cannot be perceived as continuous action. The absorption of all dualities and oppositions into an underlying commonness, the circular tensions of the dynamic schema and the multiplication of thematic games at all levels of signification, might suggest the substitution of a Nietzschean eternal return in place of the traditional temporality of pictures whose subject matter generally pointed, through mimesis, to an instant in time with eternal significance. But the possibility of a fateful return of the same is foreclosed as a theme of *The Cardplayers* because its narrated time constantly flows into narrative time, into the composite temporal significance of the shifting motif, transmutable as its intended beginning and end may be.

Once the conventional perceptions of time have been removed from this reading by the preceding considerations, it is possible to ask: What are the narrated times of the dissociated images of *The Cardplayers*? The most prominent dissociated image is, of course, that of the players; its temporality is that of communion. Concentration on the game unifies the single consciousnesses of the participants by extending their action, beyond the vicissitudes of their present engagement, to the vicissitudes of the game of life represented in the cards. But the time of the game is always necessarily the time of *one* realization of the *possibilities of life* inscribed in the figures of the cards; through *this* realization, life passes from those at play in *this* situation to any potential players. This play is not a simple instantiation of the rules of a game; the roles and the rules emerge not out of pure imaginative scheming but out of an effort to reach and transcend all experienced limits of living as a human. This effort gives its ultimate sense to the actions of the players themselves: What they attain by playing is *the time of a life* that they open for each other, a time of communion that is thus always concrete and always open to other participants.

The two additional images that can be dissociated from the overall motif, the skull and the mask, cannot be separated conceptually as they can be visually, because they embody two closely related aspects of the temporality of death-as-word. The looming skull in *The Cardplayers* is Cézanne's equivalent of Rilke's "bees of the invisible" and of Stevens's "soldiers of time." As it makes and remakes itself in time, human life becomes word, a fixed message we long to hear and whose total design we want to fit into the discordant fragments of our intentions. Thus, despite their incompleteness and openness, we can never be disenchanted about the sense of words, because we cannot give up the coherence of the course or form of life in which each completed or expressed part must be grounded. "We" are only *in* that coherence, the players are only *in* the skull, the word-in-time flows only *into* death.

The mask, on the other hand, can only exist in suspended time. The mask is the sketched coherence of a *human* sense of life that must remain ambiguous in its unlimited possibilities of realization and cannot be reanimated as such. As was explained earlier, the physiognomic quality of the mask is composed of rigidity and animation. The mask is capable of many realizations, which fulfill some of its intentions and betray others. But it is never realized as a mask. When reanimated, it ceases to be a mask; it becomes a particular actor who speaks through it or someone who listens very attentively to those who have spoken by it. Besides bringing the mask back to life *in* the human conversation, speech and listening reactivate the mask as mask, adding features to its inhuman features without making it human; the mask as such neither lives nor dies in human time.

This discussion of narrated time must be situated in the context of the clarification of the dissociated images as formed by signs. Time is not visible in images considered as arrangements of sensations in space; hence if it is perceived in the dissociated images, these must be signs for the phenomenon of time. The meaning of these images can now be fully understood: They have indeed no straightforward *figurative* content; their *figural* content coincides with the thematic significance of the nonfigurative signs and exhibits various states or moments of these signs as constituted in and by qualitative duration. The game, the skull, and the mask not only are made up by signs, but they variously present the temporal substance of a particular dynamic schema.

With this reference to the dynamic schema, the analysis of time passes beyond the level of the narrated to that of the narrative flow and enters again into human time, which is itself constituted in and by signs. The temporality of the shifting motif of *The Cardplayers* is that of the dynamic schema from which all its partial images arise; as a unique sense of time, this schema is an achievement of Cézanne's consciousness and concentration on the meaning of his life. As stated earlier, that concentration is manifested in the interpenetration of the images of the play, the skull, and the mask that have been separated from each other for the purposes of surface description only. The unity of these images is a distinct achievement of Cézanne, an achievement that was foreshadowed in previous moments of the history of pictorial creativity and would be shared in an intimate way by all the modernist masters.

On the other hand, this unique temporality of death and the word gathers, and transcends, all the emotional and psychic tensions lived by the artist in the various stages of his painting. In the temporality of the shifting motif of *The Cardplayers* are fused the distorted psychological time of Cézanne's symbolist images, the elevation of instantaneous impressions to the rhythmic endurance of his plastic images, the integration of various cosmic and psychic rhythms in his contemplative montages, and the dimensions of the word-in-time/ atemporal/intertemporal word in his visionary collages.

But the time games within the shifting motif are not to be lost in evolutionary change without a proper ending. As participants in these games, all the elements in the vision, including the local objects, the skull, the players, the painter, and, of course, *us* the viewers, share in a common time flow that is not a present moment constructed in the painting nor even an imaginative extension of this present in the various intentional directions assignable to each element; it can be stated with all rigor, using a formula of Alfred Schutz, inspired by Bergson, that all the participants "grow old together"[107] in the common temporal flow of the shifting motif of *The Cardplayers*. Perhaps the best proof of the authenticity of this masterpiece as atemporal and intertemporal word is contained in the following description of the presence of death in the late works of Cézanne:

> Je me suis juré de mourir en peignant. Just as in an old picture of the dance of death, that's the way death seized his hand from behind, painting the last stroke himself.[108]

NOTES

I.
Cézanne and the Unity of Modernism

1. Harrison, *English Art and Modernism, 1900–1939,* 46–48.
2. Nicholson, "Post-Impressionism and Roger Fry."
3. Roger Fry's "Essay in Aesthetics" (first published in *Art Quarterly* in 1909) was reprinted in Fry, *Vision and Design,* 12–27.
4. Bell, *Art,* 1–41, 135–44; also Fry's "Essay in Aesthetics" and "Paul Cézanne," both in *Vision and Design.*
5. Gasquet's conversation is contained in Doran, *Conversations avec Cézanne,* 110. I translate thus: "The landscape becomes reflective, human, and thinks itself through me. I make it an object, let it project itself and endure within my painting . . . I become the subjective consciousness of the landscape, and my painting becomes its objective consciousness."
6. Pablo Picasso made both of these statements. See Picasso, "Statement by Picasso: 1935," in *Picasso: Fifty Years of His Art,* translated by Alfred H. Barr (New York: Museum of Modern Art, 1946); and Gyula H. Brassaï, *Picasso and Co.* (New York: Doubleday, 1966), 79.
7. Émile Bernard, "Paul Cézanne," *L'Occident,* July 1904, 17–30. See also Reff, "Cézanne and Poussin." Even Cézanne referred to himself as a "primitif": resigned . . . to being the Primitive of the way that I discovered" (quoted in Émile Bernard, *Souvenirs* [Paris: La Renovation Esthetique, 1921], 65).

8. See especially Shiff, *Cézanne and the End of Impressionism,* 3–8 for a discussion of these labels.

9. Kurt Badt, *Art of Cézanne.* See especially pp. 132–37, where Badt compares Cézanne to other "great Romantics" (i.e., Constable, Friedrich, Delacroix, and Baudelaire) and discusses what he calls the "Romantic impulse."

10. Reprinted in *Modern Artists on Art,* edited by Robert L. Herbert (Englewood Cliffs, N.J.: Prentice-Hall, 1964), 4. Also see Pierre Francastel, *Du cubisme a l'art abstrait* (Paris: S.E.V.P.E.N., 1957), 72.

11. Novotny, *Cézanne* (a translation by Raymond Ockenden of parts of this book appears in *Cézanne in Perspective,* edited by Judith Wechsler [Englewood Cliffs, N.J.: Prentice-Hall, 1975], 96–107); Merleau-Ponty, *Sense and Non-Sense,* 9–25; Badt, *Art of Cézanne.*

12. See George Heard Hamilton, "Cézanne and His Critics," in Museum of Modern Art, *Cézanne: The Late Work* (New York: Museum of Modern Art, 1977), 135–49.

13. Schapiro, *Paul Cézanne,* 118.

14. Geist, "Secret Life of Paul Cézanne," 7–16.

15. Hamilton, "Cézanne, Bergson, and the Image of Time," 2–12.

16. Sidney Geist, "What Makes the Black Clock Run?" *Art International,* February 1978, 8–14.

17. Rewald, *Paul Cézanne,* 164–74, for a discussion of this period of withdrawal.

18. Geffroy, *La vie artistique,* 248–60.

19. Denis, "Cézanne," in *Théories, 1890–1910,* 23–25.

20. Lawrence Gowing, "The Logic of Organized Sensations," in Museum of Modern Art, *Cézanne: The Late Work,* 155–56.

21. Lilian Brion-Guerry, "The Elusive Goal," in Museum of Modern Art, *Cézanne: The Late Work,* esp. 79.

22. Schapiro, *Modern Art: Nineteenth and Twentieth Centuries,* 1–38.

23. Badt, *Art of Cézanne,* 30, 140, 151.

24. The skull has a triple function: It is first a prethematic (iconological) material of the imagination and later transformed into a thematic (iconological) image that stands for a certain (iconographic) state of the sign, that is, the word-in-time. The mask, on the other hand, as a total physiognomic property of the signs of the overall motif (the immediacy of life in its unity) of *The Cardplayers,* has no prethematic function and is not subject to thematic transformation from an allegorical to a semiotic meaning. Its thematic significance within the overall motif is the thematic (iconological) function of the signs in a particular (iconographic) state, the state of the atemporal/intertemporal word. Because these functions, and their full differentiation, will not emerge until the final reading of the overall motif in chapter 5, the mask will not be considered again until that reading exhibits it as metaphorically used with, though distinct from, the skull.

25, Albert Silvestre, "Un peintre genevois a rencontré Cézanne," *Vie, art, et cité,* December 1939, 319; quoted in Theodore Reff, "Final Decade," in Museum of Modern Art, *Cézanne: The Late Work,* 37.

26. Herbert Read, quoted in *Modernism, 1890–1930,* edited by Malcolm Bradbury and James McFarlane (New York: Penguin Books, 1976), 20.

27. C. S. Lewis, "They Asked for a Paper," quoted in Bradbury and McFarlane, *Modernism, 1890–1930,* 20.

28. See especially Bullock, "The Double Image," in Bradbury and McFarlane, *Modernism, 1890–1920,* 58–70, which discusses the tensions that make up this historical period, e.g., nostalgia/avant-garde, revolution/technology.

29. Bradbury and McFarlane, *Modernism, 1890–1930,* 192–205.

30. Ibid., 71. For discussions of the effects of this desire for transcendence, see Ortega y Gasset, *Dehumanization of Art,* 3–50; Wilhelm Wörringer, *Abstraction and Empathy,* 3–25; and Heidegger, *Poetry, Language, Thought,* 91–142.

31. Émile Zola, *Le roman expérimental* (Paris, 1880); quoted in Bradbury and McFarlane, *Modernism, 1890–1930,* 30.

32. Jayne L. Walker, *The Making of a Modernist: Gertrude Stein* (Amherst: University of Massachusetts Press, 1984), esp. 1–18.

33. Roland Barthes locates the beginning of modernism in the midnineteenth century and identifies it with the pluralization of worldviews derived from the "problematics of language," in *Writing Degree Zero,* 9. Also see Todorov, *Theories of the Symbol,* 255–84; and Phillipson, *Painting, Language and Modernity,* 43–97. For more general references on linguistics and language, see Saussure, *Course in General Linguistics;* Michel Foucault, *The Order of Things: An Archaeology of the Human Sciences* (New York: Random House, 1970), esp. chaps. 4, 7, 8; and Heidegger, *Poetry, Language, Thought,* 17–78.

II.
From Impressionism to Cézanne:
Psychological Theories

1. Louis Leroy, "L'exposition des impressionistes," *Le Charivari,* 25 April 1874, published in English as *The History of Impressionism,* translated by John Rewald (New York: Museum of Modern Art, 1961), 323–24.

2. See Venturi, "The Aesthetic Idea of Impressionism," for a thorough discussion of the impression as medium. Also see Clive Scott, "Symbolism, Decadence and Impressionism," in Bradbury and McFarlane, *Modernism, 1890–1930,* 212–13, 219–27; Shiff, *Cézanne,* 14–20, 39–52.

3. Shiff, *Cézanne,* 14–20.

4. These principles (association, complementarity, and empathy) are from, respectively, Gustav Fechner, Niels Bohr, and Theodor Lipps; see James McFarlane, "The Mind of Modernism," in Bradbury and McFarlane, *Modernism, 1890–1930,* 74–77.

5. In his letters to Gustave Geffroy, Claude Monet discusses the passivity of his reactions; see especially those of 20 June 1890 and 7 October 1890;

reprinted in Gustave Geffroy, *Claude Monet: Sa vie, son temps, son oeuvre* (Paris: Les Editions G. Crès et Cie, 1922), 188–89.

6. Shiff, *Cézanne,* 27–38; Gilbert and Kuhn, *History of Esthetics,* esp. 524–49.

7. Shiff, *Cézanne,* 14–20.

8. Ibid.

9. On this subject, see Scott, "Symbolism, Decadence and Impressionism"; also Phillipson, *Painting, Language and Modernity,* 99–123.

10. Alan Robinson discusses the following "misconceptions" in his *Symbol to Vortex,* 2–6.

11. McFarlane, "The Mind of Modernism," 84.

12. Bergson, *Time and Free Will,* 70–72, 85–87, 105–6.

13. David Lodge, "The Language of Modernist Fiction: Metaphor and Metonymy," in Bradbury and McFarlane, *Modernism, 1890–930,* 481–95; Bergson, *Time and Free Will,* 1–74. Also see Robinson, *Symbol to Vortex,* 2–6.

14. Robinson, *Symbol to Vortex,* 15–57.

15. Alan Bulloch, "The Double Image," in Bradbury and McFarlane, *Modernism, 1890–1930,* 69; Robinson, *Symbol to Vortex,* 15–57.

16. The notion of dwelling I have borrowed, of course, from Heidegger. For a discussion of "the four-fold relations" of dwelling that realize "being," see Heidegger, *Poetry, Language, Thought,* 213–29, 145–61.

17. Pierre Francastel, *La réalité figurative,* 201. Emphasis added. Translation is my own. "L'Impressionisme est-il une mode, un moment de la chaine des formes, sans rupture de la tradition culturelle séculaire du monde occidental; ou bien est-il un style commençant, la découverte, fragmentaire encore, d'une manière neuve de percevoir le mond extérieur par le vue, d'analyser les sensations optiques, de proposer au spectateur un champ de réflexion sensible et une problématique neuve de l'imaginaire? Dans le premier cas seulement, il est licite de parler d'une fin de l'Impressionnisme. Dans le second, il apparaîtra comme l'introduction d'un nouveau type de relation signifiante à l'échelle, sinon universelle, du moins de ce qu'il est convenu d'appeler une culture ou mieux une civilisation."

18. Shiff, *Cézanne,* 27–38, 21–26.

19. Ibid., 21–26.

20. Robinson discusses this in *Symbol to Vortex,* 15–57.

21. Malcolm Bradbury and James McFarlane, "The Name and Nature of Modernism," in Bradbury and McFarlane, *Modernism, 1890–1930,* 48–49. Also see Bergson, *Time and Free Will,* esp. 11–18, 140–221.

22. Gilbert and Kuhn, *History of Esthetics,* 479–82.

23. Shiff discusses Taine's psychologism in *Cézanne,* 39–40, 45–46, 245–46.

24. Hippolyte Taine, *D'intelligence,* quoted in Sartre, *Imagination,* 21.

25. Sartre, *Imagination,* 22.

26. Ibid., 22–23.

27. Ibid., 23.
28. Ibid., 24.
29. Shiff, *Cézanne*, 39.
30. Ibid., 40.
31. McFarlane, "Mind of Modernism," 74.
32. Cassirer, *Problem of Knowledge*, 248.
33. Croce, *Theory and History of Historiography*, 66–67, quoted in ibid., 252.
34. Shiff, *Cézanne*, 39.
35. See Bergson, *Time and Free Will*, 165–70, 235–40, for a discussion of the concept of "free and spontaneous consciousness."
36. For discussions of the subject/object dichotomy in modernism, consult H. Stuart Hughes, *Consciousness and Society: The Reorientation of European Social Thought, 1890–1930* (London: A. A. Knopf, 1958), esp. 34. Also see Lodge, "Language of Modernist Fiction," 481–95; Shiff, *Cézanne*, 27–38; and Robinson, *Symbol to Vortex*, 1–14.
37. See Gilbert and Kuhn, *A History of Esthetics*, 525, 527–37, 539.
38. Ibid., 527–37.
39. Ibid., 529.
40. Peters, *Brett's History of Psychology*, 587.
41. Ibid., 584.
42. Todorov, *Theories of the Symbol*, 147–221.
43. Gilbert and Kuhn, *History of Esthetics*, 536. The quote from Fechner comes from *Vorschule der Ästhetik* (Thiele, 1876), vol. 1.
44. I am referring to Merleau-Ponty's concept of "lived world." See Merleau-Ponty, *Primacy of Perception*, 159–90; see also David Carr, "Maurice Merleau-Ponty: Incarnate Consciousness," in *Existential Philosophers: Kierkegaard to Merleau-Ponty*, edited by George A. Schrader (New York: McGraw-Hill, 1967), 396–429.
45. See Gilbert and Kuhn, *History of Esthetics*, 536, for a discussion of Fechner's "principles."
46. Gilbert and Kuhn, *History of Esthetics*, 537.
47. Ibid.
48. Theodor Lipps's *Ästhetische Faktoren der Raumanschauung* (1891) and Viktor Basch's *Critique sur l'esthétique de Kant* (1896) are both cited by Gilbert and Kuhn, *History of Esthetics*, 537.
49. Indeed, it transforms the perceptual image into a *natural sign of, and for, the response*. This natural relation between sign and signified had disappeared in most of the linguistic theories of modernity and was gradually eroding in late-nineteenth-century art theories, which were increasingly substituting expression for imitation as the source of the meaning of the artwork. Empathetic theories reconstruct, on the basis of affective and intentional equivalence, the natural connection of signifier to signified without appealing to rudimentary mimesis. Therefore they will be as adequate for the motivation of nonrepresen-

tational art as theories of arbitrary connection are. The potential convergence of these two forms of motivation has been ignored by most critics and art historians of modernism; however, it is central to the interpretation of this movement offered in this study.

50. See Sartre, *Imagination*, 32.

51. Ribot, *L'évolution des idées générales* (Paris, 1897), quoted in French in Robinson, *Symbol to Vortex*, 61. My translation: "Anything abstract is a corpse. It might be less picturesque but more exact to say a skeleton; indeed, scientific abstraction is but the bony carcass of phenomena. Thus, at bottom, the antagonism of the image and the idea is that of the whole and the part."

52. Ribot, *Essai sur l'imagination créatrice*, 6th ed. (Paris, 1900), quoted in Robinson, *Symbol to Vortex*, 71. My translation: "which has as its distinctive characteristics the neatness and precision of its forms—more explicitly its materials are strictly *images* (whatever their nature may be) approaching perception, giving the impression of reality, and in them associations by objective and precisely determinable relations have the predominant place. . . . this is an *external* imagination, that arises more from sensation than from feeling and that must necessarily be objectified."

53. This aspiration to "classic" stability in perception was recorded by theorists (e.g., Denis, Hulme) in the first few years of the twentieth century, when it had become a commonplace ready to be carried to an extreme by various trends of modernism. See, for example, T. E. Hulme, "Romanticism and Classicism," in *Speculations*, esp. 25: "I remembered being very surprised, after seeing the Post-Impressionists, to find in Maurice Denis's account of the matter that they consider themselves classical in the sense that they were trying to impose the same order on the mere flux of new material provided by the impressionist movement, that existed in the more limited materials of the painting before."

54. Ribot, *La vie inconsciente et les mouvements* (Movement and the life of the unconscious), 113 et seq., cited in Sartre, *Imagination*, 32. "Reduced to itself alone, thought is an activity that disassociates, associates, apprehends relations, coordinates. We may even suppose that this activity is by its very nature unconscious, assuming a conscious form only by way of the data which it elaborates. . . . To conclude, the hypothesis of pure thought without images and without words is most unlikely, and in any case unproven."

55. This is discussed by Merleau-Ponty, *L'union de l'âme et du corps chez Malebranche, Biran et Bergson: Notes prises au cours de Maurice Merleau-Ponty à l'École Normal Supérieur* (1947–48), edited by Jean Deprun (Paris: Vrin, 1968).

56. The first two chapters of this work, his doctoral thesis, were devoted to a demonstration against the claim by Fechner, among others, that the presumed intensity of psychical states was not quantitatively measurable but was instead a quality characterized by the pervasiveness of attention that it is capable of achieving. See esp. pp. 8–18 on desire, hope, joy and sorrow, and aesthetic feelings, and pp. 67–70, on the mistake of regarding sensations as magnitudes.

58. Bergson, *Two Sources of Morality and Religion*, 41.

59. The key of this original and surprising doctrine is Bergson's claim that energy, when reaching the level of concentration that qualifies it as action, becomes sensory-motor, with the sensory part always constituted by arranged or mapped cosmic energies and the motor part always constituted by self-preserving impulses that *choose and mark* their paths through the environment.

60. Bergson, *The Creative Mind*, 103.

61. Merleau-Ponty, *Signs*, 166: "When my right hand touches my left, I am aware of it as a 'physical thing.' But at the same moment, if I wish, an extraordinary event takes place: here is my left hand as well starting to perceive my right. . . . The physical thing becomes animate. Or, more precisely, it remains what it was (the event does not enrich it), but an exploratory power comes to rest upon or dwell in it. Thus I touch myself touching; my body accomplishes 'a sort of reflection.'"

62. Bergson, *Matter and Memory*, 332, quoted in Alexander, *Bergson*, 43.

63. Alexander, *Bergson*, 43.

64. Bergson's theory of consciousness was extensively criticized by Sartre in *The Imagination*. Chapters 4 and 5, pp. 37–59, are devoted to Bergson and his school. Also, Merleau-Ponty severely criticizes, in *L'union de l'âme et du corps*, the separation of duration from the image that leaves the former at times in a theoretical limbo. It can be said that the above problem is less serious in a philosophy of action, such as Bergson's, than in a reflective philosophy of pure consciousness. In fact, Merleau-Ponty came closer to Bergson in his later work, as his 1959 essay, "Bergson in the Making," in *Signs*, pp. 82–92, clearly suggests. In general, these severe critiques of their predecessors by recent French philosophers (Sartre and Merleau-Ponty, but also Lévi-Strauss, Lacan, Foucault, Barthes, and Derrida) are not as serious as their emphatic tone would indicate. This tone might actually be an attempt to hide the considerable borrowings by those critics from the doctrines they criticized.

65. These are therefore, within Bergson's theory, the equivalent of the cathexed or emotionally bound images that psychoanalysis has discovered and interpreted.

66. I am using the Saussurean categories here; see Jonathan Culler, *Ferdinand de Saussure* (New York: Penguin Books, 1976), esp. 29–48.

67. Bergson, *Matter and Memory*, 32.

68. Alexander, *Bergson*, 92.

69. Bergson, *Matter and Memory*, 185, 187.

70. Bergson, *Two Sources of Morality and Religion*, 41.

71. Bergson, *Matter and Memory*, 203.

72. Ibid., 207–8.

73. Ibid., 209.

74. Ibid., 193.

75. Ibid., 158–59.

76. One could include here the category of "repressed actions," with psychoanalysis in mind.

77. Bergson, *Matter and Memory*, 154.
78. Ibid., 158.
79. Ibid., 161.
80. Ibid., 170.
81. Ibid., 171.
82. Ibid., 169. Emphasis added.
83. Bergson, *Creative Mind*, 191, 87, 110.
84. Ibid., 192, 3.
85. Ibid., 195.
86. Bergson, *Matter and Memory*, 169.
87. Bergson, *Creative Mind*, 195.
88. Bergson, *Time and Free Will*, 136–37. Emphasis added.
89. Ibid., 165.
90. Whatever the value of such analysis of "historical influences" for purposes of identification and attribution of works, exclusive emphasis on it would give art history a semblance of justification and even glorification of plagiarism. In some important respects what is *of value* in artists or works is not what they may have in common with their sources but what is *uniquely synthesized* in the author or work. Such novelty and uniqueness are often seen better by disciples than by critics, yet, in appropriating them, the followers of great masters tend to drag them down to a level where influence becomes again more important than creativity. It will be claimed below that the uniqueness of a synthesis, whether in art or in meaning or in a form of life, can be found and properly analyzed only within the framework of the hermeneutical method, hence the importance of this method for the integrated understanding of art and of history that constitutes art history.
91. For a thorough elaboration of the concept of effective history, see Hans-Georg Gadamer, *Truth and Method* (New York: Crossroad, 1982), esp. 287ff.

III.
From Impressionism to Cézanne:
Aesthetic Theories

1. Alexander, *Bergson*, 33.
2. Wörringer, *Abstraction and Empathy*.
3. Unfortunately, these questions were turned over uncritically to present aesthetics, often neglectful of the critical conquests of modernism.
4. Merleau-Ponty, *Primacy of Perception*, 160.
5. Ibid., 161–62.
6. Jules Antoine Castagnary, "L'exposition du Boulevard des Capucines: Les impressionistes," *Le siècle*, 29 April 1874; quoted in Mathey, *Impressionists*, 59.
7. Shiff, *Cézanne*, 14–20.

8. See, for instance, Pissarro's letter to Louis Le Bail, cited in John Rewald, *History of Impressionism,* 458; also "Monet in His Old Age," in Nochlin, ed. *Impressionism and Post-Impressionism, 1874–1904,* 44–45; Pierre-Auguste Renoir, "La société des irregularités," in Lionello Venturi, ed., *Les archives de l'impressionisme* (Paris: Durand-Ruel, 1939), 127–29.

9. See Robinson, *Symbol to Vortex,* 12–14. Also see Merleau-Ponty, *Sense and Non-Sense,* 9–25. Wörringer calls this "apperceptive activity" (*Abstraction and Empathy,* 5).

10. Taken from Gaston Poulain, *Bazille et ses amis* (Paris: La Renaissance du Livre, 1932); also included in Rewald, *History of Impressionism,* 136.

11. From Edgar Degas, *Notebooks,* 101 (1863–67) (Paris: Bibliothèque Nationale); reprinted in Jean Sutherland Boggs, "Degas Notebooks at the Bibliothèque Nationale," *Burlington Magazine,* July 1953, 243.

12. Proust, *Le temps retrouvé,* 249.

13. Charles Baudelaire, *The Painters of Modern Life* (Paris: Pléiade, 1863); reprinted in *Baudelaire: Selected Writings,* 390–435.

14. André Gide, *Les nourritures terrestres* (Paris: Le Livre de Poche, 1917–36); quoted in Kronegger, *Literary Impressionism,* 35.

15. Maurice Denis's "definition" of painting emphasizes the surface as the primary expressive element: "It is well to remember that a picture—before being a battle horse, a nude woman, or some anecdote—is essentially a plane surface covered with colors assembled in a certain order" (Denis, *Théories,* 1).

16. See, for instance, Henry G. Keller and J. J. MacLeod, "The Application of the Physiology of Color Vision in Modern Art," *Popular Sciences Monthly* 83 (November 1913): 450–65.

17. Texts that deal with color theories appropriate to this time period include Ralph M. Evans, *An Introduction to Color* (New York: John Wiley, 1948); Maitland Graves, *Color Fundamentals* (London: McGraw-Hill, 1941); M. Luckiesh, *Color and Its Applications* (New York: Van Nostrand, 1921); and James P. C. Southall, *Introduction to Physiological Optics* (London: Oxford University Press, 1937).

18. Michel-Eugène Chevreul, *De la loi du contraste simultané des couleurs,* translated by Charles Martel as *The Principles of Harmony and Contrasts of Colours* (New York: Reinhold Publishing, 1967); see Homer, *Seurat and the Science of Painting,* 20–28, for a discussion of this very important technical treatise and its influences on art.

19. Claude Monet, *Impression: Sunrise,* 1872, Musée Marmottan, Paris.

20. See "An Interview with the Artist in 1900," reprinted in Nochlin, *Impressionism and Post-Impressionism,* 36–43; also see William C. Seitz, *Claude Monet: Seasons and Moments* (New York: Museum of Modern Art, 1960).

21. Quoted by Lilla Cabot Perry, "Reminiscences of Claude Monet from 1889–1909," *American Magazine of Art* 18 (March 1927): 119.

22. René Huyghe, "L'impressionisme et le pensée de son temps," *Prométhée* 1 (February 1939): 9.

23. David Sutter, "Les phénomènes de la vision," *L'Art* 20 (1880): 216; also see Homer, *Science of painting,* 43–47.

24. Charles Blanc, "Eugène Delacroix," *Gazette des beaux-arts* 16 (January 1864): 5–6.

25. Charles Blanc, "Grammaire des arts du dessin," *Gazette des beaux-arts* (1 April 1860–1 December 1866): 373–89; see Homer, *Science of Painting,* esp. 17–18, 29–36.

26. These statements are from Blanc's "Grammaire," 373–89.

27. Shiff, *Cézanne.* 70–98; also see Boime, *Academy,* for more information on the "rules" of the Academy.

28. Émile Zola, "Mon salon (1866)," in *Mon salon, Manet, écrits sur l'art,* ed. Antoinette Ehrard (Paris: Ehrard, 1970), 60. Also see my discussion, in chap. 4 of Zola's contribution to the definition of *realisation* and the role of the temperament.

29. Émile Bernard's "Paul Cézanne," *L'Occident,* July 1904, 23; reprinted in Doran, *Conversations avec Cézanne,* 36.

30. Rewald, *Paul Cézanne,* 135.

31. See Wörringer's discussion of "reality" as "being formed by me" in *Abstraction and Empathy,* 6–7.

32. Charles Baudelaire, "The Salon of 1859," in *Baudelaire: Selected Writings,* 306–7.

33. Heinrich-Wilhelm Dove, *Darstellung der Farbenlehre und optische Studien* (Berlin, 1853); see Homer, *Science of Painting,* 142–43.

34. Ogden Nash Rood, *Modern Chromatics* (New York: D. Appleton, 1881), translated into French as *Théorie scientifique des couleurs: Ses applications à l'art et l'industrie;* see Homer, *Science of Painting,* 36–43; also see Sven Löevgren, *Genesis of Modernism,* 51, 73, 76, 90–91.

35. Charles Henry, "Introduction à une esthétique scientifique," *La revue contemporaine,* August 1885; also see Löevgren, *Genesis of Modernism,* 88; and Homer, *Science of Painting,* 182–83.

36. Henry, "Introduction," 441–69.

37. See Homer, *Science of Painting,* 188–98, for a very thorough discussion of Henry's theories and their practical application in the arts.

38. Indeed, Georges Seurat incorporated Henry's findings on dynamogeny and inhibition in his late chromoluminarist works, such as *Le cirque,* as "principles of composition" that could control, through the visual elements of the paintings, the emotional response of the viewer. See Seurat's letter to Maurice Beaubourg of 28 August 1890, in John Rewald, *Post-Impressionism from van Gogh to Gauguin* (New York: Museum of Modern Art, 1962), 142.

39. Homer, *Science of Painting,* 191–94 discusses the work of Humbert de Superville.

40. Cited in ibid., 194.

41. See ibid., 196–98.

42. See Homer's discussion in ibid., 199–217.

43. From a letter to Emile Schuffenecker, dated 14 January 1885; reprinted in Herschel Chipp, *Theories of Modern Art* (Berkeley and Los Angeles: University of California Press, 1968), 59.

44. Originally published in *Art et critique* (Paris, 1890); also included in Denis, *Théories,* 1–13; reprinted in Chipp, *Theories of Modern Art,* 94–100.

45. See Chipp, *Theories of Modern Art,* 100.

46. Maurice Denis, "Subjective and Objective Deformation," *L'Occident,* May 1909; also included in Denis, *Théories,* 262–78; Chipp, *Theories of Modern Art,* 105–7.

47. Gustave Kahn, *L'Événement;* translated and quoted in Chipp, *Theories of Modern Art,* 50. All parentheticals are Kahn's.

48. I am using here Mallarmé's notion of "presence in absence." See Clive Scott, "Symbolism, Decadence and Impressionism," in Bradbury and McFarlane, *Modernism, 1890–1930,* 209–13 for a discussion of the "negation" inherent in symbolism: "The Symbol is compounded of object and idea, presence and absence" (p. 209). See also chapter 4 n. 23 for the citation of the lines from Mallarmé's poem "Magie," in which he presents his ideas on presence and absence.

49. G.-Albert Aurier, "Le Symbolisme en peinture: Paul Gauguin," *Mercure de France* 2 (1891): 159–64.

50. Ibid. Also see Chipp, *Theories of Modern Art,* 93, from which this excerpt was quoted.

51. See Gauguin's letter of 1899 from Tahiti to André Fontainas in response to a critical review of his painting *Whence do we come . . .* Included in Rewald, *Paul Gauguin,* 21–24.

52. Fowlie, *Mallarmé,* 254.

53. In a letter dated 18 July 18968 to his friend Henri Cazalis, Mallarmé wrote the following commentary: "For instance a window open at night, with the two shutters fastened back; a room with nobody in it, despite the air of stability given by the shutters fastened back, and in a night made of absence and questioning, without furniture except for the plausible shape of vague console-tables, a warlike, dying frame of a mirror hung at the back with its stellar and incomprehensible reflection of the Great Bear, which alone connects this dwelling abandoned by the world to the sky." This translation is from Hartley, *Mallarmé,* 88.

54. From "Plusieurs Sonnets," in Hartley, *Mallarmé,* 87–88; the following translation is also by Hartley:

> Its pure nails offering their onyx on high, Anguish this midnight holds up like a lamp-bearer many an evening dream burned by the Phoenix and not received in a cinerary urn
> on the tables in the empty drawing room: no shell, abolished trinket of sonorous emptiness (for the Master has gone to gather tears in the Styx with this single object on which nothingness prides itself).

55. Also from Hartley, *Mallarmé*, 88, comes the completion of the translation of the sonnet:

But near the empty window to the north a gold is dying perhaps corresponding to the setting of unicorns rushing from the fire towards a water nymph, she, a dead, naked girl in the mirror, although, in the forgetfulness enclosed by the frame, at once the septet of twinkling stars is fixed.

56. Paul Gauguin, *Self-Portrait*, 1889, National Gallery of Art, Washington, D.C.

57. See chapter 2, the section entitled "The Bergsonian Synthesis," for a discussion of the formation of new and fresh images.

IV.
The Path into Modernism:
Four Modalities of Imagery in Cézanne

1. Honoré Balzac, *Le chef d'oeuvre inconnu*, vol. 14 of *La comédie humaine*, edited by Furne, J.-J. Dubochet, and J. Hetzel (Paris: Lacrampe, 1846).

2. Émile Bernard, *Souvenirs sur Paul Cézanne*, 44.

3. See Merleau-Ponty, *Sense and Non-Sense*, 18.

4. For additional discussion of the importance of the Frenhofer story for Cézanne, also see Badt, *Art of Cézanne*, 202–5.

5. Ibid., 204.

6. Ibid., 202.

7. Quoted from Merleau-Ponty, *Sense and Non-Sense*, 18.

8. Arsène Alexandre, "Claude Lantier," *Le Figaro*, 9 December 1895. Cited and translated in Rewald, *Paul Cézanne*, 118.

9. Quoted in Theodore Reff, "Painting and Theory in the Final Decade," in Museum of Modern Art, *Cézanne: The Late Work* (New York: Museum of Modern Art, 1977), 13.

10. Paul Klee, *Diaries*, translated by Felix Klee (Berkeley: University of California Press, 1964), 237.

11. Cézanne used this term in a letter of November 1878 to Zola. See the discussion below in the section entitled "Realization of Sensations."

12. See Badt's discussion in *The Art of Cézanne*, 201–9.

13. Ibid., 200–201.

14. Ibid., 209–11.

15. Eugène Delacroix, *The Journal of Eugène Delacroix*, edited by Hubert Wellington and translated by Lucy Norton (Ithaca: Cornell University Press, 1980), 407ff.

16. Ibid., 317–18.

17. See Badt, *Art of Cézanne,* 206.

18. See ibid., 209.

19. One of Delacroix's few painted bouquets, *Roses and Hortensias,* was owned by Cézanne and, as will be indicated in chapter 5, played a very important role in his theoretical development.

20. Émile Zola, *L'Oeuvre* (New York: Howell, Soskin, 1946). Also see Badt, *Art of Cézanne,* 210–11. Quotes from the novel are taken from Badt.

21. Émile Zola, *Therese Raquin,* translated by Leonard Tancock (New York: Penguin Books, 1962), 21–27.

22. Ibid., 23.

23. Fowlie, *Mallarmé,* 12.

24. Cézanne, *Letters,* 129. *Realisation* is translated in this edition as "expressing."

25. Cézanne's last letter to Zola was dated 4 April 1886 and thanked him for sending a copy of his novel *L'Oeuvre.* John Rewald believes that Cézanne felt betrayed by the characterization of the failed painter Lantier, who "resembled" Cézanne. See Rewald, *Paul Cézanne,* 153–63.

26. Cézanne, *Letters,* 111–12. This letter refers to Zola's new publication, "Un page d'amour," which had just appeared; the "persons" to whom he refers are the protagonists Hélène and Henri.

27. From Doran, *Conversations avec Cézanne,* 36. The following English translation is from Lawrence Gowing, "The Logic of Organized Sensations," in Museum of Modern Art, *Cézanne: The Late Work,* 62: "There are two things in the painter, the eye and mind; each of them should aid the other. It is necessary to work at their mutual development, in the eye by looking at nature, in the mind by the logic of organized sensations, which provides the means of expression."

28. Rewald, *Paul Cézanne,* 95–96.

29. See Theodore Reff, "Cézanne's Constructive Stroke," *Art Quarterly* 25 (1962); also see Gowing, "Notes on the Development of Cézanne."

30. The concept of the work as bringing or setting forth the truth of the world is explained by Heidegger in *Poetry, Language, Thought,* esp. 62.

31. Bergson, *The Creative Mind,* 14.

32. Merleau-Ponty, *Sense and Non-Sense,* 16–17.

33. Ibid., 18.

34. It was Wilhelm Wörringer who first called attention to the affinities between abstraction and a diffident or insecure attitude toward the world. See Wörringer, *Abstraction and Empathy,* 3–48.

35. On 26 May 1904.

36. Gowing notices this in his essay "The Logic of Organized Sensations," in Museum of Modern Art, *Cézanne: The Late Work,* 62–63. Badt also refers to this misinterpretation in *The Art of Cézanne,* 212–13. By translating Cézanne's phrase as "realization after nature," Badt tries to avoid the possible implications of representationalism. However, the preposition *after* has a common use to

signify imitation. Although Gowing's intentions in using the translation "real-ization on nature" are not clear, his terms will be respected in the present study, and its Bergsonian undertones indicating the interaction between artist and world will be emphasized throughout. The phrase *realisation sur nature* occurs often in Cézanne's letters; see, for instance, *Letters,* 258.

37. Joachim Gasquet, "Le Motif," in Doran, *Conversations avec Cézanne* (Paris: Collection Macula, 1978), 109. See Gowing, "Logic of Organized Sensations," 63, for a discussion of this. The following translation is by Gowing: "What is one to think of those fools who tell one that the artist is subordinate to nature?"

38. Doran, *Conversations avec Cézanne,* 109.

39. Quoted from a letter to Émile Bernard, 15 April 1904; see *Letters,* 233–34.

40. Gasquet, "Le Motif," 109.

41. Ambroise Vollard, "Extrait de Paul *Cézanne,*" in *Conversations avec Cézanne,* 8. Also see Gowing, "Logic of Organized Sensations," 61, for the following translation: "If my study in the Louvre goes well, perhaps tomorrow I shall find the right color to fill the white spaces. Just understand, if I put something there at random, I should have to go over the whole picture again starting from that spot."

42. There may be an echo in these words of Flaubert's celebrated struggles to find and use *le mot juste* as a polysemic sign fitting within an expressive situation.

43. Ortega y Gasset has considered "inhuman" the best aspects of the tra-dition in the visual arts, and emphasized that such inhumanity was not properly understand until the modernist revolution clearly pointed to it: "All great peri-ods of art have been careful not to let the work revolve about human contents. The imperative of unmitigated realism that dominated the artistic sensibility of the last century must be put down as a freak in aesthetic evolution. It thus appears that *the new inspiration* [emphasis added], extravagant though it seems, is merely returning, at least in one point, to the royal road of art" (Jose Ortega y Gasset, *The Dehumanization of Art, and Other Essays on Art, Culture, and Literature,* translated by H. Weyl [Princeton: Princeton University Press, 1968], 25).

44. Émile Bernard, "Paul Cézanne," in Doran, *Conversations avec Cézanne,* 36. Originally published in *L'Occident,* July 1904, 17–30. The following English translation is from *Cézanne in Perspective,* edited by Judith Wechsler (Englewood Cliffs, N.J.: Prentice-Hall, 1975), 42: "There is no such thing as line or model-ing; there are only contrasts. These are not contrasts of light and dark, but the contrasts given by the sensation of colour. Modelling is the outcome of the exact relationship of tones. . . . One should not say model, one should say modulate. . . . The more the colour harmonises, the more exact the drawing becomes. . . . The effect is what constitutes a picture. It unifies the picture and concentrates it. The effect must be based on the existence of a dominating patch."

45. See Gowing, "Logic of Organized Sensations," 69, for a listing of the varieties of brushstrokes used by Cézanne.

46. Bernard identifies this pattern as such; see "Cézanne," in Doran, *Conversations avec Cézanne,* 164.

47. See Liliane Brion-Guerry, "The Elusive Goal," in Museum of Modern Art, *Cézanne: The Late Work,* 74, for an explanation of "denatured" objects in Cézanne's paintings.

48. Gowing, "Logic of Organized Sensations," 64.

49. Schapiro, *Modern Art,* 19; originally published as an article, "The Apples of Cézanne: An Essay on the Meaning of Still-life," *Art News Annual* 34 (1968): 34–53.

50. Schapiro, *Modern Art,* 19.

51. Ibid.

52. Ibid., 87–89.

53. Ibid., 19–20. Schapiro's characterization of this attitude as "sober objectivity" is inconsistent with the Heideggerian approach he is using. The relation of "things" to man here should be precisely characterized in accordance with Heidegger as a practical, or "ready-to-hand," relation that establishes the being of an entity as its use(fulness). This being is certainly not objective: utensils are "hermeneutically" or interpretatively "understood" in reference to their overall connections to the entire workshop and, through them, against the background of the world. In Heidegger objectivity of any kind is the product of a *predicative* attitude, while the familiar objects of the human environment and the lived world in which they stand are nonobjective and *prepredicative.* This point is important, because it implies the disappearance of the traditional epistemological separation of subject from object, a disappearance that was discussed as characteristic of Cézanne and of modernism in earlier chapters and will be brought up again later in connection with Schapiro.

54. Merleau-Ponty, *Sense and Non-Sense,* 17.

55. Hulme, *Speculations,* 196.

56. Quoted in Merleau-Ponty, *Sense and Non-Sense,* 17.

57. Bernard, "Paul Cézanne," in Doran, *Conversations avec Cézanne,* 36. The following English translation is from Wechsler, *Cézanne in Perspective,* 42; "Everything in nature is modelled on the sphere, the cone and the cylinder. One must learn to paint from these simple forms; it will then be possible to do whatever one wishes."

58. Fry, *Cézanne,* 53.

59. Honoré Balzac, *Le Peau de chagrin,* in *La comédie humaine;* quoted from Merleau-Ponty, *Sense and Non-Sense,* 16.

60. Quoted in Merleau-Ponty, *Sense and Non-Sense,* 16.

61. Gasquet, "Paul Cézanne," in Doran, *Conversations avec Cézanne,* 111.

62. See Heidegger, "Hölderlin and the Essence of Poetry," in *Existence and Being,* translated by D. Scott, with introduction and analysis by W. Brock (Washington, D.C.: Regnery Gateway, 1949), 282. See also "Towering up

within itself, the work [of Art] opens up a *world* and keeps it abiding in force" (Heidegger, *Poetry, Language, Thought,* 44).

63. Schapiro, *Modern Art,* 25. Emphasis added.

64. Quoted in Heidegger, "What Are Poets For?" in *Poetry, Language, Thought,* 128–29. The text is from a letter written at Muzot on 11 August 1924.

65. For a discussion of being-in as "dwelling alongside," see Heidegger, *Being and Time,* translated by J. Macquarrie and E. Robinson (New York: Harper & Row, 1962), 80. For the positioning of poetic indwelling, see Heidegger, *Poetry, Language, Thought,* 148–49.

66. Heidegger discusses the characteristic tension or intensity of the "rift-design" of the artwork and its gathering of world horizons in *Poetry, Language, Thought,* 63.

67. The definition of fundamental mood as *Befindlichkeit,* a dimension of indwelling that is open to a world, is explained by Heidegger in *Being and Time,* 172–79.

68. Heidegger, *Poetry, Language, Thought,* 44, 48.

69. Ibid., 49.

70. Wallace Stevens, *The Collected Poems,* 512.

71. Heidegger, *Existence and Being,* 233–69.

72. Bergson, *Time and Free Will,* 136.

73. The "suggestive shapes" in the paintings of Mont Sainte-Victoire have been "found" and explained as unconscious in the following: Rewald and Marschutz, "Cézanne et Provence," *Le point* 1 (August 1936): 27, 31; Schapiro, *Paul Cézanne,* 118; Loran, *Cézanne's Composition,* 72, 117–18; and Reff, "Painting and Theory in the Final Decade," in Museum of Modern Art, *Cézanne: The Late Work,* 26.

74. Many of the most important interpreters of the abstract, plastic image insist in reading sensory and emotive harmonies as psychoanalytic fables.

75. Geist, "Secret Life of Paul Cézanne"; Badt, *Art of Cézanne,* 88.

76. Perloff, *Futurist Moment,* 44–79. The quotes in the text are from, respectively, William C. Seitz, *The Art of Assemblage* (New York: Museum of Modern Art, 1968), 150; and Jean-Jacques Thomas, "Collage/Space/Montage," in *Collage,* edited by Jeanine P. Plottel (New York: New York Literary Forum, 1983), 85.

77. Perloff, *Futurist Moment,* 246 n. 5. See also Ulmer, *Anti-Aesthetic,* 84.

78. On the patterning of (imagist) poetry after the modifications of the visual image in early modernism, see Pound, *Gaudier-Brzeska,* 82–83.

79. Perloff quotes Benedikt Livshits's reproaches of Marinetti's destruction of syntax: : What is the point of piling up amorphous words, a conglomeration which you call 'words at liberty'? To eliminate the intermediary role of reason by producing disorder, right? . . . is it worth destroying the traditional sentence, even the way you do, in order to reinstate it, to restore its logical predicate by suggestive gestures, mime, intonation and onomatopoeia?" (Perloff, *Futurist Moment,* 64).

80. For a discussion of the notion of the materials of the imagination and of their extraction, see Sartre, *Imagination,* 25.

81. See, for example, Kozloff, *Cubism/Futurism,* 105–7.

82. Quoted in ibid., 107, from Bergson's "Essay on Laughter."

83. Stevens, *The Collected Works,* 371.

84. In his essay "The Immediate Stages of the Erotic or the Musical Erotic" in *Either/Or,* Søren Kierkegaard uses as a motif Mozart's opera *Don Giovanni* and compares it with some motifs in *The Marriage of Figaro* and *The Magic Flute.* See *Either/Or,* 43–134.

85. Kierkegaard, *Either/Or,* 63.

86. Ibid., 73.

87. Ibid., 74.

88. Ibid., 79.

89. Ibid., 83, 128.

90. Roland Barthes presented many valuable insights into the relations of semiotics and eroticism in *The Pleasure of the Text,* translated by Richard Miller (New York: Hill and Wang, 1975). See, for example, p. 56: "Figuration is the way the erotic body appears (to whatever degree and in whatever form that may be) in the profile of the text. For example, the author may appear in his text (Genet, Proust), but not in the guise of direct biography (which would exceed the body, give a meaning to life, forge a destiny). Or again: one can feel desire for a character in a novel (in fleeting impulses). Or finally: the text itself, a diagrammatic and not an imitative structure, can reveal itself in the form of a body, split into fetish objects, into erotic sites. All these movements attest to a *figure* of the text necessary to the bliss of reading."

V.
Death and Non-Figuration:
Cézanne's Ultimate Synthesis

1. The common focusing on the pragmatic and *linguistic* aspects of sign making explains the proximity of positivist art theorists, such as Semper, to neo-Kantians, such as Riegl or Wölfflin, and the emergence of the use of paradigms in art history with the neo-Kantian art historians such as Panofsky or Edgar Wind. See Podro, *Critical Historians of Art,* esp. chaps. 4–6, 9.

2. Heidegger's "Dasein is assailed by itself as the entity . . . which it constantly *is* as having been" (*Being and Time,* 376).

3. One of the most forceful recent theories of modernism can be found in Perloff, *The Poetics of Indeterminacy;* the theory can be summarily represented by the following quote (pp. 33–34):

> Modernism was itself a time of tension between rival strains, the
> Symbolists or 'High Modern' and the 'Other Tradition' . . . in

painting and sculpture. . . . From the early days of Cubism in 1910 through Vorticism and Futurism, Dada and Surrealism, down to the Abstract Expressionism of the fifties, and the Conceptual Art, Super-Realism, assemblages, and performance art of the present, visual artists have consistently resisted the Symbolist model in favor of the creation of a world in which forms can exist 'littéralement et dans tout les sens,' an oscillation between representational reference and compositional game. To put it another way, William Empson's famous 'seven types of ambiguity'—that is, the multiple layers of meaning words have in poetry (and, by analogy, images in painting)—give way to what we might call an 'irreducible ambiguity'—the creation of labyrinths that have no exit.

This concept of modernism originates with the critics and theorists of the October group, principally Rosalind Krauss and Gregory Ulmer, who agree with the "Yale critics," principally Harold Bloom and J. Hillis Miller, in their consideration of "high modernism" as an extension of romanticism. The October group, and Perloff in her studies of "the Other Tradition" in art and literature, however, think of many of the modernist masters as the last exponents of a mimetic art that has run its course and given way to the fresh spirit of nonreferential, nonsymbolic invention characteristic of postmodern pluralism. See Krauss, *Originality of the Avant-Garde;* and Ulmer, *Anti-Aesthetic,* 83–110.

4. See my chapter 2 above.

5. See my article "Matisse and the Signs," *Art Papers* (January/February 1986): 29–30.

6. Both Vollard and Venturi accept the dating as 1890–92; see Vollard, *Paul Cézanne* and Venturi, *Cézanne.* Badt and Gowing date the series 1890–99; see Badt, *The Art of Cézanne,* 88–89, and Gowing, "Notes," 191. Theodore Reff dates the series as being completed between 1890 and 1895, in his article, "Cézanne's 'Cardplayers' and Their Sources," *Arts Magazine,* November 1980, 104–17, but does not discuss the Orsay *Cardplayers.*

7. Reff, "Cézanne's 'Cardplayers' and Their Sources," 104; Reff, "Painting and Theory in the Final Decade," in Museum of Modern Art, *Cézanne: The Late Work,* 17 n. 29; Badt, *Art of Cézanne,* 88–89.

8. For example, V559 in the collection of the Metropolitan Museum, New York, 25 inches by 32 inches; and V560 in the Barnes Foundation, Merion, Pa., 52 inches by 71 inches.

9. Charles Baudelaire, "Correspondences," in *Flowers of Evil,* edited by Marthiel Matheus and Jackson Matheus (New York: New Directions, 1962), 241. The English translation by Richard Wilbur, same source, p. 12, reads: "Like dwindling echoes gathered far away / Into a deep and thronging unison."

10. Frances Douce, *The Dance of Death* (London: W. Pickering, 1833), and Erwin Panofsky, *Early Netherlandish Painting: Its Origins and Character* (Cambridge: Harvard University Press, 1953).

11. St.-Georges de Bouhelier, "Simplicité de Cézanne," *L'echo de Paris*, 15 June 1936.

12. See Iniquez-Angulo, "Las hilanderas," *Archivo español de arte* 25 (1952): 67–84.

13. The anonymous *Ovide moralisé* was written by a Franciscan at the end of the thirteenth century. See Joseph Engels, *Études sur l'Ovide moralisé* (Batavia: J. B. Wolters, 1945).

14. See Wayne Andersen, *Gauguin's Paradise Lost* (New York: Viking, 1971), 80–81, who suggests this "hidden image."

15. See Meyer Schapiro, *Modern Art*, 87–99.

16. Theodore Reff, "The Pictures within Cézanne's Pictures," *Arts Magazine* 53, no. 10 (June 1979): 91.

17. For more on the influences of Delacroix's works on Cézanne, see Lichtenstein, "Cézanne and Delacroix."

18. This is recounted in Maurice Denis, *Journals*, 3 vols. (Paris: La Colombe, 1957–59), 29. Theodore Reff also notices similarities with *The Large Bathers;* see Reff, "Painting and Theory in the Final Decade," 42.

19. Cézanne spoke to Rivière and Schnerb about his great admiration for this painting; see R. P. Rivière and Schnerb, "L'Atelier de Paul Cézanne," 817.

20. According to Theodore Reff, the titles of some of the paintings of the Chateau Noir also referred to it as the Chateau du Diable. See Reff, "Painting and Theory in the Final Decade," 25.

21. See photographs of Cézanne's studio in Museum of Modern Art, *Cézanne: The Late Work*, 101–3 that include many of the still-life objects he posed for his paintings. Prominent among them are skulls.

22. See Badt, *Art of Cézanne*, 97–106, for a discussion of Cézanne's projection as genius or hero.

23. The canvas was painted at the artist's farm/studio, "Jas de Bouffan," in Aix; he used Père Alexandre, a farmworker, for the pipe-smoking cardplayer and Paulin Paulet, a gardener, for the other player. The daughter of Paulet, Leontine Paulet, recounted her recollections of having also posed, with her father, for one of the five-figure compositions. See Ratcliff, "Cézanne's Working Methods," 19–20.

24. Gasquet, *Cézanne*, 28; Reff, "Cézanne's 'Cardplayers' and Their Sources," 107.

25. For an excellent discussion of the themes in Caravaggio's paintings, see Walter Friedländer, *Caravaggio Studies* (Princeton: Princeton University Press, 1955).

26. Gasquet, *Cézanne*, 28.

27. John Rewald said that the painter's oeuvre could be divided into two principal categories: "studies from nature" and souvenirs of the museums." See Rewald, *L'Amour de l'art* 16 (1935): 283.

28. See Reff, "Cézanne's 'Cardplayers' and Their Sources," 108, for a discussion of the popularity of this painting and its reproduction in the popular presses.

29. The Louvre acquired the Chardin in 1869. See ibid., 110. For more on Chardin, see Pierre Rosenberg, *Chardin* (Paris: Grand Palais, 1979), 232–34, and J. McCoubrey, "The Revival of Chardin in French Still-Life Painting, 1850–1870," *Art Bulletin* 46 (1964): 39–53.

30. Charles Sterling suggests this in "Cézanne et les maîtres d'autrefois," *La Renaissance* 19, nos. 5–6 (May-June 1936): 12.

31. Theodore Reff suggests these as sources. See his "Cézanne's 'Cardplayers' and Their Sources," 115.

32. Kirk Varnedoe, *Gustave Caillebotte* (Houston, Tex.: Museum of Fine Arts, 1976), 142–43; also see Reff, "Cézanne's 'Cardplayers' and Their Sources," 115.

33. Reff, "Cézanne's 'Cardplayers' and Their Sources," 106, has noticed this. Also see V. Greard, *Meissonier: His Life and His Art* (London: W. Heinemann, 1897).

34. The following have noted Cézanne's admiration of Daumier's lithographs: Gasquet, *Cézanne,* 107; Bernard, *Souvenirs sur Paul Cézanne,* 23; Denis, *Journals,* 29–30.

35. Reff, "Cézanne's 'Cardplayers' and Their Sources," 112–13, suggests these as sources. Also see L. Delteil, *Honoré Daumier* (Paris: Orrouy, 1930); and K. E. Maison *Honoré Daumier* (Greenwich, Conn.: New York Graphic Society, 1968).

36. Maison, *Honoré Daumier,* 207.

37. Denis, *Journals,* 30.

38. See Rewald, *Paul Cézanne,* 170.

39. For more on optical illusions, see E. H. Gombrich, *Art and Illusion: A Study in the Psychology of Pictorial Representation* (Princeton: Princeton University Press, 1969), esp. 307–8; and Rudolf Arnheim, *Art and Visual Perception: A Psychology of the Creative Eye* (Berkeley: University of California Press, 1969), esp. 114–16.

40. Sidney Geist includes this postcard in his discussion of *The Large Bathers* in his essay "The Secret Life of Paul Cézanne," 11.

41. See Elizabeth du Gue Trapier, *Goya and His Sitters: A Study of His Style as a Portraitist* (New York: Hispanic Society of America, 1964); and José Lopez-Rey, *Francisco de Goya* (New York: Harper & Row, 1950).

42. Hoffmann, *Playing Card,* 29–35; and Hargrave, *A History of Playing Cards,* 31–87.

43. Douglas, *Tarot,* 85–88; and Hoffmann, *Playing Card,* 36–37.

44. Douglas, *Tarot,* 87.

45. See Reff, "Painting and Theory in the Final Decade," 25.

46. J. K. Huysmans, "Cézanne," reprinted in Wechsler, *Cézanne in Perspective,* 31.

47. Hargrave, *History of Playing Cards,* 79, 80, 83.

48. Ibid., 80–83, discusses this.

49. Ibid., 71.

50. The role of fictional and autobiographical plots (repetition and reproduction) in binding libidinal energies unbound by traumatic crises parallels in
Freud the Bergsonian collaging of diverse images in the visionary image. An
excellent discussion of plots, repetition, and the working together of eros and
death in narrative and artistic texts can be found in Peter Brooks, *Reading for the
Plot: Design and Intention in Narrative* (New York: Vintage Books, 1984), 139–
42.

51. Paul Cézanne, *Correspondance,* edited by John Rewald (Paris: Grasset,
1937), 21. This drawing and letter are in the collection of J. Leblond, Paris.

52. Dante Alighieri, *Inferno,* in *The Divine Comedy,* translated by John D.
Sinclair (New York: Oxford University Press, 1981–82), 401–9.

53. Ibid., 407.

54. Ibid.

55. Ibid.

56. Ibid., 409.

57. Ibid., 407.

58. On the accusation of cannibalism, see F. De Sanctis, "Il canto XXXIII
dell' inferno," *Letture dantesche* (Florence, 1968), 1:651–71; and M. Sansone,
"Il canto XXXIII dell' Inferno," *Letture dantesche* (Florence 1966), 1:143–87.
Both are translated and discussed in Lonergan, *Dante Commentaries.*

59. Cézanne, *Letters,* 291. Translation from Kurt Badt, *Art of Cézanne,*
98–99:

> DANTE: Tell me, friend, what are those people there?
>
> VIRGIL: It is a skull, by God!
>
> DANTE: My God, how horrible! But why do they consume
> this revolting skull?
>
> THE FATHER: Now eat heartily this inhuman mortal who let us
> suffer hunger for so long.
>
> THE ELDEST SON: Let us eat.
>
> THE SECOND SON: I am very hungry, give me his ear.
>
> THE THIRD CHILD: Give me the nose.
>
> THE GRANDCHILD: Give me his eye.
>
> THE ELDEST SON: Give me the teeth.
>
> THE FATHER: Gently, gently, children, if you eat in this way
> what will be left for tomorrow?

60. See Friederich, *Dante's Fame Abroad,* 131–33, for an excerpt of Déschamps's verses.

61. The prose translation of Pier-Angelo Fiorentino appeared in 1840 as
La divine comédie . . . traduction nouvelle accompagnée de notes; it was reprinted in
1861 with illustrations by Gustave Doré. See ibid., 165–66.

62. Victor Hugo, *La Légende des siècles* (Paris: Gallimard, 1950). Émile
Zola recalls the early fascination that he and Cézanne experienced for Hugo:

"Victor Hugo reigned over us as an absolute monarch . . . his drama haunted us, like magnificent visions." See Rewald, *Paul Cézanne,* 5.

63. This was suggested by Prof. John Howett, Department of Art History, Emory University, Atlanta, Georgia.

64. Cézanne, *Letters,* 292. English translation from Badt, *Art of Cézanne,* 101.

> I have resolved, dear friend, to shock your heart,
> To cast into it a tremendous and atrocious fear
> By the monstrous sight of this horrid scene
> Capable of stirring the hardest soul.
> Your heart, I thought, would cry out at these
> Evil sights: what a wonderful picture is here!
> From your breast I thought would issue a great cry
> Of horror, seeing what only Hell could dream,
> Where the sinner, dead without undergoing punishment,
> Suffers terribly for all eternity.

65. For a discussion of Cézanne's dependency on his father, see Badt, *Art of Cézanne,* esp. 104–5, also 97, 100, 106, 124–25.

66. Ibid., 105.

67. Cézanne, *Correspondance,* 45.

68. See Reff's excellent analysis of the influence of the Hercules legend on Cézanne, in "Cézanne and Hercules."

69. Ibid., 37.

70. Cézanne, *Letters,* 289; English translation by M. Kay from same source, p. 36: "I have chosen is not the word, they forced me to choose!"

71. Ibid., 290; English translation by M. Kay from same source, p. 37.

> Hercules one day slept deeply
> In a wood, for the freshness was good,
> For really, had he not been in a charming grove,
> And if he had exposed himself to the glare
> Of the sun darting its hot rays,
> Perhaps he would have had a terrible headache;
> Well he was sleeping very deeply. A young dryad
> Passing quite close to him. . . . [unfinished]

72. Ibid., 37.

73. Ibid., 193. English translation from the same source (p. 42):

> You will say perhaps: Oh! my poor Cézanne
> What female demon has upset your brain?
> You whom of old I used to see

Walking with a firm step
Doing nothing good saying nothing bad?

Notice that Cézanne rhymes his family name with *crâne.*

74. Ibid., 194; translation, p. 43:

Thus before my eyes there sometimes appear
Radiant beings with voices divine,
During the night. Dear friend, one might say that dawn
with its fresh sweet lustre colours them zealously.
They seem to smile at me and I stretch out my hand,
But in vain I approach, all at once they are gone;
They mount to the heavens borne along by the breeze
With a tender glance which seems to say
Farewell! I strive to approach them again,
And I try to touch them in vain,
They are no more—the transparent gauze
No longer designs their bodies and forms divine.
My dream disappearing reality comes
Which finds me groaning, my heart heavy within,
And I see before my eyes a phantom arise
Horrible, monstrous, it's LAW that it is called.

75. Geist, "Secret Life," 13.

76. The urgency and the meaning of this call is partially preserved within the symbolist tradition (Nerval, Mallarmé, Rimbaud), and, after passing through different combinations of expressionism, abstraction, and surrealism in the great modernist masters, it bifurcates in our own times into the formal games of Dada, minimalism, and neo-abstraction, on the one hand, and the thematic games of neo-expressionism, deconstruction, neo-Freudianism, and New Marxism, on the other.

77. Wallace Stevens was aware of the emergence of a new sense and experience of death in modernism; he understood that, of necessity, this emergence was bringing about a change in the traditional iconology and iconography of death, that is, in the collection of images that represent this theme and in the signs used for that representation (Stevens, *Collected Poems,* 435–36):

This is the mythology of modern death
And these, in their mufflings, monsters of elegy,
Of their own marvel made, of pity made,
Compounded and compounded, life by life,
These are death's own supremest images,
The pure perfections of parental space,

The children of a desire that is the will,
Even of death, . . .

78. This letter was written on 13 November 1925 to Witold Hulewicz
(Rilke, *Selected Poetry,* 316).
    79. Ibid., 155.
    80. Ibid., "The Ninth Elegy," 201. Emphasis is the poet's.

Here is the time for the *sayable,*
here is its homeland.
Speak and bear witness. More than ever
the Things that we might experience are vanishing, for
what crowds them out and replaces them in an imageless act.
An act under a shell, which easily cracks open as soon as
the business inside outgrows it and seeks new limits.
Between the hammers our heart
endures, just as the tongue does
between the teeth and, despite that,
still is able to praise.

81. Letter by Rilke written on 6 January 1923 to Countess Margot Sizzo-
Noris-Crouy (Rilke, *Selected Poetry,* 332).
    82. Rilke, *Letters on Cézanne,* 76–77.
    83. Quoted by Heinrich Wiegand Petzet in the foreword to ibid., viii.
    84. Such reversals are often the reconsideration of an earlier poem in the
light of a later one, a reconsideration that enriches the initial time awareness and
complicates the fundamental mood initially assigned to it. Harold Bloom has
repeatedly described such convergences and reversals of time and mood; with
regard to "Credences of the Summer," for example, he says: "The poet is sixty-
eight, and the trouble his mind lays by appears to have been desire. 'All fools
slaughtered' would include one's own earlier self as it had been on All Fools'
Day, at the start of April's green. The infuriations of spring, for those well past
meridian, are over, and yet it is still a long way to what will be the occasion of
the *Auroras,* 'the first autumnal inhalations.' Surrounded by a triumphant nature, the mind considers its own less triumphant comfort, the moment of sublimation that is held in the 'this' of 'it comes to this and the imagination's life'"
(Bloom, *Wallace Stevens,* 245).
    85. An entire poem, "A Postcard from the Volcano," illustrates this pre-
cariousness insistently expressed in parts of other poems even when Stevens
most eloquently showed the irresistible character of the—his—belief in the creative efficacy of the word: "Children, / Still weaving budded aureoles, / Will
speak our speech and never know" (ibid., 158–59).
    86. Ibid., 304.
    87. Ibid., 129.

88. Examples of this attitude are found in "Academic Discourse at Havana," "Like Decorations in a Nigger Cemetery," "Postcard from the Volcano," "Man with a Blue Guitar," and "Notes toward a Supreme Fiction." Stevens, *Collected Poems,* 142, 150, 158, 165, and 180, respectively. For a clarification of the sources of the term "the First Idea," see Harold Bloom, *Wallace Stevens: The Poems of Our Climate* (Ithaca: Cornell University Press, 1976), 53.

89. Ibid., 252–59.

90. Ibid., 296, 297, 300–301.

91. Ibid., 318, 319, 326.

92. It will, of course, have its most luminous appearance in "Of Mere Being," the poem chosen by Holly Stevens to close *The Palm at the End of the Mind.* This title is, significantly, the first line of that poem.

93. Heidegger comments on Georg Trakl's image of "going under" in "Language in the Poem," in *On the Way to Language* (New York: Harper & Row, 1971), 163–64.

94. Stevens, *Collected Poems,* 341, 342, 344.

95. "All the worlds in the universe are plunging into the invisible as into their next-deeper reality; *a few stars intensify immediately and pass away in the infinite consciousness of the angels—others are entrusted to beings who slowly and laboriously transform, in whose terrors and delights they attain their next invisible realization*" (letter to Witold Hulewicz, 13 November 1925, in Rilke, *Selected Poetry,* 328).

96. This tradition from Wordsworth to Whitman of poetic self-realization reaches its highest point in "Notes toward a Supreme Fiction," in which Stevens fulfills it and ends it. See Stevens, *Collected Poems,* esp. 404–5.

97. Ibid., 533.

98. Ibid., 159, 176, 289, 297, 477.

99. Ibid., 298, 299, 418.

100. Ibid., 489, 329, 300, 342, 344, 345, 346.

101. Ibid., 424, 425, 432, 433, 443.

102. In *The Hour of Our Death,* Philippe Aries has established four basic types of the experience of dying in the Western tradition: (1) the accepted death of the patriarch, the knight, and the peasant; (2) the baroque death in the sixteenth and seventeenth centuries; (3) the intimate death in the eighteenth and nineteenth centuries; and (4) the forbidden and hidden-away death in postindustrial societies. (Referenced in Ricoeur, *Times and Narrative,* 1:111.)

103. "At one time it consists in an expectation of images, in an intellectual attitude destined to prepare the arrival of a certain precise image as in the case of memory, at another time it organizes a more or less prolonged game between the images which are capable of inserting themselves into it, as in the case of creative imagination. It is to the open condition what the image is to the closed condition. It presents in terms of *becoming,* dynamically, what images give us as ready made, in the static condition" (Henri Bergson, *L'Energie spirituelle,* quoted

in Jean-Paul Sartre, *The Psychology of the Imagination,* translated by Bernard Frechtman [New York: Washington Square Press, 1968], 76–77).

104. Gadamer, *The Relevance of the Beautiful and Other Essays,* edited by Robert Bernasconi, translated by Nicholas Walker (Cambridge: Cambridge University Press, 1987), 80.

105. Ibid., 81.

106. Ricoeur, *Time and Narrative,* 2:77.

107. Alfred Schutz, *Collected Papers,* vol. 1: *The Problem of Social Reality,* edited by Maurice Natanson (The Hague: Martinus Nijhoff, 1962), 220: "'We experienced this occurrence together.' By the We-relation, thus established, we both—he, addressing himself to me, and I, listening to him,—are living in our mutual vivid present. Directed toward the thought to be realized in and by the communicating process. *We grow older together.*"

108. Rilke, *Letters on Cézanne,* 77.

BIBLIOGRAPHY

Alexander, Ian. *Bergson*. London: Bowes & Bowes, 1957.

Andersen, Wayne. *Cézanne's Portrait Drawings*. Cambridge: MIT Press, 1970.

Aries, Philippe. *The Hour of Our Death*. Translated by Helen Weaver. New York: Knopf, 1981.

Barthes, Roland. *The Pleasure of the Text*. Translated by Richard Miller. New York: Hill & Wang, 1975.

———. *Writing Degree Zero*. Translated by Annette Lavers and Colin Smith. London: Jonathan Cape, 1967.

Badt, Kurt. *The Art of Cézanne*. Translated by Sheila Ogilvie. Berkeley: University of California Press, 1965.

Baudelaire, Charles. *Baudelaire: Selected Writings on Art and Artists*. Translated by P. E. Charvet. Harmondsworth: Penguin Books, 1972.

Bell, Clive. *Art*. New York: Putnam & Sons, 1958.

Bergson, Henri. *The Creative Mind*. Translated by Mabelle L. Andison. Westport, Conn.: Greenwood Press, 1946.

———. *Matter and Memory*. Translated by Margaret Paul and W. S. Palmer. London: Sonnenschein, 1911.

———. *Time and Free Will: An Essay on the Immediate Data of Consciousness*. Translated by F. L. Pogson. New York: Harper & Row, 1960.

————. *The Two Sources of Morality and Religion.* Translation by R. A. Audra, Cloudesley Bereton, and W. H. Carter. Garden City, N.Y.: Doubleday, 1935.

Bernard, Émile. *Souvenirs sur Paul Cézanne.* Paris: Michel, 1926.

Blanc, Charles. "Grammaire des arts du dessin." *Gazette des beaux-arts* (1 April 1860–1 December 1866): 373–89.

Bloom, Harold. *Wallace Stevens: The Poems of Our Climate.* Ithaca: Cornell University Press, 1977.

Boime, Albert. *The Academy and French Painting in the Nineteenth Century.* London: Phaidon, 1971.

Bradbury, Malcolm, and James McFarlane, eds. *Modernism, 1890–1930.* New York: Penguin Books, 1976.

Cassirer, Ernst. *The Problem of Knowledge: Philosophy, Science and History since Hegel.* New Haven: Yale University Press, 1969.

Chappius, Adrien. *The Drawings of Paul Cézanne.* Greenwich, Conn.: New York Graphic Society, 1973.

Chiari, Joseph. *The Aesthetics of Modernism.* London: Thames and Hudson, 1970.

Coplans, John. *Cézanne's Watercolors.* Los Angeles: Ward Ritchie, 1976.

Cornell, Kenneth. *The Symbolist Movement.* New Haven: Yale University Press, 1951.

Croce, Benedetto. *Theory and History of Historiography.* Translated by Douglas Ainslie. London: Harrap, 1921.

Dante Alighieri. *The Divine Comedy.* Translated by John D. Sinclair. New York: Oxford University Press, 1981–82.

Delacroix, Eugène. *The Journals of Eugène Delacroix.* Edited by Hubert Wellington. Translated by Lucy Norton. Ithaca: Cornell University Press, 1980.

Denis, Maurice. *Théories, 1890–1910.* 4th ed. Paris: Rouart & Watelin, 1920.

Doran, P. M., ed. *Conversations avec Cézanne.* Paris: Collection Macula, 1981.

Douglas, Alfred. *The Tarot: The Origins, Meaning and Uses of the Cards.* New York: Taplinger, 1972.

Fowlie, Wallace. *Mallarmé.* Chicago: University of Chicago Press, 1970.

Francastel, Pierre. *La Réalité figurative: Éléments structurels de sociologie de l'art.* Paris: Éditions Gonthier, 1965.

Friederich, Werner P. *Dante's Fame Abroad, 1350–1850.* Chapel Hill: University of North Carolina Studies in Comparative Literature, 1950.

Fry, Roger. *Cézanne: A Study of His Development.* New York: Macmillan, 1927.

―――. *Transformations: Critical and Speculative Essays on Art.* London: Chatto & Windus, 1926.

―――. *Vision and Design.* London: Chatto & Windus, 1920.

Frye, Northrop. *The Modern Century.* Toronto: University of Toronto Press, 1968.

Gasquet, Joachim. *Cézanne.* 2d ed. Paris: Bernheim Jeune, 1926.

―――. "Le Motif." In *Conversations avec Cézanne,* edited by P. M. Doran. Paris: Collection Macula, 1978.

Geffroy, Gustave. *La Vie artistique.* 3d ed. Paris: Dentu, 1894. Reprinted in *Impressionism and Post-Impressionism, 1874–1904: Sources and Documents,* edited by Linda Nochlin, 106–7. Englewood Cliffs, N.J.: Prentice-Hall, 1966.

Geist, Sidney. *Interpreting Cézanne.* Cambridge: Harvard University Press, 1989.

―――. "The Secret Life of Paul Cézanne." *Art International* 19 (November 1975).

Gilbert, Katherine, and Helmut Kuhn. *A History of Esthetics.* Bloomington: Indiana University Press, 1953.

Gottlieb, Carla. "The *Joy of Life:* Matisse, Picasso and Cézanne." *College Art Journal* 18 (1958).

Gowing, Lawrence. *An Exhibition of Paintings by Cézanne.* London: Tate Gallery, 1954.

―――. "Notes on the Development of Cézanne." *Burlington Magazine,* June 1956.

Hamilton, George H. "Cézanne, Bergson, and the Image of Time." *College Art Journal,* Fall 1956.

Hargrave, Catherine P. *A History of Playing Cards.* Boston: Houghton Mifflin, 1930.

Harrison, Charles. *English Art and Modernism, 1900–1939.* Bloomington: Indiana University Press, 1981.

Hartley, Anthony, ed. *Mallarmé.* Baltimore: Penguin Books, 1965.

Heidegger, Martin. *Poetry, Language, Thought.* Translated by Albert Hofstadter. New York: Harper & Row, 1971.

Henry, Charles. "Introduction à une esthétique scientifique." *La revue contemporaine,* August 1885.

Hoffmann, Detlef. *The Playing Card: An Illustrated History.* New York: New York Graphic Society, 1972.

Homer, William Innes. *Seurat and the Science of Painting.* Cambridge: MIT Press, 1964.

House, John. "The Legacy of Impressionism in France." In *Post-impressionism: Cross-currents in European Painting,* edited by Alan Bowness. New York: Harper & Row, 1979.

Hulme, T. E. *Speculations: Essays on Humanism and the Philosophy of Art.* Edited by Herbert Read. London: Routledge & Kegan Paul, 1936.

Isaacson, Joel. *The Crisis of Impressionism.* Ann Arbor: University of Michigan Press, 1980.

Kierkegaard, Søren. *Either/Or.* Translated by David Swenson and Lillian Swenson. Princeton: Princeton University Press, 1971.

Krauss, Rosalind E. *The Originality of the Avant-Garde and Other Modernist Myths.* Cambridge: MIT Press, 1985.

Kronegger, Elizabeth. *Literary Impressionism.* New Haven: University Press Services, 1973.

Lehmann, A. G. *The Symbolist Aesthetics in France, 1885–1895.* Oxford: Oxford University Press, 1968.

Lesko, Diane. "Cézanne's *Bather* and a Found Self-Portrait." *Artforum* 15 (December 1976).

Levenson, Michael H. *A Genealogy of Modernism: A Study of English Literary Doctrine, 1908–1922.* Cambridge: Cambridge University Press, 1984.

Lichtenstein, Sara. "Cézanne and Delacroix." *Art Bulletin* 6 (1964).

Lodge, David. "The Langue of Modernist Fiction: Metaphor and Metonymy." In *Modernism, 1890–1930,* edited by Malcolm Bradbury and James McFarlane. New York: Penguin Books, 1976.

Löevgren, Sven. *The Genesis of Modernism: Seurat, Gauguin, Van Gogh and French Symbolism.* Bloomington: Indiana University Press, 1971.

Lonergan, C. S. *Dante Commentaries.* Edited by David Nolan. Totowa, N.J.: Rowman & Littlefield; Dublin: Irish Academic Press, 1977.

Loran, Erle. *Cézanne's Composition.* 3d ed. Berkeley: University of California Press, 1963.

Mathey, François. *The Impressionists.* Translated by Jean Steinberg. New York: Frederick A. Praeger, 1961.

McFarlane, James. "The Mind of Modernism." In *Modernism, 1890–1930,* edited by Malcolm Bradbury and James McFarlane. New York: Penguin Books, 1976.

Merleau-Ponty, Maurice. *The Primacy of Perception.* Edited by James M. Edie. Translated by Carlton Dallery. Evanston, Ill.: Northwestern University Press, 1964.

———. *Sense and Non-Sense.* Translated by Herbert L. Dreyfus and Patricia A. Dreyfus. Chicago: Northwestern University Press, 1964.

————. *Signs.* Translated and edited by Richard C. McCleary. Evanston, Ill.: Northwestern University Press, 1964.

Museum of Modern Art. *Cézanne: The Late Work.* Boston: New York Graphic Society, 1977.

Nicholson, Benedict. "Post-Impressionism and Roger Fry." *Burlington Magazine,* January 1951.

Nochlin, Linda ed. *Impressionism and Post-Impressionism, 1874–1904: Sources and Documents.* Englewood Cliffs, N.J.: Prentice-Hall, 1966.

Novotny, Fritz. *Cézanne und das Ende der wissenschaftlichen Perspektive.* Vienna: Schroll, 1938.

Ortega y Gasset, José. *The Dehumanization of Art.* New York: Doubleday, 1956.

Perloff, Marjorie. *The Futurist Moment: Avant-Garde, Avant Guerre, and the Language of Rupture.* Chicago: University of Chicago Press, 1986.

————. *The Poetics of Indeterminacy: Rimbaud to Cage.* Princeton: Princeton University Press, 1981.

Peters, R. S., ed. *Brett's History of Psychology.* Cambridge: MIT Press, 1967.

Phillipson, Michael. *Painting, Language and Modernity.* London: Routledge & Kegan Paul, 1985.

Pleynet, Marcelin. *Painting and System.* Translated by Sima N. Godfrey. Chicago: University of Chicago Press, 1984.

Plottel, Jeanine P. *Collage.* New York: New York Literary Forum, 1983.

Podro, Michael. *The Critical Historians of Art.* New Haven: Yale University Press, 1982.

Pound, Ezra. *Gaudier-Brzeska: A Memoir.* New York: New Directions, 1970.

Proust, Marcel. *Le temps retrouvé.* Paris: Le Livre de Poche, 1954.

Ratcliffe, Robert. "Cézanne's Working Methods and Their Theoretical Background." Ph.D. diss., University of London, 1960.

Reff, Theodore. "Cézanne: The Enigma of the Nude." *Art News* 5 (November 1959).

————. "Cézanne: The Logical Mystery." *Art News* 62 (April 1963).

————. "Cézanne and Hercules." *Art Bulletin,* March 1966.

————. "Cézanne and Poussin." *Journal of the Warburg and Courtault Institutes,* 1960.

————. "Cézanne's Bather with Outstretched Arms." *Gazette des beaux-arts* 59 (1962).

————. "Cézanne's 'Cardplayers' and Their Sources." *Arts Magazine,* November 1980.

———. "Cézanne's Constructive Stroke." *Art Quarterly* 25 (1962).

———. "Painting and Theory in the Final Decade." In Museum of Modern Art, *Cézanne: The Late Work*. New York: Museum of Modern Art, 1977.

Rewald, John. *The History of Impressionism*. New York: Museum of Modern Art, 1973.

———. *Paul Cézanne: A Biography*. New York: Simon and Schuster, 1939.

Ricoeur, Paul. *Time and Narrative*. 2 vols. Translated by Kathleen McLaughlin and David Pellauer. Chicago: University of Chicago Press, 1984–85.

Rilke, Rainer Maria. *Letters on Cézanne*. Translated by Joel Agree. Edited by Clara Rilke. New York: Fromm International, 1985.

———. *The Selected Poetry*. Translated by Stephen Mitchell. New York: Vintage International, 1989.

Rivière, George. *Le Maître Paul Cézanne*. Paris: Floury, 1923.

Rivière, R. P., and J. F. Schnerb. "L'Atelier de Paul Cézanne." *La Grande Revue*, 25 December 1907.

Robinson, Alan. *Symbol to Vortex: Poetry, Painting and Ideas, 1885–1914*. New York: St. Martin's Press, 1985.

Sartre, Jean-Paul. *The Imagination: A Psychological Critique*. Ann Arbor: University of Michigan Press, 1972.

Saussure, Ferdinand de. *Course in General Linguistics*. Translated by Wade Baskin. London: Fontana, 1974.

Schapiro, Meyer. "Cézanne as a Watercolorist." In *Cézanne Watercolors*. New York: M. Knoedler, 1963.

———. *Modern Art: Nineteenth and Twentieth Centuries*. New York: George Braziller, 1978.

———. *Paul Cézanne*. New York: Abrams, 1952.

Shiff, Richard. "Art and Life: A Metaphoric Relationship." *Critical Inquiry* 5 (Autumn 1978).

———. "The Art of Excellence and the Art of the Unattainable." *Georgia Review* 32 (Winter 1978).

———. *Cézanne and the End of Impressionism*. Chicago: University of Chicago Press, 1984.

———. "Impressionist Criticism, Impressionist Color, and Cézanne." *Yale Review*, 1973.

Sloan, Joseph C. *French Painting between the Past and the Present*. Princeton: Princeton University Press, 1951.

Stevens, Wallace. *The Collected Poems*. New York: Vintage Books, 1982.

Todorov, Tzvetan. *Theories of the Symbol.* Translated by Catherine Porter. Ithaca: Cornell University Press, 1982.

Ulmer, Gregory. *The Anti-Aesthetic: Essays on Postmodern Culture.* Edited by Hal Foster. Port Townsend, Wash.: Bay Press, 1983.

Venturi, Lionello. "The Aesthetic Idea of Impressionism." *Journal of Aesthetics and Art Criticism* 1 (Spring 1941).

————. *Cézanne: Son art, son oeuvre.* Paris: Paul Rosenberg, 1936.

Vollard, Ambroise. *Paul Cézanne.* Paris: Gallery A. Vollard, 1914.

Waldfogel, Sidney. "A Problem in Cézanne's *Grandes Baigneuses.*" *Burlington Magazine,* May 1962.

Wechsler, Judith, ed. *Cézanne in Perspective.* Englewood Cliffs, N.J.: Prentice-Hall, 1975.

Wörringer, Wilhelm. *Abstraction and Empathy.* Translated by Michael Bullock. New York: International Universities Press, 1980.

INDEX

245